# Glass Planet 3
# Apocalypse

by NM Reed
McCarthy Preston
http//:NMReedBooks.com

# Dark Angel

Hell hath no government than that fatal law
(death)
which punishes perversity and corrects error,
for the false Gods only exist
 in the false faiths of their adorers.

Book of Solomon the King




….and in the end,
god is our hope
 that there can be a better world.
And hell is our punishment
 for when we fail to try.
(author)

## Chapter One
## Discovery

**Present**

The sun was just cracking through the dense layer of fog, and lifted Gwydion's mood as he stepped off the boat. He wouldn't call it a fun trip. Interesting certainly. But his young mind was not fully able to make out what happened nor take in much of its meaning really.

All he could really remember was the cold stone crypt, the black press of damp dark stones, and the sound of hurried footsteps following him relentlessly up those stairs. And the close call as angry arms reached for him from behind in the dark echoing crypt.

But that was behind him now. And he was here is San Francisco to start again. A new school in America with American kids, just like him, he thought naively. His grandfather had work with the Historical Language Institute and his younger professor friend, Will Smithershins, too. And even his weirdo mother, Mags, had been asked to work there. His grandmother Bethany was proud of her little group of erstwhile explorers. And they were all happy to get off that boat, after their long sail up from Panama.

And Gwydion was relieved to step onto firm ground and to have arrived at what he would call home for hopefully some years now. If only he could get rid of the dreams. Those dreams that haunted him just before he woke up, bubbled up in his mind sometimes during the day. Golden eyes glaring at him, a voice in an unfamiliar language taunting him, ringing in his ears just before he would wake from it with a chill.

**Nile Delta, year: 367 A. D.**
Sestnost found himself jogging through the streets, his robes beating about his legs, almost tripping him more than twice.

"Slow down," he admonished himself. "It's very unseemly for a friar to be seen running."

"But, I have to hurry," another voice spoke into his head. "We have to hurry or it will all be destroyed! We will all be destroyed!"

And his short legs sped up along the cobble stones with new vigor.

His master needed to know. He needed to hear what Sestnost had just over heard from the Bishop of Pachomia. He had presented the paper from Hippolytus of Rome, that the Gnostic writings would be reviewed, and all heretics and their heresies would be destroyed. He had even called them liars. He had said the members of Sestnost's brotherhood had falsely attributed their writings to an earlier time by falsifying their dates, thus falsifying their validity.

But this just wasn't true! How could the Bishop say that about his honest brethren and their studies? Some of these documents were actually ancient. They were written by some important brothers in the distant past. One of them they had called the Teacher of Light. And he had given his life for the struggle to enlighten all of them. Some even called him a Savior. But this new Bishop and his followers had their own, newer savior, and they distrusted anyone else. So of course they believed this story of an older savior had to be a falsification, because this newer one was the one and only.

His exhausted legs beat the stones until they were fatigued and gave way. He landed on the hard road with a thump and fell into darkness. And in this darkness rose a shadow, its dark wings beating about its legs like the robes of some mad priest, like the wings of some dark Angel. He peered into Sestnost's eyes with amber flames. "Getup, you fool!" it screeched into his frail human ears like a demon wind. "Get up and carry your message. These scriptures of wisdom, bury them now or all will be destroyed!" The demon's yellow eyes and hot breath held over Sestnost's face. "Get up." As it turned into a blinding ray of light, it screeched incomprehensibly into poor old Sestnost's ears, "Get moving!"

Sestnost then found himself peering into the blinding light of the setting sun glancing down the dirty street. The scent of flowers hung in the air and soothed him, he thought, half dreaming. He rose wearily, dusted himself off and began to make his way again toward the monastery, the memory of the dream of the dark angel running it's cold fingers up his sweating back.

Sestnost finally reached the courtyard of his monastery running.

"Quickly," he breathed, "the Monseigneur," as he worked to gain his breath.

And when the man arrived, hurried reluctantly along by two of Sestnost's brothers, the Monseigneur looked down at Sestnost and cried, "What is this hurry?"

"Father," hissed Sestnost, "They must all be destroyed. Quickly!"

"What?" cried the older man.

"The Books! They must all be destroyed! Or we will be destroyed with them!"

In a few days, cooler minds had prevailed and their ancient written words of knowledge and wisdom were decided to not be destroyed, but rather hidden. They placed the treasured books in large earthen jars, said an impassioned incantation for angelic protection, and closed them each with a ceramic lid, and plastered that closed with mud. And into these jars they sealed their fear and hatred these dedicated monks felt for their task, against these tyrants of wisdom.

Into a cleft between huge boulders just at the high-waters' reach of the Nile, the greatest river that fed these people, these old books were buried deep in the sand and mud in these giant ceramic jars, so they could be found again by these monks when the inevitable happened once again and these despots of wisdom and tyranny were over-thrown by saner men.

But history that flowed in that river had her own plans. These despots of wisdom and their savior did not fall so easily. In fact their sect grew and flourished and began to systematically stamp out all thought that challenged her. And the great river seemed to be in compliance with this flow of history and she made other other plans. She flowed deep and heavy the next year, depositing great amounts of silt and black earth onto the cache of ancient books in the sealed jars. If those monks had survived and even wanted to find those old texts in those jars they had so carefully sealed and hidden, they would not have been able.

So, destroyed, no. But, hidden, most definitely, yes. But so hidden as to be lost. Lost for almost two thousand years. And when the course of the river changed just slightly over the course of the 2000years, and the minds of men were ready to be opened, and when a people had been ravaged enough by drought and starvation that they needed to dig into the black earth for sustenance, these jars were inadvertently uncovered.

And when these jars were broken open by the curious discoverers, these men unwittingly unleashed the powers imprisoned there. Where this fear and hatred sealed in those jars for two thousand years with those ancient books of wisdom had swirled and coalesced into a cold wind of vengeance.

**1930's**

The River Nile flows, in some quirk of geologic fate, from south to north, and empties into a great sea. And along it's way it carries a very important load within it's waters. People, fish, and nutrients are carried with it, along with a deep history embedded into the soul of this ancient birthplace of humanity. This rich river valley, the fertile Nile Delta, provides northern Africa with life-blood. Each year the monsoon season floods the delta with rich green waters, and deposits a layer of black silt higher into the red earth country, bringing rich nutrients for growing food high into the red lands of Egypt.

And the Egyptian Copts of the Red-Lands harvest this black soil and take it back to their homes to fertilize their farms.

One such falladin brother, Mahmud, was gathering black soil next to his hobbled camel, when he unearthed a large ceramic jar, sealed at the top with a bowl. He and his younger brother, Hasyin, discussed what to do with this old jar.

The older brother argued for the possibility of riches.

The younger brother prudently warned of an evil Jinn imprisoned within the jar, and argued of only bad things that would happened if they set him free.

But the thirst for treasure won out, and Mahmud raised his heavy mattock and struck the ceramic jar, crashing it into bits.

And into the air around them flew a cloud of golden dust, thus confirming both the older and the younger brothers' wisdom. But the golden cloud of dust swirled for but a moment, then disappeared with a crackling sound off into the bright blue sky above the cliffs of Jubal al-Tarif.

"What was that, brother?" said younger brother, Hasyin.

"I don't know, but I am glad it flew away!" cried the elder brother, Mahmud.

And they both turned and regarded the jar that had just

crumbled to bits on the black earth. They tipped over the broken jar, and out fell... books.

Old crumbling books.

Two tired dark faces fell in disappointment.

"Well, it's something," said the prudent younger brother, Hasyin.

"Not much," said the greedy older brother, Mahmud. "But at least it's big enough to share." And with that, he grasped the large stack of bound folio pages in his strong hands.

And his prudent younger brother watched with half disinterest, while his older brother pulled with his strong gnarled hands and tore the thick stack of dirty old papers bound like a book in half. He stared at his brother with the other half of his disinterest as Mahmud handed him one half of the old crumbling book.

He held out his own dark gnarled hands in the air, and said to his older brother, "Thanks, but no thanks, Mahmud. I think it is time we headed for home."

Not wanting to waste even this worthless old book, Mahmud took off his turban fabric, wrapped the pieces of the old book and some other junk they'd found in it, and packed it away on his camel, and they headed home.

By the time they had ridden their worthy steeds all the way back home, it was getting dark and very cold with the approaching night time, and Mahmud had forgotten about the worthless old book he had torn in half and wrapped in his saddle bags, so he emptied his turban into the midden pile out with the animals in the yard.

A cold wind began to blow in from the south, and soon froze the ancient book laying there with the goats. A page fluttered in the wind, and an old goat grabbed the page and began to chew it. But he found the ancient pages too tough and tasteless for even him, and he spit it back out. The wife of the prudent younger brother tried in her frugality to use a couple of the old pages to start the fire. But the pages were reluctant to burn and gave off such a foul smell, that she gave up and threw it back outside with the goats. Where if froze and blew in the cold north wind.

A few days later the elder brother, Mahmud, with his capitalist nature, decided to make a trip into Luxor to make some trades. Just as he was leaving the courtyard, he spied the old torn book, amongst the gourd rinds and the goat nuggets, pages blowing in the breeze and he decided to take it with him to see if he could make a trade of some kind. Maybe he could get a piastres or two for it in the old antiqua dealers. And in this he was moderately successful, and he unloaded the dirty old thing for the price of an American watch for his father.

## Chapter 2
### A New City

**Present**

The Jacobs family landed in San Francisco on a foggy wet autumn afternoon. The big ship, The Happenstance Three, landed against the black wooden pier with a lurch as the ship's motors grew quiet. Her passengers were ready to disembark in no time as they were looking forward to solid land after some weeks at sea. Their journey north from the Isthmus of Panama was uneventful for the most part, which they were grateful for. But soon the fatigue of laying at sea began to set in. So the flashing lights and the clanger of the city was a strange and welcomed change.

They had been informed by radio of their destination, and their preparedness for their arrival. The secretary of the Happenstance Foundation assured them of a safe place to stay once they arrived in San Francisco. They had never seen the foundation's new home base, now that Aloeatious was no longer a man living. But they'd heard tales of the city of San Francisco and were excited to explore.

When they stepped off the ship Gwydion 's eyes were wide with wonder. He looked around himself at the bustling Pacific ocean port town of San Francisco and saw more than was there. He saw tall rigging ships swaying in the tide, but this must have been a trick of his imagination. Sailing ships were long gone except for several historical relics that were being maintained and used as tourist attractions. But once this place thronged with the sailing ships come round the southern tip of South America first with Magellan, and then with Cortez, who purportedly landed here and establish this, a port for the Queen of Spain. But then for some years this isolated peninsula of San Francisco languished, surrounded by natives who did not care for imports. But when the Panama Canal was built some 50 years before Gwydion's time, this port and the city swelled and flourished as the trading and delivery business flourished for the onslaught of the gold rush days of the 1850s.

But since then the city had modernized and become a fashion trendsetter and center of commerce on the West Coast of America. History Gwydion saw, what was once life here, 100 years ago. The history was deep, and Gwydion could feel it seeping into his bones along with the cold from the fog. When he looked around at the cars driving on pavement streets, he instead saw tall black narrow cabriolet with tall spoke wheels pulled by snorting horses wearing blinkers tossing leather harness. But the cars of today could wheel circles around the horse-drawn carts of yesteryear. And Gwydion saw it all at once as a clangor of information in his mind's eye.

In his teenage mind this layered complexity put him on a plane different from everyone else. It set him apart and gave him an appearance of dreaminess to others. It was often misunderstood to be aloofness or snobbery. But it was nothing of the sort. In fact usually he just felt confused and at a disadvantage to these other people he could tell did not doubt their reality, as he did.

"Ah, yes, this will be the way," Will Smithershins said loudly as he made his way towards a long black car parked against the curb. "They've sent a car round for us, as I knew they would." They all the small group began to make their way towards the shiny black car.

And Antony Jacobs looked over at Will Smithershins, with a wry glance, thinking to himself, "that guy seems to know too much sometimes." Will always seemed to Antony to be where he needed just when he needed to be. It almost seemed to him to be a prater-natural ability to predict what was going to happen. His head frightened Anthony at first when he'd encountered his old friend the former associate to Aloeatious Happenstance at the Foundation, when they met again this last summer at the anthropology gathering in southern Mexico. He seems to be just where Antony would've expected him to be if he just thought about it. And there he was at his side just when he needed him. And then again when Gwydion had gotten lost at the Temple site. And then here now, will seem to know just where to go.

Will glanced over at Anthony looking at him, and seemed to anticipate what the older man was thinking. And he said, "I have been here before remember. In fact I helped ol' Aloeatious set it all up for you."

Antony just stared at the younger man, then said, "Set what up?"

# Chapter 3
# Death Feud in al Tarif

**Egypt 1930's**
Mahmud's father was a loyal working man. Each night he served as night watchman for the small town of al-Qasr.

One night a cold evil wind blew through the small town, when Mahmud's father was on watch, and with it the wind brought an intruder with mal intent from the near-by village of Hamradum, the village at the foot of the cliffs where the ancient jar was found. Where the evil force had been released when they had broken the ceramic jar. And this breath of wind, this power of hatred and fear, had lodged itself in the breast of a young man who wandered into Mahmud's small town of al-Qasr late that night.

And when this intruder crept into the town streets late in the middle of the cold black night, Mahmud's father was faced with the dilemma of being loyal to his god and church and never taking another man's life, or of following orders and protecting the town and kill the intruder.

His need to keep his job to feed his family won out, so he shot the man and killed the intruder. But his loyalty was repaid quickly, and he was shot in the head a few nights later. It was vengeance of someone from the family of the man from the other village who he, Mahmud's father, had shot and killed. And such was unleashed a feud of vengeance that it made the pages of history. And Mahmud's mother, now widowed of her husband of forty years, told the brothers to keep their digging mattocks sharpened to a bright edge, for someday they would have the opportunity to avenge the murder of their father, her beloved husband.

And about six months later, Mahmud was to recall, six months after finding the jar near the cliffs of Jubal al-Tarif, near the small rival town of Humradum, that opportunity presented itself. The two brothers found the sleeping murderer of their father alongside the road late one evening. And with little hesitation, then and there, they wielded their heavy sharpened mattock, and slew the young man to bits. But revenge was not nearly enough for them, for fear and hatred had ripened in their hearts with time; they wanted complete humiliation. So they tore the young man's heart from his chest and shared it between them, consuming it then and there on the spot, with the cold wind blowing in their bloody beards.

And thus was unleashed a blood feud that passed with that dark cold wind between the two small towns on the banks of the Nile. Mahmud recalled much later both these events, that they were forever connected in his mind, the finding of the book in the old ceramic jar, and the revenge he was able to exact on his father's murderer.

But Mahmud in his passion for avenging family did not once connect the breaking of the jar, and the golden apparition he had released into the bright blue sky that day.

For what Jinn had he released? A Jinn, is there such a thing? An ancient idea of spirits captured in a bottle, then released inadvertently by some curious treasure seeker? Is such a thing possible? Or is it just an old tale of ancient warning, of evil spirits that travel from man to man, possessing them with blinding powers of fear, hatred, and revenge.

Or was the Jinn something very different, something Mahmud would never know of in his short life. Mahmud would not live much longer, not long enough to know that that old crumbling book that he sold for a few piastres held a Jinn far more powerful that just a man's hatred and fear shared between one another. For that old book was the first of what was to be found there at the base of the cliffs of Jubal al-Tarif in the black blood of the Nile. That crumbling old book would set off a wildfire of hunting for more jars and more manuscripts at the base of those cliffs. Because what the treasure hunters and anthropologists were to find there in the following years of hunting and digging would unleash powers of greed, hatred and fear, not for vengeance, but for the ownership of wisdom and beliefs.

For that old crumbling book would be the first to be found of what would soon be called the Treasure of the Nile, ancient Gnostic writings and scripture never before seen in 2000 years, the Nag Hammadi Library.

## Chapter 4
## Voices in His Head

**Present**

Far to the south another young man stared in disbelief around himself. He had headed south in a fog. 'Get away, get far from here', a voice had ranted in his head. So he had boarded a bus. And it had brought him here to a new country.

The city thronged with life. But around him voices spoke but he did not understand. He knew he had suffered a shock. But he was afraid more probably he simply did not speak the language. Maybe he was safe from what he had just done. But how was he going to get along not being able to speak the language.

He walked for a while and looked at his shoes striking the pavement. Litter and an occasional animal body part littered the sidewalk. What strange world had he just landed on?

He had traveled such a long way from home, with a group of students and professors, all to come to this other continent to study and learn from one another.

Ah, but the things he had learned were not in the syllabus. No this was his classroom of survival. Again. He thought to himself, I have to do this again. Survive where I was never meant to be.

He walked along and found a newspaper stand. He looked at the headlines. All indecipherable. He looked up at the stand keeper. It was an older woman. She stared him straight in the face. And then a smile broke over dirty cracked teeth. She tilted her head and said something in their indecipherable language. He just shrugged his shoulders and gave her a pitiful look. He decided to give it a try. And he asked her if she spoke English, in his halting strange accent. Her body wagged back and forth as she said, "Si, si. I speaka good Englesh. Si!"

And he smiled and laughed because he did actually understand her. On a whim he asked her, "Where is the University?"

"Ah, yes. Student." And she shook her hand free from her robes and pointed down the street and mumbled some directions about turning right and left, and he wasn't sure, but thought he could give it a try. So he thanked the gal and turned to head down the street and she stopped him with , "Wait!"

When he turned back she was holding a map of the city. He lifted his hands up, for he had no money. But she shook the map at him and smiled. A beguiling smile if he didn't know better. Even from this old woman. And he remembered, that even in his most disheveled state, he often had this effect on women. On men too actually. So he smiled at her daftness of not knowing what lay inside his heart, and grasped the paper map and said, "Gracias."  She gave him a quizzical look at him using her native language, but none the less nodded and watched him as his tall form strode off down the street.

## Chapter 5

## A Setup

"This was set up for us?" Asked Anthony..

And Will answered cautiously," Well, yes. The old man knew he was dying and he did not have children, not that he knew of anyway," Will said with a wink, "so his foundation had to go somewhere." Will turned towards the car and opened the back door for the Jacobs family. And as he helped Anthony in last he said under his breath "I think you'll like it here. There is much more here than meets the eye. He will find the happenstance historical foundation quite accommodating to you and your family."

Will gently shut the door step forward a couple steps and opened the passenger door in the front and slipped inside next to the uniform driver. It seemed a strange formality to Antony, who had never known opulence or luxury in his life. This car and driver seemed almost a parody of something he would never have expected, except perhaps in an old movie. But he settled back in the seat and placed his warm hand on his wife's cold one, and looked at her as she looked back at him with mild surprise. The children, Mags and Gwydion were enthralled with the city passing them by as the car drove through town.

After a few moments, the window between the driver's compartment in the passenger area slid open with a snap. And Will Smithershins craned his head around and said into the back compartment, "are we going to dinner?"

The two children cried out in unison, "yeah!" The two adults in the back however groaned a little and said, "are we?"

"Well, why not," asked will rhetorically. "It's on the foundation anyway. So in San Francisco, I suggest seafood. Martin?" Said will looking at the driver, "how about Pier 45."

"Yes, sir," said Martin the driver in a flat voice. In the small group drove for a few more minutes and parked along the edge of the bay at one of the dark wooden piers jutting out into the dark water.

Lights were strung along the boardwalk between the piers bustling with people about their evening in the settling darkness. Visibility was hampered by the increasing strength of the famous San Francisco fog, and on occasion a fog horn could be heard, often from various directions. The clanging of belled buoys rocking unseen somewhere in the shrouded waters mingled with the cries of seagulls wheeling overhead. The smell of the ocean mingled with and complemented the smells emanating from kitchens cooking their evening fair. Ah, seafood being prepared in a bay-side restaurant. Not that they hadn't had any on their trip north in the yacht. But somehow seafood eaten while on solid land seem different.

They selected a small restaurant with bright lights small tables and steam clouding the corners of the windows. They chose a small table in the corner for the five of them, Martin was waiting in the car. And sat down to a basket of steaming sourdough French bread wrapped in white linen set before them.

They ordered and tucked into their food before any of them said much of anything. As fatigue began to dissolve with warm food some white wine and a cup of coffee, they began to chat wondering of their adventures to come. The children wanted to know where they were going, where they would be staying. And Will assured them that they would enjoy the lodging the foundation was providing for them. Antony had understood he would be working for the foundation, but had not been given specific information as to what they would be researching. In affiliation with a local university, Will assured them there was a teaching position available for him, and Mags too if she wished. There was a local high school that Gwydion would be attending, and he groaned and rolled his eyes at the thought.

"Now I know Gwydion, that you have some difficulties in your last school. But I assure you San Francisco be different for you. You'll see," Will assured him.

Gwydion just looked at him then looked down at his food without saying a thing.

## Chapter 6
## The House

Will Smithershins paid the bill with the company card and the small family ventured out of the restaurant and down the boardwalk back toward the car. The black night had deepened and seemed to fade into gray in the distance as if the night had vanquished the fog and only where the lights of the city penetrated was space.

They embarked into the black sedan and headed on their way towards parts unknown. Only Will was privy to that knowledge, and there was no way for him to prepare the family for what they would find when they arrived on Beacon Hill. Only when they got there and began to sum up what their new life had in store for them with this tension inside Will subside. Perhaps that was so, he chided himself, perhaps not. This tension for this project might never subside. And even if he were allowed to divulge that information just yet, honestly he probably wouldn't know where to start. He would not have known where to start on this long tale, even if he were the teller of the story, and not me.

But that information, the reader cannot know yet. And I, the narrator of the story in the far future, will remain a secret fathomable only by those infinitely capable of dissecting a mystery before it's time.

But all in due time, as in all happanstance history, shalt mystery be revealed.

Through the city they wound in their comfy quiet ride, surrounded by lights and tumult of the city that rarely slept. The city was not asked sleepless as the one they had come to know on the other side of the continent. But close.

In the city seem to have a greater mystique. Mystery hanging in the fog between streetlights. In the street at beckon the soul to wonder at new depths never before imagined. The mystery that beckoned to the soul of Young Gwydion, his mind just emerging from the slumber of childhood into the tumultuous hormonal years of teenage. And as they drove through town he pressed his nose against the cold glass occasionally wiping away the steam from his breath so that he could look out across the street and into the Windows were other people dwelt. Strangers he could only in the lights of their home going about their evening activities. He wonder if they wondered what life was like outside the glass of their Windows the solidity of their walls. He saw them comfortably enclosed and wondered if they knew the un-moorings he knew, of travel, of the change of space, of something of the confusion he felt at the actions of others. He assumed they felt as he did similarly confused and disoriented at all of the mystery. It would not be until many years later he would come to understand just how different his perceptions were.

They drove through winding streets some lined with old Victorian buildings and some lined with new skyscrapers disappearing up into the fog. They crossed market Street and to the right was a tall thin building shaped like a tall slice of cake with Windows like different layers of frosting. As they drove people flashed by his window and stared back at him with ghoulish smeared faces in the fog, and Gwydion wondered if he was seeing things. Things past or future that haunted these busy streets were past present and future seemed to meld and coexist.

"Oh look at that," his mother kept saying. "Oh, look at

that Gwydion," she would say every few minutes. And he would look and see nothing but the normal people or cars. He wondered that she did not see what he did the fog and the lights played tricks with their faces, the horses and their narrow spoke wheel Cabriolet's snorting in the fog. A horn blared and he was jolted back to the present as the black sedan swerved to miss a yellow taxi running a red light.

"Are we almost there?" He said plaintively.

"That's a nickel," said his grandfather. Gwydion groaned. Such a dumb game. He never had any money anyway. But he tried to staunch his automatic tendency to ask if they were there yet. It was something he knew he had to grow out of knew that he was a teenager and going to high school. Things are going to be different. He could feel it in his stretching bones. He shook his forelock over his eyes, shrugged his shoulders, and blew a puff of air from between his lips. Will turned and looked at him and said, "Yes actually. Almost there".

The streets took turns in the family knew they'd need a map to go anywhere the next day. Food and exhaustion had softened their memories. And no way on these convoluted streets would they ever find their way to anywhere without a map.

They turned onto a small street going crosswise on the hill above town. Gwydion noticed street sign, "Alexandra," it said. And he thought how interestingly Egyptian that was.

The long black sedan pulled to the curb and stopped. And will couldn't help himself but then down and look out the drivers window and say, "and there it is. Your new home in San Francisco." Everybody turned and looked out the side window across the street to a huge Victorian pile.

"Wow. What a beaut," said Antony.

"Oh my. That's lovely," said Bethany. "That will do just fine," she said as she took in the many high narrow Windows framed with lace curtains, the shingled sides reaching up to a third floor and several pointed cabled roof. Mags let out a squeal of glee and reached across Gwydion and popped open the car door, and gently hurried him out, without waiting for the driver to open the door for them.

They stood in the street and looked up at the mansion the windows lit brightly in the dark of night. "Wow," said Mags.

"Let's get our stuff mom," said Gwydion impatiently.

Martin popped the trunk and the family gathered around to pull out their travel belongings.

They carried everything across the street and waited for Will to unlock the front door. Inside was a vestibule lined with rock slabs. Several well tended plants grew in china pots on the floor and stone shelves. And a steep set of stone stairs lead up to what would be the first floor. They waited at the top for Will to squeeze by and unlock that door too. He opened it and the family stepped into their new home.

"Oh, look. There's upstairs, too!" Cried mags excitedly.

"The upstairs is closed off." Said Will. She looked at him with disappointment. "I know. But sorry. It's just full of junk and dust. And we haven't had time to clean it out. So it's off-limits for now."

"But I still get dibs on the bedrooms!" cried Mags as the thumped down the hall.

"Actually I think we do," said Bethany about her and her husband. And she glanced at Antony who winked. There were many rooms in this rather unoccupied old Victorian. "so many rooms, " said Bethany quietly.

"This place has been largely unoccupied for many a year," said Will. "Aloeatious got it for a steal. Seems there were some rumors of haunting or something. I've never seen anything amiss myself. But then again I'm not much a superstitious kind of guy. Ghosts and such." He turned and shrugged his shoulders at Antony and Bethany. And Antony chortled. Bethany was too busy looking at the rooms to notice what he had said. She chose the largest, the one with the biggest bed and the huge windows facing the city to the north, which beamed with bright glow through the fog and the night. She plunked down her bags and turned to will and her husband. "This is really something," she said to them in a hushed voice, almost reverently. "What a change from Egypt. that was like a cookie box in comparison."

Will just smiled and said, "Glad you like it; Aloeatious would be happy. Rest his soul in peace," he added in a quiet voice.

Antony just smiled and beamed at his wife, perhaps hoping to pick up some of the credit for this advancement in their quality of life. And he accepted gratefully her tight hug and kiss on the cheek. Couldn't be better.

## Chapter 7
## New Jobs

In the morning the all met in the kitchen. After years of living in the cramped apartment in Cairo, they had learned to synchronize their sleep and wake patterns. and the family always seemed to wake up at the same time to start their day. Will was cooking breakfast. making eggs and toast for everyone. "we have a long day ahead of us today." he said to the small group around the table.

"What are we doing? I thought we would be sleeping in. taking in some sights." said Mags.

Outside the fog was just beginning to burn off. The light of day was bright but still you couldn't see much past the street outside. But you could tell it was clearing and would be a clear day.

"We are going to the university to start things with the foundation. School starts in 2 weeks and we need to get a head start."

Gwydion yawned and stretched and said in his sleepy morning voice, "It would have been better if you guys hadn't been running down the hall all night."

Everyone just looked at him with wide eyes. He realized his mistake and said quickly "Just kidding." Then he put his head down and started in on some eggs.

"Well I don't know about yo all, but I slept like a rock," said Bethany to the group.

"Ya, me too," said Antony as he picked up his steaming coffee cup and then slurped down some of the dark brew.

"i didn't hear anything last night, Gwydion," jabbed his mother. "More of your dreams I suppose."

"They're not dreams," he shouted at them., them looked back down at his plate.

Mags just groaned and rolled her eyes. She had heard all kinds of weird stories from Gwydion through the years. and she'd learned to take them all with a grain of salt.

"There's no one else in this house, Gwydion. But its old. You must have just heard the floor boards creaking, that's all." said Will knowledgeably.

"Ya, sure. whatever. I didn't hear anything." Gwydion was getting surly in his teenage years and he didn't care so much what they thought anymore. Or he tried to think that anyway. He was trying to learn to say what they expected him to say so they wouldn't bug him about stuff. But he never knew which stuff they would believe and which they wouldn't, although it all seemed real to him, so it was still hit or miss .

"We are going to go drive out to the university and get things rolling," he said to his captive audience. Gwydion rolled his eyes and flipped his hair to the side. Will looked at him for a moment and said, "You, Gwydion, start high school next Monday. Are you ready?"

Gwydion did not have any idea what he was talking about so he shrugged his shoulders and looked at his fork. "We'll drive by there today and have a look so you know where it is. There's a bus that will take you straight there."

"A school bus?" asked Antony.

"No. A city bus. Lots of mass transit around here. Bus or rail line right by the high school. Pretty cool."

Gwydion shrugged again and acted like he didn't really care. But inside he was excited that he was going to have the freedom to move around and do things on his own. And in an American city, where everybody looked like him and spoke like him. what a change from Egypt that would be. Or Mexico where he had not spoken any of the language at all.

They piled dishes in the sink and got packed to head out. Will cleaned up the food and dishes while they went and got ready. Gwydion closed his door and changed his clothes again for the third time that morning. he was more nervous than anyone realized. He had awoken several times in the night to noises or what he thought where noises upstairs in the old house. Maybe it was creaking of the floor boards. But in his sleepy mind last night it had been much more. Not that he would tell any of them though.

As they got back in the car, the fog had begun to really clear and they could see that this house was high up on the side of the hill. there were other Victorian houses surrounding this one. But this one was larger and more ornate than the others. And it was purple, something they couldn't see in the gloom of the night before when they had arrived. And as they headed down the hill, they could see the city sweeping out before them, with patches of water and the bay peeping in between hills.

They drove through town in the long black sedan and Gwydion rolled down the window and breathed in the fresh air. It wasn't as salty flavored here as it had been the night before when they had dinner. But that was right on the wharf. Here it wasn't so strong.

But as they drove, it began to get salty tasting again. They were getting nearer to the ocean again on this drive. And after a few moments, they came over a rise, and there it was. The dark blue Pacific stretched out before them again. After months on the sea, and one night on land, Gwydion had not missed the presence of the sea and it seemed now a stranger to him. He closed his eyes and breathed deeply and heard the call of some seagulls overhead.

They wound down the coast a ways and then turned abruptly inland to the left. Up they drove into a cleft in the steep hills and found the university nestled there in tall dark green trees. Martin parked the long sedan and Will leaned over and said something to him, and Martin answered, "Yes, sir." quietly. Antony saw the subtlety of this and wondered if there was more to the simple seeming relationship of driver and boss. How much does one know about the nature of one's bosses business? Sometimes maybe it's a fine thing to not know too much. Even simple anthropology has its secrets. And Antony had been involved in enough controversy for anyone's one lifetime. He envied Martin's simple imperatives; Park here, wait such and such, simple things.

The Institute was small but beautiful. The red brick buildings were not old, yet the copper roofing had earned its classic verdigris drippings within its short life time. There was, Antony noticed, a wrought iron fence that surrounded the entire institution which had pointed finials all along the top. Perhaps decoration, perhaps protection. But in all Antony gathered that this was probably more privately funded than not. And he wondered how much exactly was provided by the Happenstance of Historical Foundation.

The group was taken into the front room and introduced to Prudence the secretary and principal Mr. Hillard that presided in a side office that adjoined. Anthony was impressed by their cordiality and their seeming happiness that they had arrived safe and sound from their journey. Will then led them down along carpeted hall into the rooms towards the back. One of the rooms had lettering already installed on the pebbled glass window that said Dr. Antony Jacobs. And will grasp the brass doorknob turned it and opened the door for them to enter.

What a nice room, thought Antony right away. Mags skipped into the room and flopped herself down onto the sickly padded dark leather armchair. There were dark wooden bookcases on the shelves holding all manner of anthropological texts in scientific journals. Gwydion strode in and sat down on the other padded armchair, while Antony walked around in awe to the heavy wood desk with a black leather rolling office chair behind it, and sat down with a squeak. His wife Bethany stood opposite him and beamed.

"New chair," he said casually. But inside he was thrilled to have such nice digs. He looked across the room and saw a stack of old boxes and crates that he recognized. Will watched his gaze and said, "Oh, yes. This just came in from Egypt. All your stuff you left behind in a hurry. All here and accounted for."

"Well, thank you, Will did you arrange all that?" Said Antony. "I suspect you did. I figured it was lost to time when we left in such a hurry." He thought about his former colleague that had died while they were in Cairo at the university there. Under mysterious circumstances, it had actually been deemed a murder, although the details had remained largely undisclosed. He had whisked his family away quickly when things had gotten intense, and hadn't learned of the murder until after they had reached New York, after their stop in England to attend the service of the just-passed Aloeatious Happenstance, Antony's colleague and mentor. That was a tough period for the Jacobs family. And the memory of it occasionally surfaced violently and unexpectedly on Antony. Like now, seeing those simple beat-up boxes of his old office stuff. He wondered at the old manuscripts he had been translating back in Egypt. He wondered how much of that was still hidden in those boxes. He had taken the most important infrared photographs of the ancient documents with him when he fled. But he knew when he opened those boxes ghosts of memories would come flooding back to him.

"I think I'll wait a little while to get to those boxes, Will. They could wait another day."

"Yes, they can. In fact today we have a conference call scheduled. In about an hour," said Will. "So let's take a tour," he addressed everyone in the room.

They went back outside the room and down the hall and out the back into an open courtyard of red brick surrounded by landscaped plants. The air is fresh and bracing so near the coast here and Antony knew he would enjoy working here has a fresh change from the harsh climate of Egypt. He hoped he'd be here for quite a while.

Will led them across the courtyard and pointed off to the right and said, "That there Gwydion is the library." And Gwydion's eyes lit up, he gave a small quirk of his mouth and walked in that general direction and push through the solid wood doors to the sound of Will saying, "we'll come get you when were done." Gwydion didn't even glance back.

Mags chuckled; she understood her sons love of libraries and books and the solitude they entitled. "What about me?" She asked out loud.

"How about the children's room?" Said Will.

"There's a kindergarten?" Mags asked with wonder.

"Yep. All the young children of the teachers and staff attend here instead of public school, if they wish. Most do. It was Aloeatious' wish that all children be treated to a rich education afforded usually only to wealthy children. He found they responded well, unexpectedly well."

Mags looked at him with almost tears in her eyes. But didn't say a thing. Will looked at her for a moment, then turned and they walked in the other direction toward the sound of children's voices. He opened the door to the children's room and all heads turned towards them. "Mrs. Fredrickson," he directed towards the teacher at the head of the room. "I'd like to introduce to you the Jacobs family. And Margaret here, would love to help with the children."

Mrs. Fredrick beamed and said, "I've heard so much about you. Glad you came."

"Oh, call me Mags, please."

"Mags, nice to have you aboard. Have a seat, we are reading the Iliad." And with that she turned back towards the class of children and began reading from the thick book she held in her hands again.

The three adults turned and exited from the room. They headed across the causeway again to another room which when they entered it became apparent was the cafeteria. "Let sit a moment then I'll explain some things to you," said Will.

Chapter 8
The Superintendent

The three of them selected a table in the mostly empty room. As in most cafeterias, the sounds echoed off clean hard walls. The scuff of a chair could be heard clearly across the room. But in this one there was a difference. The colors were warm and there was art on the walls. Made it a little more homey, to Antony's eyes anyway.

"Would you like something to eat or drink?" Asked Will of his two guests.

"I think I'm too excited to eat anything," said Bethany.

"Why don't I get you some coffee honey," said Antony to his wife.

"Maybe some decaffeinated tea, with honey and milk, perhaps might settle my stomach," she answered. She grasped her hands in her lap and shrugged her shoulders and smiled it will. "This is also beautiful and exciting," she said.

"I'm glad you're happy with it. Some of this was prepared for you," said will.

"Yeah, I could tell by the lettering on the door. That was very welcoming," said Antony.

"We are all glad to have you here." He walked over to the coffee bar and poured himself some coffee and Antony made himself and his wife each a big mug of Earl Grey tea with honey and milk. "That ought to do it," said Antony to will, and they turned and walked back to the table and joined Bethany again.

After a few moments of silence while they enjoyed their hot beverages they both looked up at Will with expectation in their faces.

"Ya, this is a lot isn't it?" said Will. "We set this up pretty fast, Aloeatious and I, and a few others. It was always his dream to have this kind of an educational facility. And I don't think his mortality ever set in and to the last minute, when he was dying."

"Ya, he went too fast for my comfort," said Antony.

"Actually, he knew he was dying for a really long time. He just didn't tell anybody. So although the Happenstance Historical Foundation might be only a few years old, this brick-and-mortar institution is about 10 years old. They have been working on this for a while."

"They?" Antony has caught that word use.

"Yes, there are a few of us involved in this project. One of them you can meet in a few moments. By phone anyway. She's one of Aloeatious' more ...." and here Will hesitated just briefly, Antony noticed, "reclusive Associates. I've only met her a couple times. She is a little different. The positively brilliant. A real guiding light for this institution."

"That sounds fascinating," said Bethany over steaming mug of tea.

"She thinks it's important that you be there to Bethany," said Will. "So important to history. Husbands and wives. Families"

"Well, thank you. I feel honored to be a part of this project," she shrugged her shoulders and giggled. "Whatever it is." She felt the importance of this undertaking although she didn't quite know why. But she wanted to respect the seriousness of it and felt that something astounding was about to be revealed to them. So she just looked at Will, the slightly younger man, about the age of her daughter Mags actually, and felt pride in curiosity for the importance he seemed to serve.

"Does this 'she' have a name?" Asked Anthony.

"We call her Azra."

They finish their drinks, stood up and headed back to Antony's plush office. Will picked up the phone punched the button and spoke quietly into the receiver. He replace this is receiver in the cradle and looked at his guests. Who were no longer guests really. This was now Antony's office, and technically, Will was now the guest. That made him smile. He felt satisfied that having brought his quarry here successfully. Now for the strange part.

In a few moments the phone rang. Will picked it up listened and then spoke quietly. He punched a button on the front of the phone and set the receiver back in the cradle. And a voice came over the speaker.

"Hello? Is Antony and Bethany there?" Said a soft but succinct voice that sounded neither male nor female.

"Yes, this is Antony."

"I'm here too, this is Bethany."

"A pleasure to meet you, Anthony and Bethany. You can call me Azra. I have other names but that's the easiest. I'm glad you're here; I've heard a great deal about you. "

"We are glad to be here, too," said Antony into the air above the phone, hoping his voice was carrying. The speakerphone was a new gadget to him. He'd never used one before. They had no such thing in Egypt. But modern marvels were all the rage. If not confusing. It made him feel like an old man, but he was trying.

"Yes, thank you for having us," said Bethany. "We would like to be involved in whatever we can do for you."

"For me, no," said the voice. "For us, this is a project for all. Aloeatious Happenstance has given me discharge to develop new ways to enrich human life. We saw in his last days is frailty and he wanted to ensure that there was a continuance of effort. I accepted the challenge and would like for you to join me on this journey." There was a brief silence. And then the voice continued.

"Is your son there?" she asked.

"Gwydion?" Bethany asked stupidly.

"Is he with you there now?"

"No, he's in the library. His favorite place," answered Antony.

"Well, we are glad to have him aboard too," said the voice on the speaker phone.

"Well, he'll be going to high school at the local public school," said Bethany informatively.

"Yes, that's fine. That's great. It will be a normalizing experience for him."

"He's had problems before in public schools. He's... different, you know," informing the person behind this voice as if she would not know this about her son.

"Different, but special," said Azra on the speaker phone. But Bethany didn't take umbrage to it this time, she took this to be a comfort, not pitying condescension like she usually got from the school administrators about her grand son. And as if sensing Bethany's train of thought, Azra said, "Yes, we think he's very special. He has unusual talents others don't."

"Talents?" asked Antony. He'd never heard anyone say that before. although he had often thought it himself .

"Yes. Talents. A special insight. He learns really quickly doesn't he?" she asked his grandparents.

"Yes, he learns scary fast sometimes. But he's not great with communicating with words." Said his grandfather.

"We are not unfamiliar with this type of learning. But it seems to be special or unusual with humans, uh, people for the most part. You see , we've come to believe that children are born open to more levels of reality and consciousness then were previously thought, uh, understood. And as they grow into young people a part of their brain that receives information from what is sometimes called the collective consciousness, that part of the brain begins to shut down as the child assimilates into the strictures of society. But with some children this doesn't happen. A rare few maintain the "open doors" as we call them, to the messages from the greater planetary good, as we like to call it. But sometimes this makes them appear strange, mal-adjusted, social outcasts, even."

Picking up on her distanced word usage, Antony asked

somewhat defensively, "Is he going to be a part of some study of yours?"

"No. Nothing is specific as that. It's just, these traits, talents, fall among family lines."

"We don't believe in that spiritual mumbo-jumbo," said Bethany skeptically.

"I'm a scientist, and I rely on hard fact," said Antony.

"Oh," said Azra. "Of course you do." She waited a beat for them to feel that she was considering what they had just said. Then she continued.

"But how can these, as you call "spiritual", aspects of human experience become facts if we don't study them?"

She left it hanging at that for a moment for these people who she knew were intelligent, but who were also defensive, having just been brought into this completely new situation and whose outcast grandson they were talking about. Then continued, "And we are very happy to have your family with the Happenstance Historical Foundation. Very happy, welcome, Jacobs family."

Antony and Bethany looked at each other and then looked at Will's blank face and raise their eyebrows. Will just shrugged nonchalance.

"And that brings us to our next project. Now, Antony, I know you and your family have traveled the world to many different locations, and you've encountered various obstacles and controversy in your studies. But we think you're strength in dealing with adversary makes you the perfect person to direct our hyper human studies." There was a break in her narration as she let these ideas settle on her small audience. Then she continued, "Next summer there is a conference in Italy we will be attending. It will be on the anthropological archaeological findings in the Nile Delta. We think that within these ancient scriptures is evidence for the transmutation of the human soul into energy. It's a new study of the human mind, and it encompasses the human spirit, religion, alchemy... All of the things we've been studying up to now, with the new ideas of space travel and teleportation, and demonology thrown in for good measure. "

This was almost too much for Antony. He was old-school anthropologist, and sometimes wondered how he had even gotten into the field of the translating of ancient scriptures. He was told it was because he was unusually adept at translating languages, and was not an expert in any one field, which usually hindered scholars when they entered the area of biblical translations.

But this talk of demonology and space travel. This kind of talk usually turned him into and ice cube. He wasn't sure any of this stuff was real. They were beginning to call this "supernatural phenomena". And most didn't even consider it a science.

But then again he wasn't ready to poo-poo this stuff yet either.

"So, how does this involve me? I'm just an anthropologist."

"Actually it involves the translations that have recently been uncovered, some of which you have been working on already. I understand you still have some of them in your possession, from your time in Egypt."

Antony wondered if that was vaguely a threat. Like maybe she thought he had stolen them. Or left the country illegally with the ancient transcriptions in his possession. But he had never been contacted by anyone in that regard. And it didn't seem like she was accusing him now. Maybe she regarded his possession of those certain transcripts as an advantage over other institutions that were trying to get an edge on publishing translations of important ancient scriptures.

And maybe that was partly why he was here. This Azra saw him as an asset to her institution.

But he still didn't think there was any of that sort of information in any of those stories he had possession of in his file or briefcase. He didn't know how it related to her fields at all.

"But still, that all sounds like spiritualism, or supernatural studies," he said. "They are calling it "Supernatural Phenomena" I think. That is an unrelated field of study."

"You wont think so after ….but, well, I get ahead of myself. There are some artifacts that have not been released to the public yet. And Aloeatious was very excited to start publishing. But anyway. It stands to be quite fascinating, as I'm sure you understand. The five of you will attend the nine day progress of this convention next June, after the high school year for your son Gwydion ends."

Antony and Bethany sat looking at each other. Despite his arguments, they realized they were being given a new anthropology linguistics project. Which meant full time work and housing.

And another travel journey. Which meant more travel. And they weren't sure how they felt about that, after their recent return, umm, flight, from Egypt.

"You will think about this among yourselves. But I am sure minds like yours will find the idea enticing." There was a shuffling sound over the intercom and they became aware that their conference call was coming to a close. They hadn't given their acceptance of the project yet. But all parties could see that it was something that they simply could not refuse.

"We will be expecting papers published by the both of you, Doctors, either together or separately. And Bethany, you are encouraged to contribute as well. In fact , your son Gwydion shall be encouraged to begin his paper writing career also."

Now Antony and Bethany really blinked at each other, as Will sat and watched their surprise. They were not used to this sort of language from anybody really. Educators usually had their way of speaking eloquently about their dreams for enriching mankind. And no one had ever flattered them, surprised them, with talk of Gwydion contributing.

But no, something about this voice was more than the

usual enthusiastic administrator. Richer and less strident. Concerned but less strained. They felt soothed and carried by this voice and were speechless, incapable of adding any thing coherent to the discussion. And they were grateful to have a new direction, to be wanted on an interesting new project.

So they just said thank you.

"With time, more of the professor Happenstance program will be revealed. But for now this is probably enough. I'm sure you are tired from your journeys. Thank you."

With that, the line clicked and a dial tone sounded a solid buzz. Will reached forward and punched off the intercom button. Antony and Bethany just looked at him. He smiled a wan smile and shrugged his shoulders slightly. "Like I said, enigmatic, reclusive."

"No, that was great." said Antony. "I like looking forward to another trip abroad."

"We just got here," said Bethany quietly.

"Look, it's September. That's not till late June next year. We'll get settled and have a good school year. And that will be our vacation next summer. Imagine, Italy," said Will.

Antony and Bethany just nodded. But inside they were just beginning to bubble with the excitement of their new lives.

After the three of them had refreshed themselves and grabbed a quick drink in the cafeteria, they walked over to the library to retrieve Gwydion. They found him sitting on the stairs leading to the reading loft of the library, the sun streaming in through the indoor ficus trees that reached up against the windows. He looked up from some thick old book and saw his grandparents approaching, and wondered at the glowing looks on their faces.

"Come, Gwydion. Let's fetch your mother and will be on our way home."

Gwydion looked at his grandfather and smiled, and knew his grandfather would not forget that they needed to stop by his new high school, so he didn't mention it.

They walked back outside and across the courtyard and entered into the children's day room. Again all eyes turned towards them as they opened the door, and Dr. Fredrickson laid her thick book down and smiled at them.

"I suppose you've come to reclaim your daughter now. She has been wonderful; thank you for lending her to me for a time. I hope she can return on a more permanent basis, professor Jacobs. Bethany."

Mags beamed like a child herself. "Oh, I'd love to come back. Can I come back and help?" She asked enthusiastically.

"In fact, I think something might be able to be arranged with principal Hillard, if we ask nice," answered Dr. Fredrickson.

Mags just beamed and followed her family out the door.

She put her hand on Gwydion's head gently tousled his hair. He bent away from her touch, he was getting too old for that stuff, but couldn't help himself from giggling.

The black sedan gradually turned inland and made its way back towards the city. The way was unknown to them the city being new to them and all, and only noticed that they were stopping somewhere new when they pulled alongside the curb and saw the brick institution that would be Gwydion's new high school. His eyes your wide as he saw the teenagers his age caring book bags and coffee cups, and chatting together in pairs or clusters in the school choir. He felt fluttering in his chest that was part mingled fear and apprehension, and excitement at what this place held for him. Nobody said anything for a few minutes as the car quietly hummed and they sat and watched the high school campus life.

Then Will said, "you'll start school on Monday. I'll show you the bus route when I get back to the Institute house."

Another young man had found himself in a new school too. Only this one far far south of where Gwydion was. And he realized when he found it and walked up its great steps that perhaps from American standards, this was as much a school as a church. The stained glass windows told the story. He recognized the angels and the Christ, with his halo and white robes. He recognized the lines of benches and the black books and the small shelves on the back of each wood bench.

The young man walked up to the front of the church, just before the steps and the alter that he knew were the area of the priest. This was not so different, he thought, than his place of worship back home. He had been told that the white devils practiced witchcraft and bloodletting and that he would never go into one of their damned churches.

But here now he didn't see any of that. In fact it really looked quite the same as from what he remembered from as a boy the few times he went to a mosque back home. And in Egypt too when he was studying there, he had visited a church with his patron there and had felt relieved that it was not all that different from what he was used to. Not that he went to church mosque very often when he was young. But his mother had taught him the importance of piety, of careful living and speech. And to read the Koran. Here they called it the Bible. But when he had read some way through it, it seemed really quite similar, except that there were strange language affectations in the western book.

He bowed his head and mumbled a prayer for thanks that he had arrived here safely, when he heard steps next to him. The priest must have realized that he was not a regular student. He was here alone at an odd time of the evening, when no one else was around.

The priest said something to him in their unfamiliar tongue, and tears sprang to the boys eyes. He was so tired and so fatigued that he wasn't sure if he could even explain what he was doing here. And the priest's kind words, even if he couldn't understand what he was saying, brought forth the strangest passion of relief in the boy's chest, that he wept with silent wet sobs.

The priest reached forward and touched this child on the shoulder, and said something again in his soothing voice.

The young boy sniffed and said in crackling voice, "English."

"Oh, my," said the priest quietly. "May I help you, young man?" said the priest as he stood behind the praying boy. "Are you lost?"

"Bless me father for I have sinned," he said instinctively.

"Oh, no, young man. You are not in confessional. although we can do that if you like. I can have someone..." And the young man turned toward the priest. He stood up and faced the older man, who gasped and took a step back.

"I'm sorry. I didn't mean to intrude," said the young man. He thought quickly with a story. "I am traveling and was trying to find the university. I want to study but my parents reject your faith..."

The priest was mute for a moment. Then collected his thoughts and said, "Oh. Do I know you from somewhere?" he asked as he looked stridently into the young man's face.

## Chapter 9
## High School

Gwydion found himself in the cafeteria. It was lunch time and he had just sat himself down at a long white table with a bunch of other kids. He didn't know anyone. But it was clear that some of these kids knew each other. They sat yelling and gesturing at each other. The noise was terrible. But in the Gwydion found a solace; he had anonymity. In fact no one was even looking at him.

He saw kids of all shapes and sizes and different ethnic background. He felt comfortable in the tumult that was freshman high school group mentality. He had never had that before. No one was paying him any attention.

He looked around the area where he sat and realized that someone was looking at him. and suddenly he felt the cold grip of fear. Someone was watching him. A girl over on the other side of the table. she was pretending to eat out of her tray of food, but she was facing right at him and he could feel her eyes on him as he ate. Or tried to eat ; his stomach was turning into a knot of fear.

What could she want with him? Who was she? Did he know her from somewhere else?

He kept his eyes down and tried to finish his lasagna. But his eyes darted to her between bites. She had dark hair and dark eyes. And she was wearing a purple dress and had a black hat on her head. and her face. Her face was dark, like there were dark circles around her eyes. Like she was sick. and her mouth was red. He thought maybe she painted that color with lipstick like his grandmother wore.

He looked back down to find he had eaten everything. He hadn't noticed he'd done that. He slammed down the last of the tepid, stinking milk, set the empty carton down on his tray and began to stand up to return it to the lunch counter. But he found his lags weren't working so well. He was terribly conscious of the movement his legs made. Each step felt like his legs were turning inside out and his feet weren't hitting the floor right. What was wrong with him?

He walked stiffly to the counter, set his tray down and turned to walk out. Then he noticed the purple girl was staring at him. Oh, god, what now? he thought to himself. Just keep walking in a straight line, and out the door.

When he reached the door frame and stepped out into the sun, his legs began to function correctly and he walked down the side walk. He stopped and pulled out the worn piece of paper that was his schedule and the campus map and studied where his next class was. Down the steps to the right then into the building and the first door on the left. got it.

He strode forward and ignored the people around him. They seemed to be ignoring him too. such quiet. Kids in their own tumult were so much quieter than adults always trying to peer into your soul, always wanting to know what was going on inside your head. The peace and quiet of peers; he had never known that. At the university in Cairo, he had been mostly with students that were quite a bit older than himself. Mostly college students and some of them quite a bit older than him. At first then he hadn't noticed them, but soon he had begun to feel a pressure growing inside his head, with these more adult students always looking at him and always studying his movements. This was a relief to be surrounded by kids his own age. Kids who looked like him, Americans he guessed, although there were all kinds of kids here. They all seemed happy. And no one seemed to be following him, No one seemed to be mad at him. It had seemed constant back in Egypt. there was that one kid who had followed him. and Gwydion had never known why. And it had gotten worse.

Gwydion reached the door to the room and stopped thinking about that. It was something he thought about at night when he was alone. In fact he still had nightmares about that boy, the boy with the crossed eyes. Nightmares, banging noises, clutching at his coat, running, slipping, falling, and he would always wake up. Sweating.

But here the art room opened up before him. The smell of paint assaulted his nose and the noise chanced from outside. There was a murmur of soft voices and the tip tap sound of tools being used in an art room. He chose a stool at the back of the room and waited for the teacher to lecture. But that never materialized. The teacher walked over to him, and for a moment he thought he was in trouble, and his heart began to pound. But the teacher asked him his name and then explained the assignment. Draw or paint on the easel a scene from summer vacation. That was it.

He looked at the easel dumbfounded. What was he supposed to do? He looked around at the other student sin the room and became aware that they were all pretty busy doing their projects. So he set his backpack under the stool and sat looking at the paper on the easel.

Just then the door behind him opened and in walked, guess who, the girl in the purple dress. He looked abruptly away and studied his paper and picked up a paintbrush. She walked past him and chose an easel to the side and slapped her backpack underneath the stool and began to move tools around. She seemed to know what she was doing, as Gwydion watched her furtively. Then all of a sudden she turned right toward him and gave a tiny smile. and he quickly looked away. Maybe she didn't notice he had been looking eight at her. He felt a burning in his chest and a tingling in his fingers. What was with her? he thought to himself and he fiddled with his tools. How can she know about him? what had she heard?

In his confusion he started painting and soon found his paper covered with a rough sketch of the three pyramids of Giza.

After a while he looked up from his work. He had failed to notice that some people were standing behind him, watching him work. "That is so cool." "Where'd you get that idea?" said another. Gwydion felt his face turn hot as he bent down a little more to hide.

The teacher stepped over and asked, "Have you been there?" And Gwydion just nodded his head a little, then he flipped his hair back out of his eyes. He noticed a pair of combat boots step over and stop right near his easel. it was the girl in the purple dress. Now he could barely breathe. His hand jerked and he made a black smear on the page. But no one noticed but him and kids oohed and ahhed at his painting. They soon went back to their own smudgy paintings for a while and then the bell rang. "I will let these dry and put them in back for next time. Be sure to put your name on them at the bottom, folks, so we know whose is whose!" said the teacher loudly as the noise level tripled in the room as the kids began to pack up their bags and shuffle out the door. Gwydion moved onto the rest of the day, but it was a blur after the intensity of art class. and soon he found himself on the bus going home.

There was a writing assignment in his English class. He had never really written anything before. And Gwydion thought it was too advanced for anyone to do. It was too vague and everyone had groaned as the teacher gave it out. Write a short story of something scary that happened to you. Halloween was coming up and the teacher was trying to get everyone into the mood. He had read in front of the class The Tell-Tale Heart, by Edgar Allen Poe, and Gwydion, like the other student's had been entranced. So much so that he had gone into the student store and bought himself his own copy of the works of the writer. He read all the stories, but the "Tell Tale Heart" was the most vivid, the most scary. So when he wrote his short story for the class assignment, he was inspired, he thought he might do something scary like that.

"As I walked down the cold stone steps, the air around me turned to a bracing chill". The teacher told him to use lots of adjectives with each noun, at least one, anyway. so he tried hard.

"I could hear the tick tick tick of the water dripping from the damp stone ceiling, as the steps took me deeper into the cavern. I pulled my new yellow coat closer around my shoulders. I had left it on the stairs earlier and had come back to get it. My mother would have been mad at me if I had lost it for good.

"So here I was being drawn into the dark depths of the stone temple deep in the jungle. Mysteries surrounded the history of the stone temple. And no one knew it's true purpose. There were no real rooms in there. Only a deep stair case and one small room at the bottom where it is told they held human sacrifice, and stored the hearts in the stone tomb."

And here on the paper, the teacher had written, "Gwydion, stick to the facts" in red ink. and Gwydion thought how unfair; these were facts, according to his professor grandfather. Just wait till I tell him about my dumb teacher.

"I continued down the steps, drawn by some unknown force, into it's black maw. Then a sound began to penetrate my consciousness. A deep thrumming sound I could not locate. It seemed to emanate..." he liked that big word, "...from the very rock surrounding me. Boom, boom, boom, it resonated until he felt it might be my very own heart banging on my chest. Or was it the sound of the many still-beating hearts stored in the stone tomb?"

And here the teacher had written, "Oh, I see, like "Tell Tale Heart" !" Boy, was she slow, he thought.

"I stepped down into the dark and heard a rustling in the corner. A rat, perhaps? I listened and heard it again, only louder this time. Too big for a rat. What could it be?

I called into the dark, "Who goes there? Anyone there?" And suddenly out of the gloom materialized a face; a white moon of a boys face, with a grimace full of sharp teeth. And it was the face from my nightmares. For each night a ghoul haunted my dreams, a face jeering and grimacing, its foul breath bathing me in its horrid stench.

I jumped back and landed on my rear on the cold stone floor. "Who are you?" I screamed.

It just laughed a menacing laugh and said, "I'm your worst night mare!" And with that it began to stride towards me, boney fingers reaching out. I turned and began to bolt up the stairs, the menacing form scrabbling right behind.

My feet felt like lead weights as I tried to flee. The harder I tried, the heavier my feet. I could feel it's cold hands clutching at my coat. The thing caught the hem once with its steely fingers.

"I will get you. I will kill you! I will end your still- beating heart that echoes on these walls of terror!"

The monster from my nightmares screamed at me in its rage. And still I climbed the stone stairs, my terror ripping the air from my lungs, stripping the strength from my limbs. More that once his cold fingers grasped my new coat, and still I ripped it free.

Just as I reached the light at the top of the stairs, I felt his hand grip the back of my coat. I squirmed and let out a terrified groan as the specter behind me tripped, and yanked the coat from my shoulders and fell backwards with it. I heard him scream as he tumbled back down the cold stone stairs, his cry of agony fading as he fell, until it was quieted by a sickening thump as he hit bottom."

And what was written at the bottom in big red ink letters by his teacher changed the course of Gwydion's life, although he wouldn't realize that for many years to come. "That is very good short fiction, Gwydion!"

## Chapter 10
## Stack of Scriptures

"It seems," answered Antony, "that those monks would later, years after the Christ was dead, issue edicts, warning devout people of heretics and the heresies they espoused as ancient truths. They decided that some of the Gnostic writings were not worthy of including in the big book because they were falsified as to the date they were written."

"It was just a way of denouncing things they didn't want," added Will.

"Right," said Antony. "But more, they were refuting the

actual age of these ancient documents, saying the dates were falsified and not really good old ancient wisdom. And therefore not worthy of being included."

"Well, they were calling them not true wisdom because they really weren't old," said Will.

"Oh, I see, " Said Mags. "So they were saying that if they actually were old, that then they would be "better" wisdom. So they refuted their age there by refuting their worth."

"Right," said Will. "That was their own implication."

"Which of course we know now that they *are* actually older than most of the new testament," said Antony.

"And now that our new dating machines are saying that they really are older than most of the New testament writings, and that they actually date from *before* the time contemporary with Christ, now that its been proven that they are older, now they say they are worthless *because* of it."

"So two-faced," said Mags.

Will snickered. He enjoyed Mags commentary. She always brought things down to earth in an everyday way of understanding these erudite things.

"Maybe. Definitely frustrating," said Antony. "But now I think we are finally between these two places, in the middle between this bigotry that has some ulterior motive. Between these two hard places and we have to work it out."

"As a society, you mean," added Will. "I agree. Our awareness has been forced open. We can no longer close our eyes to this reality of the existence of these ancient documents that the church has been suppressing for so long."

"I think we are asking questions we never could have before," said Bethany. "People are beginning to see from the outside that this is just another era, we have left the one, the one that believes that religions are the only way to see existence. We only believe it at the time that it is the only way. "

"Right," said Will. "We are gaining that eastern mystic

perception of an outsider that can observe the phenomenon of what we can call religious belief."

"Well, looking at ourselves from the outside, and observing our behaviors," said Bethany. "Did you know Dr. Freud said that?"

"What?" asked Will.

"Dr. Freud said we do not know ourselves, and that results in oppressed thoughts and impulses, and that results in psychoses and hysteria."

Antony looked at his wife. "I did not know he said that. What have you been reading?"

Bethany just smiled and shrugged her shoulders.

The group gazed at the stack of copied manuscripts on the table before them. "So that's it, then?" asked Antony.

"We have gathered all of them together," answered Will.

"Even the Berolinische Gnostica?"

"Yup. They even agreed to have it translated by our people, any people for that matter. Any one who wants to take it on," said Will. "They seem to have completely lost the will to fight over who looks at it."

"They've had long enough to get over it, that's for sure," added Antony.

"Is that the one found by the Thule at the turn of the 20th century?" asked Mags.

"That's right," said Will. "They hid it for a while, then the curse of the Egyptian Zombies returned and brought them to a screeching halt."

"Ya, so they went to South America and wreaked havoc on our dig," said Bethany.

Antony chuckled, "Yup that's the one. But, from what I have read so far, I'm just not that interested in any of this so called library," said Antony.

"What?" said Will in a shrill voice.. "Seriously?"

"i am kind of sick of the holier than thou stuff this seems to be, what I have read so far," said Antony. His wife looked at him dumb struck. Not like him to not take a translations job.

Antony continued, "I mean really, and I quote 'They praise the second and so then the first; the way of ascent is the way of descent'. It is New Testament hog-wash re-write. I feel like I'm in catechism again."

"It's not all like that. Take the Gospel of Mary for instance," said Will.

"Sure, but we had that in the older stuff from Egypt , the Dead Sea documents. That gospel is really old. Predates the Christ birth. But this new find is almost all rewritings of that. Even the secret Book of John is all rewritten into patriarchal sexist hog wash. I can hardly read it. "When they learned of the expressions of the father, they knew, they were known, they were glorified, the gave glory." HUH? What silliness. Maybe sounds good from the pulpit, to sound menacing to an ignorant audience."

"Honey!" said Bethany.

"The really sad part," he continued, "is people feel uplifted by reading that tripe. They really feel they've learned something and have been up lifted toward saintliness by reading something that is essentially essential-less. Meaningless." Antony let out an exasperated breath at his diatribe.

"My, haven't we gotten spoiled over the existential finds of earlier," said Will sarcastically. "Maybe we can find you some things here that might interest you. I mean you are a valuable asset and we should like to keep you interested, keep you on."

Now that was starting to sound a little like a threat to Antony, and he put his hands on his hips. But in his mind he was thinking maybe it just wasn't worth it anymore. He had to be interested in it to do it. And most of this wasn't even catching is attention at all. Except to irritate him.

"We will find you something you want to work on, don't worry. There's plenty out there. You have this in your brief case, right?"

"Ya, its been sitting there for a while, yes," answered

Antony. "Did you know?" he started in, and stopped himself. Did he dare he tell Will this. Why not, the jerk. "Do you know that I used to read those Dead Sea stories to Gwydion at night?"

Will just looked at his older colleague and friend.

"Those stories were really kinda beautiful. But you know, not one of these, not one! would I read to him. With that Gothic language they were dreaming up and the sexist crap, no way. He used to sneak into my case and read them when we weren't around. Most boys grab a playboy. But no , not Gwydion. He grabs grandpop's old documents and goes for a 2000 year old spin in weird land. He actually like the Dante-esque apocalypse of Peter. He was fascinated." He shook his head vigorously. "But this stuff, no way I'm locking it up."

"Now you are over-reacting," said Will.

Antony breathed deeply. "Ya, I know I am." He looked at his wife and daughter, who both looked uncomfortable and about ready to leave. "Don't worry about me. I'll find something productive to work on."

"Well, remember," added Will as they were all walking out the conference room door, "The conference in Italy is in a few months. We'll have to have something."

"Oh," said Antony. "I'll be ready."

## Chapter 11
## Oh, Hallowed E'en

Gwydion wondered what he was going to do with this huge picture. He noticed that the girl in the purple dress was working on her painting already. But he didn't want to work on this one anymore. He was kinda embarrassed it was so big. And graphic. He hadn't even thought about it and the picture had just appeared. Then he was embarrassed it had caused so much attention. He never meant that. People in the class thought it was good. And they wondered where he got the image. But they didn't know that he was actually there last year. They knew almost nothing about him after all. The Jacobs family was very new to the area.

But does she always wear that purple dress? He wondered to himself. She had her black combat boots on too. Like a uniform.

And what was that she was painting. He stared at her paper up on her easel. It looked like a giant skull. With a dagger going through it. And a red rose. How strange.

He rolled up his now dry acrylic painting of the pyramids and laid it next to his back pack. Maybe my mom might want that. She probably hang it up and think it was wonderful. He smiled. So silly.

He slapped on a new big paper to his upright easel and stared at it for a minute. Then he looked over at the girl in the purple dress painting black into the background of her giant skull picture and an image flashed in his mind. Stone steps surrounded by deep green. He picked up a thick brush dabbed it in watered down acrylic paint and began to sketch shapes on the paper.

After a while he seemed to come out of a trance. He

looked around and there was some activity in the room. The girl was still painting, finishing the very red rose in the skull's mouth. He got up and stood behind her. She had a book open on a stool next to her left knee. It looked like a medical manual.

She felt his presence standing behind him. "I like skulls," she said. "The bones are really beautiful, sculpted like art."

He grunted and shuffled his arms across his chest. "Do you like it?" she asked him.

"Oh, sure," he said defensively.

"Death fascinates me," she said turning toward him and looking into his face. Her irises were light colored tan, and her eyes he could see now were drawn in with black pencil with shadows painted under them to make her look sort of spooky. So she wasn't sick, after all, thought Gwydion, just painted to look that way. He wondered at this death child here, and noticed how the irises were lighter, like yellow almost.

She turned back to her painting and held the brush up and tilted her head. "All done, I think."

Just then the teacher said loudly, "OK, class is dismissed. Sign your art work and leave it there to dry. Remember, it's Halloween tonight so be careful and be safe! See you on Monday!," she called to the class as they began to make noise packing up to get out of there.

Gwydion packed up his things. And as the girl in the purple dress was walking by, she stopped and said to him, "Are you going to the Halloween dance tonight?" When he just looked at her, she said, "It should be fun. Wear a costume, dress up in something. It starts at 8." When he didn't say anything, she just smiled, hoisted her backpack onto her shoulder and walked out of the art room.

He had never been to a dance before. He kinda didn't know what it was. Dancing? He didn't dance. He had no idea what that was. The image of dumb boys gyrating stiffly to canned music from the LP was just a little nauseating. And girls were there too? Dancing with them, expecting them to dance and act casual. That sounded dumb, he told himself, but inside Gwydion was terrified.

But the girl in the purple dress had asked him to go, sort of. Implied he should be there anyway. He should go. She was interesting, in a weird kind of way. What would he wear? A costume? What would that be?

Well, he reasoned, I have to ask permission anyway, so I'll ask my mom about costumes. She will probably think I'm stupid for wanting to go, he thought to himself.

Mags tried really hard to control gigantic smile and a giggle when Gwydion asked her if he could go to the dance that night. She didn't care that it was a last minute thing; she was sure it had been planned for a while. But that he had just not known about it, or wasn't paying attention, seemed kind of a typical boy-thing to her.

Or had just simply never gone to a dance before; that much she was sure. Things like that did not happen back at the school in Egypt. Well, he really wasn't in regular school. He pretty much attended the audit's college courses at the University with the college students. But here, this was different. These were his peers, and mags was really happy about.

So when her son asked her if he could go to the dance that night, which meant him riding the bus alone at night both there and back, worry was pretty far from her mind. She was actually thrilled that he was interacting with the other kids, and wanting to go to an after school event, by himself no less.

And in a costume? Now that was encouraging. Maybe her little boy was starting to fit. Such a consideration was thrilling after all of the tumultuous years of this child, and Mags struggled to keep a somewhat straight face, and not squeal out in glee and reach out and grab and squeeze her son like she wanted to. Because she knew that would totally turn him off. She knew that he wouldn't want to please her too much.

"Well, let's see. A costume," she said scratching her chin. "We really don't have all that much stuff around here. Maybe some junk from Egypt I stashed away. Most of that got left behind. Then let's go get them box of clothes and see what we can find".

They dug through the box and found mostly clothes that his mother wore, things handmade in Egypt, with mirrors and stitching and jingles on them. Things no one in America would wear, at least not for another 10 years. But when they got to the bottom of the box, there was a pile of hair. And Gwydion grabbed that and pulled it out.

"Oh, that nasty old thing," said his mother. "It was a gag gift from one of your grandmother's bridge friends. Somehow it has stayed in the bottom of the box all this time. To Egypt and back again."

Gwydion pulled it out and shook it loose, for it was crushed and packed together in a wad. And as he shook it long green snakes shook free, their red tongues rattling in the air. He screamed and dropped it to the floor. Then he realized the snakes were just rubber although very realistic, and both he and his mother burst into gagging laughter at the silliness of this black wig with green rubber snakes dangling from it.

"Oh dear God, that's perfect," she said to her son, as Gwydion wiped tears from his eyes from laughing so hard. He grabbed the wig, dragged it over his dark curls in front of the mirror. And stood looking at himself gaping as a parody of Medusa. Transformed into a demon.

"Really," she said, "you wouldn't have to wear anything else. That is so perfect."

And indeed it was, thought Gwydion. So perfect. He selected from the pile of clothes a bright colored cape with black and orange designs stitched in it with tiny reflective mirrors. "I'll wear this too. Can I wear this too, mom?"

"Oh, my cape," she said. "I guess. Be careful with it, I like that one. It's kind of, I don't know, magical. Just don't lose it like you did that yellow jacket in Honduras last year."

He frowned at her with her remonstration. Why did she have to bring that up. What a scary day. And he lost that stupid yellow coat, too. Twice, actually. And he shuddered at the thought of the boy who had chased him down and dragged that coat off his arms as Gwydion had fled up those stone stairs into the light of day. Where had that boy gone? Was he still wearing that ugly yellow coat that belonged to him?

She saw has frown, and said, "Sorry. I know that was a hard day. But we will forget about all that soon, it will all be in the past."

How wrong she was.

## Chapter 12
## New Translations for Antony

Will and Antony had gone through some of the stack of copies of the manuscripts they had managed to get a hold of from the Nag Hamadi Library. There was many varied stories and scriptures in this large stack of infra-red photo-stat copies. There was really no one place to start, as the so called "book" had been merely all kinds of folios stacked together, and sewn with gut into a pile of skins that would have to be called a book. The outer cover was a fully intact goat skin, crudely cured in the manner of two thousand years ago, with the front and back covers thickened and secured with stacks of what were news stories of the day. This was often how these ancient documents could be dated, was by the dates on these various pieces of paper that were sewn into the covers of these ancient books.

But when viewed together the book was very coarse and strangely shaped. So Antony was actually glad that they had before them the copies of said book, because the actual book, the stack of pages wrapped in the ancient goat skin, probably stunk. And it probably was dirty. And it was probably falling apart, and then that would be Antony's fault for handling it until it was ruined. Ancient documents just weren't handled by hand any more these days. Copies copies, a stack in his brief case.

So just the better that they had clean photo stat copies of the pages. Where they wouldn't be distracted by the quality of the pages themselves, the texture and the colors and hand written ink strokes were mesmerizing in their own way. As if you could feel the person long dead bent over some wooden table that was now dust, with some ancient writing implement, writing those letters 2000 years ago. Those delicate pages were now packed away in some thermostatically controlled cold, light-less room somewhere, where very few people could get near them or ever touch them.

But the knowledge was here for them to review. Some of it had been translated by others. And some of those published papers were here in front of Antony and Will as they sat at the round table in the office at the Foundation.

But where to start. Antony had reviewed some of the already translated material and was dismayed at it verbiage. There was such a huge difference between the writings, if he sampled a tiny bit from each of the currently translated bits. So he simply started at a place where no one else seemed to have. His frustration seemed to evaporate as he got into the words themselves, and seemed to be drawn in and mesmerized by the ancientness of the languages.

"I was given a great task by my fore bearers.
They to me a garment of Yellow made fit.
And they wrote a covenant in my mind,
that in my journey I shall not forget.
'You shall to Egypt go,

and the white pearl to find,
it lay in the devouring serpent's lair,
under a garment you shall don,
your earthly appearance unbind.' "

He read another short verse:

"The leader of the authorities was blind.
In his arrogance he shouted,
' I am one and only god!'
His blasphemy echoed down to father Chaos,
and down to mother Abyss,
as he followed it down
at the suggestion of Pistis Sophia.
For the visible was born of the first invisible."


"How am I supposed to pick anything?" said Antony in an exasperated way. "There is so much stuff here. And it is all so different!"

Will just nodded his head. "I know. Its kinda nuts. There is simply so many different kinds of writings here. That's why they called it a library. There were many books, but each bound book contains lots of different kinds of things."

"I really had no idea," his said spreading his hands apart in the air, "last time I guess I had sampled such a small amount. And the Dead Sea group was so similar throughout. The stories had a certain flavor." Will just nodded his head at Antony's apology about his last rant.

"I don't think it matters which one. Just choose something that hasn't been started by anyone else and go with it. There's different languages too, so you are going to have to be comfortable with that dialect and the individual style. Just include all that you do translate with the folio if you do give up and switch. Then the next translator can start from there."

"No wonder they just gave up with their exclusive rights to translation. It'd never get done."

"I'm working on this one," and he handed Antony a page with his name and the single work he was translating. On the page was a long list of names and titles. "And the rest is the most current list of participants from the museum list. They are trying to keep track so there wont be too much overlap. Be nice to get this project done before the turn of the millennia." Will smirked as Antony looked up at him and smiled.

"That's 45 years away," laughed Antony.

"Ya, but you've seen this pile of stuff." Will put his hands in his pockets, and said, "and that is if all these scholars stay organized and work together."

"Hopefully," smirked Antony. "What a nice change from last time that would be."

## Chapter 13
## Dead Dance

At 8 o'clock Gwydion stepped into the High School auditorium. He was right on time and there was almost no one there. How embarrassing. What a stupid party. No one was even there. And the music blared in the hollow auditorium dolefully.

So he walked over to the counter with refreshments and got a big cup of punch. It was bright red and thick and tasted really good. He drank down one cup of it and then had them fill him up again.

As he was sipping his second cup of blood red punch, he turned around and looked at the crowd. It was growing. People were flocking in the doors. And they had the wildest assortment of costumes on. He was glad then that he'd worn something for Halloween, even if he didn't feel weird wearing and Egyptian Cape, and a plastic wig with green rubber snakes.

The blaring music wasn't so bad now that the auditorium was filling up. And voices made a clanger against the auditorium walls and bounced off the ceiling to make a tumbled blurry sound.

It wasn't long before some people gathered around him people he knew from his art class mostly. People he barely knew, but who are like him in that they were somewhat outcast and not part of the cool athletic group. The girl with the purple dress was there, and so was her purple dress and combat boots, and he thought to himself, well she didn't have to dress up much. But her makeup was heavier and somehow she had a fixed too long fangs onto her eyeteeth and they hung out onto her lips when she closed her mouth and dangled menacingly when she laughed. And her tongue looked black when she opened her mouth.  The others laughed and seemed to feel less strangely than Gwydion, and he figured that it was better to be in a group of strangers than to be alone. But they were loath to dance. Not many of the kids danced. Some couples that were established boyfriend and girlfriend couples spent the entire evening on the dance floor together. And were unaware of anyone else.

Not this group of artists and strangers. They sulked in the corner, and then they sulked by the punch table, and then slunk back to the corner and sulked some more. But it was a quiet friendly kind of consolation that they found in each other's presence. And they had never spent any time together other than in the art room classroom anyway. All freshmen, all slightly afraid of this new status as a high school student. And most of them were new to the area, so they had not brought friends with them from elementary school or Junior high.

After a while one of them said, "Do we want to go

outside?" The air was getting stuffy and hot with of so many students panting and dancing and talking. So this small group of students friends now, struggled outside and gathered on the large cement covered porch of the auditorium. A couple of them lit up cigarettes, which surprised Gwydion, it seemed strangely adult occupation for high school students to be smoking cigarettes. But they seemed actually to be very comfortable doing it as if they had been doing it for years so he said nothing. It didn't seem to be fakery.

After a while one of the boys said, "Do you want to see something?" And this of course intrigued everyone. The dance was becoming very dull, and the music was very loud and they were not interested in going back inside. So there were a couple of voices that chirped in, "Sure." Another said, "What?" And the tall boy answered, "There's this house down the street."

And so this group of kids who barely knew each other from the art class, walked together as a group down the street. Several of them peeled off and went back, not wanting to leave the safety of the school auditorium and the dance where they were supposed to be, where they had told their parents they were going to be until 10 at night, when they were, then, supposed to walk home.

Halloween night. When most young children dress up in goofy costumes concealing their identities, and walk around town with a big shopping bag begging for treats from any door that seem to be lit with a pumpkin and a candle. But these children had grown beyond that now, and would've felt ridiculous doing trick or treat. So down the street they headed together in the dark the cold brisk on their bare fingers, making their breath into puffs in the night.

They walked down the street, and their leader turned the corner and headed into a dark area of town. There they found and stopped at the front of an old mansion with boarded up windows with broken glass.

"This looks a little scary," said one of the girls.

"Ya, well, it's Halloween," said the boy that had led them there.

The five of them stood and looked at the old house, mustering up courage. It was obviously abandoned and people were not supposed to be in there. But all the better to be spooky on Halloween Night.

So they walked around the back. And sure enough, the door on the back stoop was ajar. "Hey, Eric, what is this place?" So obviously one of the students knew their leaders name to be Eric. And Eric was leading them into trouble, Gwydion was sure. But he could not back out now. But all too fascinating and strange. A new adventure he'd never had before.

So the group slowly made their way up the creaky steps of the back stoop. And Eric their leader pushed open the creaky door. And went in.

The others followed. "This is a mistake. We should not be in here," said the girl of the purple dress and Gwydion stopped walking.

"What? Are you afraid?" Taunted Eric.

She didn't say anything in response. But the other girl did. "Ya. Just a little, Eric."

"Oh shut up Linda," said Eric with an edge to his voice.

"Oh, you shut up Eric," said the girl called Linda.

The other boy said quietly," Shshhh, what was that?" And he froze in his steps and looked up the staircase into the upstairs.

"Oh, knock it off John," said Linda.

He just laughed, then said, "What, are you afraid?"

Gwydion tried to memorize their names, realizing he'd been invited with the small group of friends. They knew each other but they really didn't know him. He thought they might not even know his name. But then John said, "Are you afraid, Gwydion? Do you want to go back?"

And Gwydion threw his head back and gave a snort chuckle. Afraid? This was kind of nothin'. If only they knew that some of the things that he'd heard and seen.

The boy named Eric led the way up the stairs, and that little group followed, the stairs creaking under each step. Someone produced a small flashlight and helped light the way up the stairs, it's weak light showing an old worn carpet on dark wood of what was once a regal mansion, now having fallen into disintegration.

When they reached the top landing they turned and headed into what was once a master bedroom, but was now empty, looted, and littered with junk.

Eric found a place along the wall, kicked aside some junk and plopped down on the floor. The others did the same and formed a small circle in the gloom. Someone took out a cigarette and lit it, and passed it to the next person. Gwydion did not smoke so he passed it past himself.

"What is this place," asked Linda.

"Just the coolest place in town." said Eric.

"This is pretty cool, " said John, taking a drag off the cigarette. And then coughing.

"I think its creepy," offered Linda. Eric just chuckled. Gwydion said nothing.

"Speaking of spooky, what was that story you wrote in class," purple dress said in the general direction of Gwydion in the gloom.

"Hmmm?" he said non committally.

"Oh, come on. The teacher raved about it. And you got an A. Come on, what was it?"

"I just made some story up," Gwydion lied.

"But is it spooky?" Said John.

Gwydion just shrugged.

"Oh, some dumb spooky story you wrote. Who cares," said Eric.

"Shut up, Eric," said Linda sternly. "I wanna hear it. Come on, tell it."

Gwydion groaned a little. And started slowly," last summer we went on a trip. It was to an ancient temple in

Central America."

"Oh this sounds dumb," said Eric.

"Shut up, Eric," said Linda for the third time.

"Ya. I want to hear it," said Sophie.

"Ya, me too," said John. "So shut up Eric!" He said and then laughed.

Gwydion felt uncomfortable being put on the spot, but he didn't like being made fun of either. "No, it's true. It happened," he said to the group.

"Go ahead. Tell it. I want to hear a spooky story," said purple dress girl.

"Well, there's this creepy guy that was following me. Stringy haired and crossed eyes and he was tall and skinny. And he'd been following me since Egypt."

"Egypt! Now that's ridiculous," said Eric.

And the other three said in unison, "shut up, Eric!" So Eric lit another cigarette.

"Well anyway, we went to this ancient temple, and I climbed all the way as the top. It was really tall and steep."

"The temple? What kind of temple? That sounds spooky."

"It's an old Mayan temple where they used to do human sacrifices."

"That's not even true!" Said Eric. They just looked at him.

"It is true. My grandfather is an anthropologist. And this is what he studies." The two girls said wow in stereo. Gwydion was encouraged. "Ya, he travels all over the world and gives lectures. He's pretty smart. He speaks lots of languages."

"The Temple..." Said purple dress girl.

"Right, the temple. So I went up to the top and no one is watching. But there was this dark staircase made of stone down into it. And my grandfather talks about in his lectures that these people believed that they were created by a son god that flew down from the sky. That he and his brother fought in the sky lobbing balls of fire at one another, until brimstone rained down upon the people on the ground. And that this was so frightening to them that they came to worship the hero twins from the sun. And these primitive people developed a religion where they honored their gods by sacrificing humans to them."

"What you mean sacrifice?" Asked Linda.

"They killed people, stupid," said Eric.

"Shut up, Eric," said John. "I want to hear this."

"How did they do it?" Asked combat boot girl.

"They took the King's son down into this cavern of stone, and placed him on this magic altar. I saw it. It's a carved slab over a big tomb. They tie the boy down, do some ritual and chanting, and then they take knives and hack his heart out."

The girls gasped in unison. "No way," said Eric, impressed for once.

John laughed and said, "cool."

Gwydion was on a roll. "Then they took the heart out. It was all bleeding and they took the heart and placed it in the ceremonial bowl they had. I forget what it's called. My grandfather would know. And then they put it in the tomb where there's this magic, and the heart never dies. It beats, and it beats, and it beats forever in this tomb. And when I went down there, I heard it. I swear I heard it."

The other four kids were silent. They each were listening to their hearts beating loudly in their own chests.

Just then there was a loud boom, and the chandelier tinkled overhead. The girls gasped in shock and jumped to their feet. "What was that?"

The other boys just looked up, white with fear.

"Probably nothing," said Gwydion. "Just the still beating heart of the sacrificed boy knocking on the roof."

Linda screamed, and ran from the room, with two boys following her. Fang girl dove into Gwydion's lap. At that moment the chandelier began jangling, and there was loud thumping on the floor boards. "Get under my cape," yelled Gwydion. And he threw the edge of the Cape over her and his legs, and buried his face underneath. A something went on, thump thump, thump thump, thump thump, for quite a while. Forever it seemed to these two kids. Until finally grue quiet, and the two of them could hear their own breathing slow, and their hearts beat slow in their chest. And they relaxed and sat up.

They just looked at each other in the gloom. Not willing to say a word in the silence. Not willing to chance that it was their voices that had conjured up this spirit of Halloween night. The spirit conjured by Gwydion story of the still beating heart.

Slowly they stood and Gwydion led her ahead of him, both still wrapped in a cloak, out of the room and down the stairs. As they left the disintegrating mansion, Gwydion noticed the mirrors on his magical Egyptian cape were reflecting a red glow, as if they were cooling off from repelling an evil spirit.

In a church far to the south, the young man sought refuge in the pews of the huge church. In fact many people did. It was Halloween and many feared the very air around them. Outside there were revelers, practicing the ancient religion of death, wearing bones, costumes and rattling and banging musical instruments, they sought to connect and commune with dead relatives. And this was the one day of the year when the veil between life and death was the thinnest. When the ghosts of dead relatives came to visit. And many people sought out these spirits to communicate with those long gone.

But the more devout of the people did not appreciate this view of the season at all. They thought it somehow extremely unchristian and avoided the revelry like the plague. And many sought the safety of the church on this night.

The young man hung his head in prayer. His prayers were strange and mixed up. But his mentor instructed him that in time his head would clear and he would become free of his demons. His mentor father Micheal told the young man that things would get better. His evil dreams would often with time and the spirits that haunted his dreams and even his wakeful hours would diminish, if the young man practiced his verses, repeated his prayers and followed his instruction in the church closely, and was obedient to his elders in the church.

And this all had a calming effect on the young man. He had never had things explained so clearly to him. He had been beaten so many times by his father, and his uncles, brothers and cousins, that his mind had closed off. But he felt himself opening up, felt himself blooming in the warm bosom of this sacred place of learning. In fact when father Micheal had learned that this young man had lived in far away lands, he realized that he had a penchant for foreign languages. And father Micheal cursed his own vanity that he felt excitement at the shared interest that this young man held for scripture. For father Micheal secretly fascinated with the ancient scriptures of the church, and longed to travel and behold some of them from the father land himself. He longed to travel and see some of these ancient documents with his own eyes. And that his new student and disciple had once lived there and studied with some of the scriptural professors held just a bit of envy for the priest. He did not tell these interests to the young man., But held them inside himself and nursed this sensation along with his teachings of this new acolyte from off the streets.

## Chapter 14
## Late Night

The fog floated through the trees and coalesced onto the leaves like a million diamonds, and dripped on to the heads of the two young people as they made their way home after a terrifying evening of Halloween fun.

Sophie stumbled on the corner of a cobblestone and swore to her self. "What's wrong?" said Gwydion quietly.

"I don't want to go home," Sophie said.

"What?"

"I don't want to go home."

"Why not!' Its gonna be OK." Gwydion lifted her a little with his arm and she stood straighter and took a few tentative steps.

"It was just some old house," explained Gwydion. "I've seen that place by daylight and it is just an old house that no one has lived in a long time. Its falling apart and that was what we heard and saw, something falling out of the ceiling."

"No," said Sophie.

"What?" said Gwydion becoming exasperated. "An old house, ya."

"That place, its an old..."

She stumbled a few more steps. "An old..."

She let out an exasperated sigh as they tottered along like ancient people in the cold San Francisco fog, miasma swirling around inside and out of their young heads.

"...meeting place. Its dark, I can feel it."

"What are you talking about?"

"It has a history. You haven't lived in this city for very long. It has stories around it that every body tells. "They walked along in the half dark, what light there was was diffused by the swirls of fog.

"Those are just stories. Those are stories they tell to scare young people." Gwydion shook his head and let out a stream of steaming breath.

"Not just old stories. They are all true." She stopped and looked up at him. "All true. Everything you think you know is not true and everything they told you were fairy tales is absolutely true."

He held her by the shoulders and looked her in the eyes. "Now, Sophie, you're starting to sound like me. Listen to me starting to argue with you." He laughed out loud, raised his face to the sky and let out a belly laugh. "I must like you because I'm contradicting my self just to make you feel better."

"Nothing is going to make me feel better. I have to go home. That's scary enough."

"Now what are you talking about?" he asked her with a tired exasperation.

"My parents are creatures," she said quietly. "Creatures from the black lagoon."

He laughed again. "oh, come on. They can't be that bad."

"Oh, yes they can," she said looking suddenly up into his eyes with something like terror in them. "Give me the ghouls in the old IOOf building any day."

"In the what?"

"The old IOOf building. Don't you know what that is?"

"I have no idea what you are talking about." said Gwydion shaking his head.

"That building. The IOOf building. The International Order of Odd Fellows?"

"I have no idea still, what you are talking about."

"Ugh," she let out an exasperated growl. "They built buildings all over the west during the gold rush. They all look exactly the same, same square brick nonsense, with exactly the same shape windows, two floors, a door and stairs in the front and in the back with windows on either side that look like eyes staring out watching everything everybody does. It was supposed to be a brother hood of longshoreman or some such. No wait, they were Masons. Like the free masons."

She stopped and looked at him again. He said," I've been in Egypt studying ancient middle eastern religions and language."

"You have?" she looked at him with total incredulity on her young face.

"I was over there for 5 years with my family. We came back here for my high school. Well, and because of some other stuff."

"Well , I tend to be a historian of Western American culture it seems, at least in comparison to you." She sniffled and wiped her nose on her sleeve. "I always thought they were some kind of friendship group. But boy was I naive. They were religious fanatics. Oh, I know, you know about the inquisition?"

Gwydion nodded his head, his wet curls sticking to his forehead and nose. He wiped his face with his sweatshirt sleeve, catching some of his hair in the mirrors of the cape. "You know the guys with the red crosses on their white capes. They were purportedly started looking for the holy grail."

"Oh sure. The inquisition and the holy purge in the middle east of heretics." Gwydion looked over at his friend. "That's the connection?"

"They are the same group. And that was one of their buildings. They say its haunted and I think they are right. I have never been so freaked out in my life."

Gwydion shrugged his shoulders and began to walk along, pulling Sophie along by the arm. "I have. On numerous occasions." He rolled his shoulders and Sophie glanced over at him tentatively. "In fact," he continued. "I think I might take ghosts any day of over some of the junk I've seen." There was a silence between them the Sophie did not want to break right then. She wasn't sure if she wanted to know what he was talking about. His thoughts and memories hung between them like ghosts that would have to wait some time to show themselves to his new friend, if he could help it.

# Chapter 15
## Late Nightmares

They came to the corner of two streets.

"This is where I turn," she said to him in the gloom. The street light barely cut through the thickening fog.

"Ya, I go that way," he indicated with his shrugging shoulder that he turned the other way. About to separate, they became suddenly afraid and pensive, wanting to hurry home to their respective warm beds, but unwilling to break the bond that had formed between them on this freaky night. Who knows what the light of day might bring. What change of perspective might occur with sunrise. How this magic would fade with the harshness of everyday life.

"Monday at school then," he offered.

"Ya," reality setting in colder than the fog itself. They let go of one anothers arms and stepped away. That was the hardest one. Then the next ones became easier as they turned and walked down their streets in opposite directions.

His footsteps faded in Gwydion's ears as he scuffed along the damp pavement. When he couldn't hear her steps anymore, he turned and could barely make out her dark form against the fog lit by street light. Was she turned to look at him? He could not tell for sure and maybe only imagined it. He continued toward home as the cold penetrated his sleeve where her arm had been, and penetrated his heart where for a small moment in time there had been a kindred spirit.

The house was dark when he approached. He found the key under the fake rock and unlocked the front door. He stopped and listened. His awareness of empty dwellings was enhanced this night, after the experience at the old house. A house now suspected of being a once used place for ritual perhaps of an occult nature. That was tantalizing. He knew nothing of that sort of American myth. He wanted to talk to Sophie about it more sometime.

He locked the door behind him and slowly stepped up the cold cement steps of the foyer. The floor above him creaked and he froze. "Oh knock it off Gwydion," he admonished himself. "Its just this stupid old house." he walked a few more steps, and then thought, ya that's what you thought about that last place you found yourself in just a few hours ago. And just about got eaten by spirits.

He reached the upper door and began to ease it open. It creaked on its hinges. He was amazed at how all the sounds were amplified by the lack of awake humans.

Was that it? Lack of awake humans? It was so quiet, everything creaked and moaned. Or were his senses just heightened from that experience.

He gingerly stepped into the hallway and began to make his way down the hall. There was a faint light under the door at the top of the stairs. They were not allowed to go up the stairs. There was nothing up there but stored stuff.

So why was a light on?

Wasn't any of his business.

Ya you're just scared, he told himself.

I am not scared, I'm minding my own business. Besides I'm not supposed to go up there.

You're a chicken.

Am not!

Am too. Chicken.

Oh, shut up. I'll just go up there and turn the light off. No one must have noticed after going into one of the rooms when there was the light of day. And now everyone was asleep. I'll just go up and shut it off.

Slowly he stepped up the steep carpeted steps up to the upstairs level. Every other step squeaked with what seemed like a demons yowl that echoed through the house.

Or maybe he just imagined it. But he stepped on the side edges of the stairs anyway as it seemed to diminish the squeaking sounds.

When he reached the top of the stairs, he stopped and listened. He thought he heard something thump. He froze. Then the noise stopped. He took a step toward the room with the faint light under the door and he thought he heard another thump. He froze. And he stood there and listened. He thought he heard a thumping, a gentle thumping just barely stroking his ear drums. He held his breath. His heart beat seemed to become louder.

As he listened he heard the thump thump, thump thump become more pronounced as he listened. Then he realized he was listening to his own heart beat in his own ears and he sighed with disgust at himself for being so scared. He breathed easily and took the two steps toward the door and grasped the handle. It was cold. Very cold.

Brass is usually cold, but Gwydion felt like his hand had stuck to the metal. It was that cold.

Gwydion you are imagining things, the voice in his head said to him. He grasped the handle again and began to turn it very slowly. Then he heard it again. Another faint thump. And then another. The light under the door quivered slightly. Gwydion felt his ears fill with his own heart beat again, obscuring any sound that might or might not be coming through the thick old door from the room inside.

Oh stop it, he scolded himself again. Just go in and turn off the light. He turned the handle and cracked open the door. Faint light flickered across the walls and an eery red glow came from somewhere around the corner behind the door. He heard faint rustling rather clearly now as the throbbing entered his ears more directly from its source. Somewhere around the other side of the door. He looked up at the wall and noticed that there was furniture there. And an old bureau with a very large mirror on top, with a dark wood frame. It was tilted downward somewhat and he could see movement there reflected from around the other side of the room. From where the rustling noise came from.

Light flickered and there was a gasping . But not his own. But unmistakably human. The form in the mirror broke into two deeply shadowed forms as one of them turned at looked Gwydion full in the face, the old mirror reflecting it grotesquely in the candle light. But it was unmistakably the face of his mother.

The scream was his as he yanked the door closed and bolted down the stairs, ran into his room and slammed the door.

He dreamed that night. Some strange colorful dreams. The scent of baby powder permeated his senses as he struggled with the pastel images he saw in his mind. He felt a warmth he had never known before and became aware of another presence beside him in the room. 'Shalom' it said to him. He felt happy and comforted by this presence. It lifted its hands before him and there just above its hands revolved some small objects that Gwydion could not identify. Shalom giggled and smiled as she swirled the objects around in the air. Then she looked at Gwydion and said sweetly, 'hello brother'.

Gwydion bolted upright from his sleep. The sky was just beginning to clear and show the streaks of a new sun. He groaned and pulled the covers back over his head. Thank goodness it was Sunday today. He needed another day of sleep after the kind of night he had had the night before. Halloween was over.

## Chapter 16
## Morning Church

"Gwydion!" Cried a voice from the hallway. "Gwydion, get up! It's time to go to church."

The door was closed tightly, and the voice was somewhat muffled. But Gwydion was sure he heard someone say they were going to church today.

He rolled over in the covers and buried his head under his pillow's. But that couldn't be. That's not possible, they just didn't ever go to church.

So he rolled over the other way and faced away from the bracket in the hall. But again the voice of his mother persisted. "Gwydion!" The doorknob turned and the door cracked open. "Are you up?" She yelled into his room. "Are you even getting ready?" It was as if she expected him to be getting ready, as if this always happened every Sunday. As a matter of fact it never happened Sunday. Except for that day they went to the funeral for Professor Happenstance. But that was on a Sunday. But the stress in his mother's voice was enough to scare Gwydion out of bed and to begin scrambling for some close to wear.

The door cracked open again, and his mother cried, "Gwydion!" Then she stopped when she saw that he was out of bed and said to him, "What is wrong with you? I thought you were getting ready to go to church?"

"What is wrong with *you*? We never go to church!" He yelled back. He was not much for arguing with his mother but this was too much. He really did not understand her hostile behavior.

After a while he came out of his room a bit rumpled but fully dressed, and wandered into the kitchen where his mother was making coffee. His grandmother and grandfather were there too. Antony quickly cast in the furtive look. By the look on their faces Gwydion saw that they didn't understand what was going on either, but were going along with the commands.

"Maybe it's for the better," his grandmother commented offhand, seeming to understand the unusual nature of this early morning activity. "We haven't been in so long."

"For him and there was the service at Canterbury,"

commented his grandfather. "Now that was a beautiful church." And Gwydion was transported back just over a year ago, when they attended the funeral service for his father's friend. The church had been an ancient one, and Gwydion had been moved in ways you never expected. In fact he had a hard time tolerating sitting there in that huge expanse of Cathedral surrounded by memories and ghosts of the ancient past. His grandfather had told him that it was an ancient place, with more history than could ever be known. But Gwydion had not realized what exactly that meant. Egypt had always been a strong memory. But a child's memory, one involving things Gwydion could not understand in such a young inexperienced mind. But he was becoming a teenager now and the change from one ancient culture to another very distinct and different one was shock enough to awaken his mind in new ways. So the church at Glastonbury was quite a startling experience for him.

    The ancient gray stones roughly hewn and piled atop one another, not anything like the construction that Luxor. But distinctly British. Cold and strange. And vibrating with stories, memories and ghosts from eons past. A very different violent and cold history, quite apart from the golden sands of Egypt.

    And within the cold space of the Cathedral were held captive spirits all held within the ancient Catholic ritual and the gilded staring statues of Jesus and Mary and the gilded angels of wing. And in the midst of the chanting and singing within the squirrels of the smoke of incense, those gilded wooden statues of Angels had vibrated and come alive in Gwydion's mind speaking to him in whispers from centuries ago of deeds and misdeeds, potentials and dreams of the humans who came here and prayed, and of the expectations of the supernatural beings that were channeled through the Celestial portal.

    And Gwydion had hardly been able to tolerate the long time sitting in the hard wooden pew between his mother and his grandmother, his grandfather holding onto the Bible and closing his eyes. But Gwydion imagined that he was not praying so much as tolerating this strange ritual experience. But afterward nothing was ever said about him if it. Only his grandfather explaining how they were on the Glastonbury plane which was a place of ancient beliefs, of ancient people living in the wild lands of Britain who were conquered and changed by invaders from the north and east. That the ancient peoples of Britain had built monuments to their gods and goddesses of ancient times. And that these monuments still stood in their austere simplicity, hand hewn erect stones towering over their human worshipers. He called them the rings stones of Stonehenge.

Gwydion didn't know what that meant. But after the service the family had driven in a taxi northward on the Glastonbury plain and had driven by the monument of tall gray stones with wide flat Stones on top 20 feet in the air. And Gwydion had realized what he was talking about. Similar ritual artifacts as he'd seen in Egypt. But on a much smaller seemingly more primitive scale. Nonetheless Gwydion had been moved and understood now the ancient nature of man's worship of gods he did not understand. He remembered the motion of the car and the faint car-sickness that he was experiencing in the pit of his stomach. And how when he knelt up on the seat and watched the towering stones pass by as they rounded the driving circle around the monument, his car sickness vanished. He pressed his warm face against the steaming glass of the taxi and stared in wonder. "Stop that!" his mother's sharp voice had jolted out of his reverie. "Don't act so strange. Now sit quiet like a good boy." His mother had admonished him and sharp tones and instantly his car sickness had returned with a sudden vengeance.

He stopped suddenly in the shoveling of his bowl of cereal at the breakfast table at the memory, as the others were getting ready to go to church. He was going to go into a church, for the second or third time in his life. He did not want to meet those angels again today, but he feared that his awareness of their living nature and his awareness of them might draw such an encounter towards him again.

This cathedral was different. The stones were newer and the memories less ancient. He didn't feel the age of the planet so deep in his bones this time as he entered the tall metal doors of the church. Perhaps he could tolerate being in there for as long as his family would expect him to be.

It was cold, and he sat down on the wooden seats, but was afraid to look around for a long time. He did not want to invite the stares of any angel statues if he could help it.

His mother looked at him askance when they had seated and the rustling had continued for a few moments as the family got settled. She saw his look of reprisal on his face and registered shock in her own face in return. She turned and faced forward, picked up a hymnal and whispered defensively, "Will couldn't make it this morning." After a few moments she said under her breath but out of the side of her mouth nearest her son, "And anyway, that's none of your dam business."

Touche', he thought. So that's it, isn't it?

## Chapter 17
## Monday Morning

School the next day was normal, No more costumes, no more excitement. Just back to normal boring school. Except some of them had stories from their Halloween adventures. Some of the kids were staring at Gwydion off and on during the day. He wondered if he still had weird makeup on from that night. Or they could tell what was going on inside him, the way his mother was treating him like a pariah.

But when they were in painting class, one of the other boys came up and said to him, "Seen any ghosts lately, Gwydion?" then he laughed and walked off. Somehow people had heard of the adventure they had had in the haunted house. Word had gotten around. He looked over at Sophie and she glanced at him then sheepishly looked away. I'll talk to her later, he thought.

But he never got the chance. The day went too swiftly, and night time dark came all too fast. He didn't get a chance to talk to her for a while. Yes, the burning light of day had withered the delicate connection they had formed with the terrifying experience they had shared that night.

In another part of the world, a young man entered a church, but not through its front doors. He had been initiated in to the church as a budding young priest. He had never expected that, but he felt maybe he had deserved it. After all of the unfairness in his life, finally someone was taking an interest in his talents.

They had met at a conference of professors and clergy interested in the old inscriptions of the middle America peoples of old. Archaeology the scientists called it. But religious cleansing is what they referred to it in the back halls of this church. These old religions were great for understanding how peoples had gone astray. And studying them was a way to help understand their mistakes so they could be avoided in the future.

The old religions were certainly not to be studied to be understood for any information or value of understanding of the human condition. No, these were thoughts and traditions to be avoided. In fact this church used to have a policy of destroying old documents when they were found. But science had taken over and insisted that these things be taken as valuable simply for their antiquity. And some scientists had even deigned to suggest that they should be saved and studied because they might have some value for man-kind, that perhaps in these old ways there might be some valuable understanding. That these documents and artifacts could have any real information in them seemed ridiculous at best. There was only one book. And its words came directly from the big man himself. It was fact and gospel and everything else was temptations of one kind or another, to take mans mind off the beauty of God.

The young man had learned this in his religious studies in this church. But he had always felt these things in his bones. His early education., tho extremely limited, had been of the same strict nature towards thought and the great book. It was a different religion, but now as he studied this ornate one that was new to him, he felt a kinship to it. It seemed to fit. The strictness was the true path to strength. The obedience and solitude were the only path to salvation. And if he followed it correctly he felt in his chest that he would be allowed into the kingdom of the righteous. If only he could follow it and be obedient. Sometimes his mind strayed. And he castigated himself for these transgressions. He made himself suffer. He told his new mentor of the awful things he thought, confessional they called it. And he reveled in exposing these things to this strong older man. It made him feel cleansed when he did that. Often the mentor then punished him. Punished him in ways that he was not entirely unfamiliar with. But never did this mentor stray so far as did his other two mentors had. And they had suffered. For they had crossed the line. The line where the young man felt was no longer for the kingdom of heaven but for some other place that these ideas often came from. He could not put his finger on where that place was. But in his studies he was searching. Searching for that dark place that dwelt deep in his mind and in the mind of other men that sought to torture him, for he wished to rub it out. He wanted it to go away. If only he could annihilate that part of himself and of these other men, the world would be a better place. And perhaps he could find peace within himself finally.

And as he entered the darkened church and saw the ornaments of the rituals and of the sacramental worship, he sensed that he was getting closer. Closer to a resolution of this dark conflict within himself. Study, pray, debase himself. Read the old scriptures and find the heresy there and destroy it. The heresies that the other had discovered in the jungle and in the desert where he had come from. Only if he had gotten a-hold of those manuscripts first, he could have done with them what his god demanded, and what his mentor was working toward, destroy them so the heresies could never be read by human eyes again, never be misunderstood and stand against the one and only true word of god.

His prayers were answered one day soon following. He was allowed into the brotherhood of the priest's secret circle.

Father Micheal smiled gently and laid an old gnarled hand on top of the initiate's head.

"You have entered the circle, my friend. Now you are one of us."

The boy took a deep breath and felt something infuse his whole body. A warm satisfaction perhaps. Or maybe the holy ghost. He hoped it was something more like that. He was not sure.

He only knew that he felt fulfilled and vindicated somewhat by his hard work, concentration and yearning.

But this was not the real initiation, the one that would take place in public. That, he was told, was some time in coming. When he earned it. When he had done enough for the brethren itself , in sacrifice and self-debasement, then he would be able to acknowledge his acceptance in front of the people of the church.

"And how long will that be?" he asked his mentor, and brother, Father Micheal.

"We shall see," was the oblique answer. "We will see how things go and at what levels of self-sacrifice you can manage. You are young and you are new here. There are others that have been at this a lot longer that you have, my son. And they deserve to move up in rank a little faster than yourself, even thought they might be younger than you are."

The thought of this older man spending this kind of time with the other boys brought a burning into his chest. He knew it was true, but hearing it made his chest constrict and his face burn. His hands clenched tighter and he grasped at the fabric hanging in front of him.

The older man saw this and interpreted this as jealousy. "Now, don't feel that way about it. You know it is the way of things."  In a moment he continued, "And besides, someday after you are truly accepted in the churches fathers, you will have a group of your own to watch after and to help pass through the rack of initiation and acceptance."

He was always apart of some older man's ranks of young boys. Always., Back at home, always his older brothers and cousins had belittled and humiliated him. His uncles and even his father a couple times had debased him and locked him in the room of tears after ward. Why was it always that way? The younger man thought to himself. Why? Always? When it came time, he thought to himself, he would get his revenge on those younger boys. He would not treat them well but initiate them into the tortures that he had undergone as a child, and at the hands of these older men who were stronger than he.

The young man bowing in front of the older man sniffled and tried to stifle some angry tears as he suppressed these thoughts. And with a flood of pain he was suddenly filled with self-pity.  He deserved better; he deserved more just by his devotion to the cause. The old man had noticed the welts and dried scabs on his back and his privates where the boy had been debasing himself in front of the alter each night in an effort to purge his dirty sins. Surely this old man could see that? But he held it in, again. He knew he would wait and he would get what he deserved. Each of them would. He would wait.

"I know that is hard for you to accept, even at this time of exaltation," said the older man as he began to rise. "We shall see with your dedication and vigor just how quickly you shall rise in the sight of your god." He stood and stepped away from the young man still kneeling against the skirt of the alter.

The young man waited with his face buried in the tear-stained fabric, as the older man walked out and closed the door behind him, leaving the young man behind once again to clean up the candles and the rumpled covers and wet towels, and rest of the mess in the bedroom.

# Chapter 18
## A Story

"Do you want to read my story?" He was sitting on the green lawn in the Indian summer sun when the voice broke him out of his reverie from behind.

He spun his head around to face his attacker, and saw to his delight it was Sophie. He sputtered, "You have a story?"

"Yes. I have been writing it for quite a while. But I cant seem to finish it. I just keep rewriting it and rewriting it." She sat down on the grass and stretched out her young straight legs in front of her and pupped off her boots. They never seemed to be laced or actually buckled. They had buckles on them that slapped when she walked. But she never seemed to have them buckled closed. And her socks were pink striped. He tried not to stare.

He looked up at her face and smiled. "What is it about?"

"Well, its about this girl that gets lost in the forest. She was going for a walk and minding her own business, when this squirrel runs by and runs into the dark forest. And of course she follows it. But then she gets turned around and gets lost. "

"Maybe she needs a hero to help her find her way out," suggested Gwydion.

Sophie looked at him askance, "Is that a chauvinistic comment?"

"A what?"

"A chauvinistic comment. You know, male chauvinist pig and all that." They had been studying political science in civics class and this was one of the new modern terms that was being batted around in the newspapers.

"Oh, right. So you don' think that boys should rescue girls?" Gwydion asked her.

"I just think it is a knee jerk reaction to say that kind of thing. Maybe the little girl is going to help the little boy find his way out of the forest. Or maybe they cant get out and she saves his life because she knows all kinds of forest skills that he doesn't."

"Well, what does you story say?" he asked her trying to save the conversation from exploding.

"Well, they both are equally versed in forest living skills, and he wonders what she is doing there. But she starts arguing with him about the political situation in the kingdom and he realizes that she doesn't want to leave the forest. Things are getting too awful out there and she doesn't want to go home."

He looked at her for a moment. Until she said "What?"

He turned away. And said, "sounds like you."

"Well, I suppose all good fiction is a reflection of the authors wishes and dreams."

"And their denials about their own character."

"What?" she said again. Gwydion looked at her and smiled. And she punched him in the shoulder.

"So there is a kingdom. And I suppose it is ruled by a glorious King." said Gwydion after they quit laughing.

"No, actually. It is run by a queen. A good queen although she can be tough as nails sometimes. When she needs to be."

"So this is a feminist story?"

"What?" Sophie said for the third time.

"It just sounds like it is going to be a woman power story, that's all. I think boys might be bored with it."

"So you don't want to hear my story," she said flatly.

"Actually I would really like to hear your story. It sounds different than the usual tripe I hear all the time."

she looked at him for a long time. So long the bell rang and they had to part ways and go to their separate classes.

"Next time," she said as she walked away and smiled at him.

"OK," he said back as he stumbled on the sidewalk.

## Chapter 19
## Trip

The trip was set. They were getting ready to go to Italy.

After the first year of high school and all of the strange events that had happened, and the tension between the members of the family and the Happenstance Consortium, Gwydion was looking forward to this trip. Looking forward to this sojourn away from all that was now mundane and boring to him.

Everything had become boring. The people, the fighting, the school subjects. He supposed he was yearning for some travel to a new place because he had traveled so much when he was young. Well, heck he grew up in Costa Rica alone with his mother in the wilds of the jungle. His short trip through New York really counted as the side trip through the jungle, and that was interesting. But certainly did not rank as "normalcy" to him. Then those years in Egypt. That really changed him, he thought. He was there a long time and went from a boy to....well, what? He thought. A bigger boy, really.

He had no confidence in his abilities to fit in and be a part of things. He still felt that he stood outside of some bubble that other people lived in. he was a stranger. But he was finding that really only he was the one that noticed it. No one else seemed to notice that he was really that different. Except certain bullies. But he was becoming aware that they treated everybody with disrespect, not just silly little Gwydion. So he was learning that if he just stood there with nothing on his face, and acted inert, people just walked around him.

So walk around him they did and what a swirling mass of boring people it was, it seemed to Gwydion. Just leave them be in their little swirling worlds and they usually left you alone, he thought to himself, as he saw his family packing for the trip. After all they weren't so different from the rest were they?

Except for that Will Smithershins. Sometimes when that guy looked into his eyes, it was as if he knew something. There was some link through the eyeballs to the mind thinking things and the two of them connected. And that was a strange feeling for Gwydion. All those years of not holding eye contact with people. And now that he was doing it, he was picking up on information. Picking up on the information people were hiding there. And some of them, yes some of them like this Will character, had something going on in there. And if Gwydion looked too long into eyes like that, he saw begin to burn something terrifying. What, hostility? The preparation for attack?

Once you saw that in someones eyes, you learned to move them quickly away, onto something inert.

Maybe that was why I always avoided peoples eyes all those years, he thought to himself. Of course he had been a tiny child, and could not have really known any of this. But maybe there was some animal part in his brain too that had known, had alerted him to the true nature of the hostility of people that had shied him away from eye contact. From any contact really. Always glancing and running, glancing and running.

Well he wasn't running anymore. He was trying to stand still and look. Maybe be a part. At least act as if he were a part of it. His girlfriend was a part of that. She was weird and was a part of it all. She didn't seem to care what anybody thought. She did what she wanted and joined in with things whether people liked it or not. It gave him confidence. If he just acted like he was a part of things, then people would just let him be there.

In fact she had kinda done that with his family. She had showed up a couple times, and his family had hardly noticed. Then they just got used to her. although Gwydion hadn't let her come around too much. He didn't want them getting too cozy. Keep her for himself. And when he announced that she was going to come with them, they had just glanced at him and smiled, so he thought perfect. She gets to come with us. She explained that it was fine with her family and that they would even make the arrangements for her if he just told her when and which flight.

The flight over was long and a bit dull for Gwydion. Since they had made separate arrangements, the two kids were unable to sit together, and Gwydion was tuck between his mom and his grandmother the whole flight. As the 12 hour flight settled in and people got up and wondered or went to the bathroom, Sophie came back and sat down with him for a while.

They talked quietly in confidence like teenager's do, not letting his mother or grandmother into the conversation at all. Will and his grand father had moved to an isle seat when a section was vacated and spoke practically forehead to forehead and great conspiratorial tones about important things, Gwydion supposed. Sophie leaned over and spoke into Gwydion's ear. "So we are finally on our way. Are you excited about going to Italy?" she asked him over the hum and rush of the airplane engines.

"oh, ya, I'm so glad to get out of the states. So insulated

from the world." answered Gwydion.

"I totally agree," said Sophie as she sat back down looking forward. There was a few moments of silence when the two kids just enjoyed their time together on this screaming jet. Then Gwydion spoke again, "Aren't you excited?"

"Of course. What an adventure. Italy is so old, so beautiful."

"You've been there before?" said Gwydion.

She turned and looked at him with a startled look, and then her flaming eyes simmered down. "Well, I've read a lot about it. Venice is so beautiful. The Doge's palace, the Bridge of Sighs, the place were so many people were executed for religious and political treachery."

Gwydion just looked at her smooth face. She was fascinating, this child of such strange tastes. That's one reason he liked her so much. She was just so different from the other kids he knew. It was as if she had some of the same experiences as he had. Maybe some of the same horrific ones as he had, although they had never talked about that kind of thing.

The food service was announced which meant that everyone would have to go back to their assigned seats, if they want ed to get a meal that is. Sophie stood to get up and go back to her seat where ever it was in the rest of the hundreds of seats on the plane.

"I could come up and sit with you, couldn't I?" he asked her.

"No, they put me in first class. My parents spoil me sometimes. And they don't allow anyone else to go up there, not even to use the bathroom!"

Gwydion twisted his young face into one of exasperation, and Sophie got up and squeezed her way forward, Will and his grandfather came back to their assigned seats on the other side of his grandmother, and the dinner service was served.

## Chapter 20
## A City of Ancient Angels

Venice is an ancient city, built on the marshes of central Eastern Italy, on the northern edge of the Adriatic. Over a thousand years or so, the city on stilts has sunk deeper and deeper into the marshes, where now the streets are under water. Cobblestone lay many feet under the surface of the water and are buried by layers of sand and garbage. So instead of streets, now, Venice has canals. Lots of canals. In fact more canals than streets or walkways.

It is a strange old convoluted city of winding ways and decayed brick and rock work. Beautiful archways hang over sparkling waters of the canals. And many houses now have no way to get to them by barca. Picillo barca. Small boats. They line the water ways and are tied in small spaces defined by upright logs buried in the mud and silt to make what they call in America 'driveways' or carports. Except these hold the family boat. And this boat is moored securely because it is the only way to get off the little island But as in all quaint European towns, the boats are not locked. How dare someone even consider stealing someone else's boat, unless it were dire emergency. And then you would return it carefully to the rightful owner afterward.

Steps have been built down to the water level, because the water level has now risen above the foundation line. So really walking around you are really seeing the second floor. And under water, and only at low water tides do you see what was once the first floor. This has been happening to this beautiful historic city for hundreds maybe thousands of years, since it was first chosen to build this strategically located city on a swamp.

The hotel where the Jacobs family stayed in Venice was, by virtue, old. There were choices of new lodgings, and not necessarily more expensive ones by reason of boring-ness to avoid. But by their fascination with things old, this place was chosen, right in central island Venice just off St. Mark's Square..

And what a delight for the family it was. All except maybe Mags. She complained of the old pipes that made noise when you turned the spigot. And the sometimes brown water came out.

"Just drink bottled water, Mags," her mother would say. It was a luxury in America that the water out of the pipes was generally clear and sweet. Sometimes straight from the ground from a well. But not so here in Venice where the ground water was brackish, part of the ancient marsh that was sweet only to the crabs and fish that dwelt within.

But the brick work was old, and each window was framed by an arch of interesting plaster and stonework. And the view out the window was onto the balcony of the neighbor just across the narrow canal 30 feet below the window, where often was hung the wash to dry. And for more enterprising Venetians, potted plants and small gardens hung from specially made racks, where edibles and flowers could be grown and enjoyed for the ground-challenged city of canal dwellers.

The rooms were small, and the floors were wood. And in no time Gwydion and Sophie found a hidden doorway at the back of a small closet that had been boarded up long ago. It was part of an old staircase that had led down into the lower rooms. The first floor, the one that was now officially under water most times, was never used, as it was occasionally flooded. The air smelled dank and cold to the kids as they crept down the creaky stairs.

"I hope this wood doesn't give way, Gwydion," said Sophie in a shaky voice.

"You're light as a feather. It should be fine," said

Gwydion. "Just don't stomp like a monster and you shouldn't break through I don't think." Just then he stomped and growled like he was going to get her, and she shrieked in a muffled way, realizing that there were others just above them and they didn't want to get caught on their adventure.

"Did you bring them?" she asked.

He put his hand on his pocket edge and shook it a little, with a big mischievous grin, said, "Right here. Pops will never notice they are gone." He took a tentative step on the mouldering wood.

"Well, as long as I get them back before he gets back later today."

"OK, well, let's have a look." She stopped and turned and shook her hands in excitement.

Sophie opened up the comforter she had slid off the bed and carried with them down here. She folded it into a square that they could both sit on and laid it on the damp wooden steps. Gwydion sat down and folded his long legs on the step below. She sat next to him and looked expectantly as he pulled out the folded papers and spread them on his knees.

"This is some of the new stuff that he is translating. Let me see here." He shuffled a few pages around. There were the hand written pages of his grandfather's scribbling script. And there were dark smudgy printed pages that looked like the photostat copies of the originals of the ancient manuscripts.

Sophie gasped as one of those came to the top of the pile he was shuffling. "Look at that," she said, pointing.

"What?"

"Those look so old. They look moth eaten or something," she said.

"Ya, like 2 thousand years old," said Gwydion. "The originals are in some library museum somewhere. But these are the copies of them. They don't let you take the originals out anymore. But still, I bet these copies are worth something, too."

Sophie's eyes got misted over as she looked at these ancient hand-lettered manuscripts. "They must have been really meaningful back then, to someone." She looked at Gwydion. "Do you really think that those people that wrote these met Jesus? I think he really was a God or a visitor from another realm or something, don't you?"

"I really don't know," said Gwydion. "But the way everybody gets all wow oh wow over the guy, makes me wonder that there really wasn't something going on back then. Something supernatural or cosmic or something. Because the awe factor is still really strong for people. Even today. And that they found these ancient books seems to just drive everybody wild. "

"I've never really believed the bible or anything. My parents think it is a bunch of old poetry. "She put her hand on the copy of the 2000 year page of hand written words, and said, "But when I look at that, and I know how hard it was for them to write anything down, I mean they had to use skins and stuff, it must have been really important."

"And to think they went to such great lengths to hide it all, some priests put this stuff in jars and sealed it in the mud of the Nile river. And somehow it lasted just long enough and then it was found, nearly at the same instant that those were found at the Dead Sea caves.... so strange, it seems like it was planned to happen that way. That we were supposed to find these things right now for some reason."

"It's almost like people had to wait to get to a certain point of mental evolution before they could handle this discovery of these old ideas," suggested Sophie.

"Ya, the last ones they found, when my grandfather was translating them, they were all fighting and trying to kill each other over the rights to translate them, and over whose translation was right or not."

"What? Kill each other?"

"Yup. That's why we got the heck out of Egypt so fast, and left all our stuff there a few years ago. Someone tried to kill my grandfather."

"Did they catch they guy?"

Gwydion smiled and big Cheshire Cat's smile.

"What?" said Sophie, smiling now too.

"He got his own. Just by a different person and in a different way."

"What do you mean?" she asked.

"That guy I told you about? The one that attacked me?"

"You mean in the temple?"

"Ya. The same one." Her eyes widened. "Yup. He did it. He killed him."

She shook her head and laughed. "How do you know this stuff, Gwydion. You cant know that stuff."

He shrugged his shoulders and just said, "Well, I just do. That's all." He looked back down at the stack of papers and said, to change the subject, "Here. The Great Seth. He came down from the Majestic world of Yaltabaoth, and Jesus took possession of a human body, thus throwing out the previous tenant and using the body for his own purposes. It was a joke of course, and when the silly humans tried to kill him, he was somewhere else watching them and having a great laugh." read Gwydion from the hand written text he had borrowed out of his grandfather's leather case.

"No. It does not say that. You are reading that from some fiction that some crazy person wrote." objected Sophie.

"Nope. Its right there. This was found in this group of folios in what they call the Nag Hammadi papers."

"That's unbelievable. What else does it say? Keep reading!" cried Sophie.

" "Someone else, Simon, bore the cross on his back, someone else, not me, wore that crown of thorns. And I was up above watching, laughing at their errors of ignorance, at their conceit and the excesses of their arrogance." "

She just looked up at him when he paused to take a breath. "It was after all just a body that the holy spirit borrowed for the duration, and not his spirit that they crucified."

"Sounds to me like Simon was an angel doing God's dirty work, bearing the pain for one of the greater spirits."

Now it was his chance to look at her funny. "And how do you know that?'" asked Gwydion.

She gave a sheepish shrug and said, "I don't know. I just do. Angels come down and can be mortal for a while, and take the place of the spirit who doesn't need to feel pain."

"But does the angel feel pain?" asked Gwydion.

"Oh, yes, Gwydion. Angels feel pain. It is their job."

# Chapter 21
# Grande Canale

The two of them walked on the stone flags, the water lapping at their heels in the Grande Canale. The sun was setting and picked up the bits of blown glass hanging over the boats. Blown glass was one of Venice Italy's specialties. To Mags, the globes looked dark and foreboding. Primitive, like some piece of an ancient mariners boat. And she then thought that was probably true. This city had been here for centuries. Just like this, sitting in an ancient lagoon, stinking, slowing sinking.

But by god it was strange and beautiful. And she let out an audible sigh as she watched the sun set behind the crumbling red tiled roofs.

Will looked at her and wondered what was going on in there. "Don't say it," he laughed. She looked at him, then got the joke, and said loudly, dramatically, "Ahhh, Venice!"

He turned and laughed across the water, his deep voice vaguely echoing in the relative silence of the evening. A few boats came and went, shurring against the slight ocean current of the evening. The small flat boats hugged the center of the Canale, where they could speed along to the inner canals to begin making their night deliveries of produce from the mainland. Everything here was boated in. There were no huge bridges to drive trucks over in the vulgar fashion of more modern cities. Venice by Ancient Design.

They walked for some time in companionable silence. Finally Will broke the silence, a silence that had been going on longer than just then. Some subjects were very difficult to bring up.

"So, Gwydion has been pretty irritating of late," he

started trying to be diplomatic. He had his own opinions but was trying to sound like he agreed with her point of view so she might be more amenable to the conversation.

"Irritating? That's putting it nicely," she answered.

He laughed a little. "He's at those awkward teenage years," Will said again diplomatically.

"I don't know know if it's any different."

"Ya, but you seem, I don't know, like its starting to get to you."

"Maybe I just need to cut the apron strings." He was glad she said this and not him. That usually pretty irritating thing to say to a gal. A mother.

"I've wanted to do that for so many years," she said with relief, like she'd wanted to say that for many years too.

"Oh," he said, not used to someone being so direct. And not sure where to go from there.

They were silent for a few minutes as they ambled in the most romantic city in the world, along one of the world's most arguably beautiful waterways, glowing gold and blue in the setting sun. Will knew to stay silent. He wanted to talk about this, but knew sometimes it was easier for people to pick their own route, filling up an unknown void than to be pushed with questions.

She started again quietly, "After Stan left, it was really hard. I thought it would be good, that I would feel relief. But it just wasn't like that."

"That was in Egypt?" asked Will. He knew but was trying to sound curious, but not too curious.

"Ya, he went off to work and just never came back." Will almost said that they had always been curious about that but stopped himself just in time. When she didn't say anything for a minute, he decided to ask, "How was that hard?"

"Oh, not just the money thing. My parents do fine and it was good to have Gwydion with his grandparents. He and his grandfather have such a great relationship. I think it was the only thing that brought him around. He was so inside himself.

He wouldn't even look at people. He never spoke. And he shunned physical contact. What a hard thing." She hugged herself with her crossed arms, and there were tears in her eyes. No one had ever asked her these questions before. No one had been brave enough.

Will answered with his own observations. "Well, he still doesn't talk. He makes sounds and he answers in some simple body language, and you know he's listening. But if you didn't know him, you would think there was nothing in there. In high school we used to call that an air head. Not very nice, and I think probably really wrong."

"Ya, he's really smart. He just knows stuff, and remembers everything. He seems to know when things are going to happen. I don't think in an ESP way; I think he just processes the tiniest details and figures it all out, on some subatomic level and then reacts. Like an animal reacts to the slight changes in weather most people don't even perceive. And us big adults, we're so sure we know it all, talk and talk, and miss what's really happening." She was emoting now and Will smiled. He had wondered what this mother thought of strange Gwydion. But she continued before he could respond. "Costa Rica was really tough. He was always getting into things. He was just a tiny guy. No one around us spoke English and he didn't talk but I didn't think anything of it. "She hugged her arms and shivered.

"And sometimes he would just take off. He would just disappear."

Will looked at her in question. "Huh?"

"At night, I'd go in and he would just be gone. Five years old and out in the forest at night. I'd go out and find him with the dog roaming around in the moonlight. "

"What?" asked Will, a little alarmed now.

"He was so weird, it freaked me sometimes," she cried out a little, kind of defensively that Will had reacted with alarm.

Will shut his mouth; he knew that mothers often had

troubles with their little kids, especially if fathers weren't around to help and do things with them. So he tried to act detached from what she was saying. And he just kept quiet.

"And that time at the Temple, I'm just remembering this now, how strange. We went to that same Temple and he got lost there. Inside the Temple. And he came back later, after we searched and searched, and he came back later all dirty and rumpled. Like he'd fallen or something."

"Oh, you mean the Singing Temple on the Yucatan? The one we just went to?"

She looked at him in the eyes, a little spooked, both of them, "Ya, that one. I just remembered that. Weird huh?"

They walked along for a while, thinking about their experience at the Temple last year, the one called the Temple of Inscriptions, incorrectly so, because there are no inscriptions in it except the huge plaque of stone carved to depict what looks like an astronaut in a fiery vehicle of some kind. The Temple where they had all met 15 years before in the dig that went hay-wire when the war broke out.

"But I can't just lock him in his room and restrain him like I did then. He's too big for that. I guess I just have to learn to let go of him," she said in the glowing dark. She leaned a little closer to him and their shoulders touched lightly. He put his arm around her shoulders. And Will thought she probably hadn't half begun to do that, letting go of her son. But the word restraining lodged in his subconscious for later.

"He's a pretty fascinating little guy," Will said to put a little distance to suggest the conversation was about to be changed. "How about dinner somewhere?"

"He's not very little anymore," she said, her mind still far away. She laughed a little thinking of her son, now a young man. "He's taller than me now. But he still slinks around like a kid. It's kinda weird. Probably why I am kinda on edge about him. Looks like a man, but isn't yet. And he still doesn't talk. Still doesn't look at me." She sighed and crossed her arms. "Maybe I ask too much."

"Oh, I don't know. Maybe just let it go. He seems fine." Will answered diplomatically. And walked them down the Canale toward a well-lit eating establishment. And as they bent under the old sign painted with a cat over the low doorway into the warmth of the restaurant, it started gently to rain.

## Chapter 22
## Damp Stones

The two children hung along the damp stones of the ancient stairway as it began to rain outside the higher window of the cairn.

"Wait, wait, I love this part," Sophie said as she crinkled the paper in the growing darkness. Gwydion leaned over her shoulder and looked at a new typed-out translation she held there.

Drip drip drip a small formation of drops fell onto the widow sill.

"It's a tragedy of the Aeon, Sophia, before the formation of our planet in the dark chaos, she chose to produce an offspring with out the participation of her consort. The result was a monster god who had the power to create, and destroy, and he was named, Yaltabaoth. Sophia saw her mistaken creation as a malformed being. He decided in his delusions he was the one and only true God, and he set about to prove it by the creation of the Prison War planet Earth, which did not exist yet. As this tragedy unfolded, the supreme beings who watched then sent some of their own to instruct the imprisoned inhabitants of the violent blue and green planet with the knowledge necessary for their entrapped mortal souls to escape to the higher plane."

Gwydion's eyes were wide. "How old is this?"

"Pre-Bible. This is the stuff the bible stories were developed from. Or thrown away. This says Genesis 1-4."

"Where was that found?" he asked her.

She flipped the page but there was nothing written on the back. "The Nag Hammadi folders." She said with a certitude. "That's all that's here."

"I'll see if I can find more in my grandfather's case tomorrow," said Gwydion. "It's getting dark," he added. "I can hardly see."

"It's raining," Sophie said to Gwydion, smiling. "I love it when it rains, especially in ancient cities when I'm underground."

Her morbid humor was not lost on Gwydion. "Ya, we should get back. It's getting dark and I think I missed dinner."

They turned and began to walk up the ancient steps, warn smooth in the very center from a billion treadings of human feet. After eons even soft leather will wear rock down. Sophie had her hand placed against the side stone of the wall for balance when it struck the edge of something, and she stopped. "Look at this, Gwydion," she gasped. Upon closer inspection they realized it was some kind of doorway that had been boarded over.

"I bet this goes up to the other rooms. And by its placement I bet it goes to my room."

"No, let's just go back," Gwydion's fear of strange places in dungeons was beginning to take over, with the gloom developing in the evening and the drone of the rain outside on the canal and the rock walls making a humming in the air that was beginning to press on them.

"No, wait. Let me just look." She pulled at one of the boards and it popped off, and they were able to see that indeed it was a door. She pushed the handle and the ancient door began to creak away from them into a totally dark void. She wedged her skinny body through the crack and disappeared into the gloom just as Gwydion reached to stop her.

"No, wait," but she was gone in an instant. Just then Gwydion heard the front door of the apartment open and band shut and running steps into the living area of the hotel overhead. He thought he'd better get back. Just then her head popped through the slit in the door and Sophie said, "It's fine. I found it. Go on!" And with that, he turned and fled up the stairs and pushed his way through the coat-stuffed closet.

## Chapter 23
## Convocations

The door flung back with a jingle as 2 figures dashed into the foyer of the Hotel. They were laughing and shaking off the rain.

"Buona Serra!" cried the inn keeper to the two wet figures, recognizing them as the American professors. They just laughed and started running up the stairs. The Venetian just smiled and returned to some paper work on the desk. What a rainy night. A bolt of lightening lit the sky and the dark alleyway outside. 'A night for romance, or maybe one for nightmares,' he thought to himself, as a wave of thunder rode over the ancient city for the probably the millionth time in its lifespan.

Will and Mags hustled into the apartment, in a hurry to shed themselves of their drenched clothes.

"How was I supposed to know it was going to rain?" cried Will defensively. "Next time I bring a bumbershoot just for good measure, huh?" he said looking into her wet face.

Her face registered confusion. And he added, "An umbrella!" And laughed and she laughed remembering the funny British term. "You Americans!" he said with exaggerated false derision in his thick Liverpuddlian accent.

Antony and Bethany were in hearing distance and they

came in and laughed at his joke, and at how unbelievably wet they both were.

"Boy, did you two get caught in it!" he said.

Will regarded his colleague and now sort-of dad- in law. "We sure did. A nice dinner at Pas de Chat and this happened."

"Where?" asked Bethany. "That sounds French."

"Ya, I know," said Megs. "Weird, huh?" She pulled off her drenched wool blazer and hung it on a chair. "But the best darn cabbage wrapped pork meat balls I've ever had."

"It was very strange," said Will. "It was American cafeteria style, with the plastic trays and the old wizened chef serving you from a buffet behind glass. But oh, my gosh, the food.... wow."

"OK, then you'll have to take us next time, Will," scolded Bethany.

"So, you two up for tomorrow night?" Asked Antony.

Will looked up through fogged glasses and said, "Oh, ya. The reception. Ya, sure. Why not?"

"Just wondering. It's not required. But you know how that goes. We really have to be there."

"Not me, tho," said Mags. "I mean, mom, you can go. But I really don't have to."

"Well, technically, you are a teacher with the Institute now. And this trip is about them." Antony would be the one to say anything to her. She probably wouldn't listen to anyone else. Bethany turned her head and rolled her eyes so no one would see. She was pretty sure she knew where Gwydion got that part of his personality, autistic or not. Apples after all don't fall far from the tree. She retreated to the tiny kitchen to wipe dishes after their Provencal style dinner of some things she had picked up at the store. Bread, cheese, some fresh vegetables, biscuits. There was no refrigerator like back in America, but the simplicity of eating in Europe was refreshing. A clear white wine that was really from a vineyard.

The discussion continued in the main room. "Well, I'll go.

But do we have to take Gwydion?" complained Mags in a quiet voice.

"Yes, I think he should go," both Antony and Will said almost in unison. They were careful not to look at each other. Will crossed his arms.

Mags looked at her father but not at Will, but she felt him cross his arms next to her. "Fine." She stepped toward the washroom to get a towel. "What time?"

"4 PM ish. Afternoon. I don't think it's supposed to be that fancy," said her father to her back. He looked at Will and gave the tiniest of shrugs. Antony turned to walk back to the kitchen.

"Where is Gwydion, anyway?" asked Will.

"He's out. As usual, prowling around," answered Antony. Will gave him a questioning brow. Antony dismissed it with a wave. "He's fine. He always does this when we travel. You know, back at home, too, really, with his tall dark looks, they'll just think he is a local, when he rarely opens his mouth to dispel that belief."

Will smiled and nodded his head slightly. "Ya, he's probably picked up the language by now."

"Ya, but he never talks. He seems to just avoid situations where he is required to speak. He's figured it out somehow." Antony shrugged.

"He doesn't say anything, does he?" said Will. "Its funny tho, after living with him for a while, I seem to understand what he is doing and saying, almost like he is actually speaking to me." Antony looked at him funny. "No, not ESP or anything. But like a sub-verbal communication, like with an animal or pet. It's interesting. I think we could learn from that."

Antony looked at him like a stranger for a moment, then said, "No, I understand you. I've just been living with him for so long, I don't even see that that's how we communicate, he and I."

Will looked at him with interest. "I think, Professor Jacobs, that maybe your being an Anthropologist may have helped you having him as a grandson. Probably interested you in some professional way."

"Ya, you might be right. although I've never thought of it that way before."

"Probably what's allowed you to be tolerant instead of irritated at his weird behavior, like other people mostly are," said Will. "It interested you, this weird, sometimes frightening behavior of his."

Antony looked at his colleague. "I guess it is frightening. I get so caught up in protecting him and teaching him I forget people are afraid of him. And now he's turning into a handsome young lad, and people expect certain things from him. Which he just cannot fulfill, and then I think they become angry and frightened. Each time I see that, it makes me just a little bit more sad."

"Ya, I feel sorry for him too, sometimes," answered Will.

"No, not for Gwydion," Antony answered just a that person burst into the main room from the closet.

# Chapter 23
# Listening

Gwydion couldn't stand it any longer. He burst through the door and ran through the main room into the hallway.

He'd been listening to them talk, his ear pressed against the old door at the back of the coat closet. Listening to his grandfather and that guy, Will, talk for some time now. He heard his mother leave the room and go into the washroom. But he had to go; he couldn't hold it anymore. So he burst through the door, unfortunately revealing his hiding place, which he considered to be a really a bad thing to do. But he had too. Maybe if he ran through there into the hall down to the public bathroom, maybe they wouldn't think anything of it.

Once relieved, his mind turned to what he had heard them talking about. Another one of those dinners tomorrow night. And he was expected to go. He used to look forward to those things, all spiffy and shiny like they wanted him to be, show him off. Smile and be quiet.

But that last time in Egypt, with that other kid following him. And he could tell some of those other professors were openly hostile to his grandfather. How could adults get away with that kind of thing. They were supposed to be adults. And they told him to be mature and not fidget and wiggle. He was always quiet because he just didn't think he had anything to say to them anyway. With their hidden motives and their body-tells shooting off in all directions. Like animals reacting to each other, and then getting mad at him when he rolled his eyes at them and didn't want to go.

And then that other boy. The one that was following him around. And no one even cared. No one even *believed* him. He tried to tell his grand father about that mean boy that was following him. But his grandfather had given him *that look*. That look that says he not only doesn't believe him but that he thinks the Gwydion is having some kind of mental break down. Which certainly is not true. Just because I see how fake all you old people are.

Gwydion sat down on the bench outside on the walkway along the canal in back of the family's apartment with all of these thoughts rushing through his head.

But they are going to make my mom go tomorrow night too. He could just hear her complain about that too. On and on she'd go about those stuffy professors and their superior ways. And then he thought maybe they were superior to her; she didn't have all that education and stuff. But maybe he was starting to sound just like his mom. And his vision cleared a little thinking that.

He felt his stomach do a flip and make a noise and he remembered he had been down below in the wet basement stairs for a long time, and he had missed dinner. He knew his family just dismissed his being missing half the time and didn't even ask him where he was anymore. After all those years of his hiding and going off, they had gotten used to it and stopped trying to tie him down.

He walked back up to the apartment door and knocked on it because it locked behind him when he ran out. His father opened the door and let him in. "Where'd you go?"

Gwydion looked up at him sheepishly which said it all. He just walked in and made his way over to the kitchen where his grandmother was stacking some dishes. "You missed dinner Gwydion. Where were you?" she asked fully not expecting and answer, but asking anyway in a nice tone to let him know she did care about where he was, even if she didn't need a verbal answer. She put together a plate of food and he sat at the tiny table and ate dinner by himself.

The two men in the main room took seats opposite each other near the window. Will looked at Antony. "What in the world was he doing in the closet?"

"Hiding," was Antony's oblique answer. And they laughed. Their conversation turned to the subjects of tomorrow night's talks. The families could go home after the introductions, but there would be some sort of discussions afterward that were compulsory for the professors and their aids.

Gwydion listen quietly for a while and realized they weren't even talking about him. And not the closet or anything. Then his secret hiding place downstairs in the forbidden basement would remain a secret. He would check later and make sure the door was completely shut and hidden like it was when he found it the first time. No one would be the wiser.

## Chapter 24
## Dinner

The pre-convention dinner was the usual thing for Gwydion. He slunk away as soon as possible and went and stood over by the food table, where there was a buffet of strange little things on platters. He tasted every punch there was, and he really like the thick red one. It was so strong he thought maybe there was alcohol it it. Or maybe not; it was just so thick, almost like bright colored blood. He fascinated with for a while as he sipped it and he became a little dizzy from the red additives in it. He wandered over and filled one of the little plates with strange little food parts that were arranged on the large silver platters.

There were all kinds of people here, some of them dressed in weird clothes, like people from all around the world wanted to be identified with the country they were from. Otherwise people wore regular clothes, the men in black suits and the women is dresses. Everyone stood around and laughed and held drinks. Soon people wandered to tables were they sat talking in groups and then someone got up on stage and started talking about stuff. The convention and what they were all there for. Gwydion scanned the room for anyone he knew. There were almost no faces he recognized besides his family and Will and Doctor Hillard from the Institute. And maybe a couple professors form their past trip to Egypt. His grandfather approached with one of these men from their past trip. They walked right up to him. Gwydion thought maybe they were just getting food and would pretend not to see him, but his grandfather was beaming at him and leading this older man straight for him. He tried to look away, but his grandfather said, "And this is my grandson who is now going to school in San Francisco. Gwydion, this is professor Shallot, you remember?" Gwydion allowed his hand to be taken and squeezed by the very old professor, he smiled into his face. Gwydion knew he seemed weird to people and knew that when people smiled at him like that, they had been told all about him and his disease, and they were trying to be nice, but inadvertently showing pity for his 'condition' as his mother was now calling it to people behind his back. When he didn't answer, the professor looked at his grandfather and waited for him to pick up a conversational thread.

"We will be hearing some short reports from some of the linguists on the new discoveries from the Egyptian Nile find. You might actually find this interesting, Gwydion." He did not return his grandfather's gaze. So Antony looked at the Professor Shallot and said, "Gwydion is quite a fan of the things we are studying. He enjoys reading some of the stories we find and translate," he turned to Gwydion and added, "Don't you Gwydion?" His face flushed hot red and he looked even further away. He wasn't sure if he was in trouble for reading what was in his grandfather's suitcase. Maybe it was a test to see if he would admit that he dug around and read those forbidden pages. But he wasn't about to give any of it away. It was his, and now Sophie's, secret. It was his secret domain, with his grandfather and with his friend from school,

Sophie. He thought about Sophie and that she had not wanted to come to this tonight. He had wished he could bring her like a little angel on his shoulder, so she could see all of these people forced into this charade, and the way they always put him on the spot. She would have rolled her eyes and said, "Oh, Gwydion. Just ignore them. They are just adults."

He felt better when he thought that, when he thought about having her as a friend, where she never judged him for what he was and seemed to not be able to help being.

"Well, it should be interesting," continued his grandfather, Professor Jacobs to this older man, Professor Shallot, from Egypt. "We have a pretty big contingent from the Ecclesiastical community." He turned toward Shallot who had a big grin on his face. "And that promises to be quite a stir." And Antony's grin widened and the two men shared a look and a chuckle. Gwydion took it to mean that these other men from the church were insulted about something and would argue about a whole bunch of things just to get a rise from the professors that were more like his grandfather and professor Shallot.

Some people came onto the stage and moved some chairs around. One of them stepped to the podium and the micro phone and tapped it to see if it was working. "Tap*Tap" was the microphone's loud response, and all heads turned toward the stage, and people began to wander to tables and sit down. Gwydion hurried over to a table and sat down near the back. Easier for escape, he thought.

"Good evening, ladies and Gentlemen, Madams et Messieurs. Welcome tonight to the special convention of minds, the International Archaeological and Anthropological Society of Study. Tonight we welcome the best minds in the fields of the study of ancient man, with guests from around the world." Gwydion listened with half an ear as he watched the colorful persons walk around and take chairs at tables, and set their drinks down and look up at the man on stage speaking into the microphone.

"I am professor Amin Teklat from the Museum of Antiquities of Luxor, Egypt, and I welcome all of you into the celebration tonight of the discoveries of the Ancient books of Jubal al Tariff, that special place on the Nile delta." He adjusted his bow tie and cleared his throat away from the mic, then turned back and said, "With no further ado, we shall commence with tonight's speakers in their short presentations of field notes and thoughts. First up for the introduction is our renowned professor from Prague, Poland, Dr. Rushlav Shitzlew...." Gwydion's mind turned off at the pronunciation of that name. The new speaker replaced the first one amid a round of applause, and began to speak with a deeply intoned voice, his accent so strong that Gwydion tried for the first few words to follow him, but could not, so he turned away and began looking at people again. He noticed the way some people fidgeted, and some people were smiling and enraptured with the talk of the Polish gentleman doctor. A small group dressed in church garb were all scowling at the stage, and visibly fidgeting at the professor's words. Gwydion noticed the gentleman professor had doffed his black bowler and placed it upon the podium in front of him and was staring at it as if it divined the words of his speech there in. He droned on in his hypnotic thick accent. Then Gwydion noticed he was understanding the thickly accented professor now, and he could follow the meaning of his words, if he didn't focus on them or try too hard. "...Latin and Greek also were found in this ancient collection of folios, as in the several works of the Greek, Plato, most of them were pious in tone, not herseolgical in voice. This would seem to indicate that these texts were even older, and had been saved not to be read and studied, but to be held onto and preserved, valued for their already antiguitous status *then*, in the year 367 A.D. when they were buried, which was the latest dates found on any document, of course no later date, no more recent date, would be found than the burial date."

Gwydion did quick math in his head and came up with about 1600 years; that long they had been buried in the Nile banks. About 350 years after the Christ was born. Time enough for his story to become popular.

"But why, we ask ourselves, were they buried and not simply destroyed? Why did someone go to the effort to seal them in jars and hide them in rocks in the sand of the Nile? Whoever "they" were, they were very careful and meticulous in hiding and preserving them, as if these documents would have certainly be destroyed if not been sealed and hidden and buried?" He let that hang for just a moment. Then continued.

"Perhaps an answer can be found in that significant date. In that year, 367 C.E., the Archbishop of Alexandria issued a canon, one that was to define the 27 books of the New Testament just being compiled and formalized.  He decried that all other works were heretical, all Apocryphal works would be considered heresy. He cited these works were all written by heretics and had been falsely dated attributing them to an earlier time, falsely giving them more credence..."

And Gwydion wondered at this. Would that mean that if written before the birth of Christ meant they were true? Or only if they were really written between the birth and then this Bishop's canon they were true? He felt that somewhere in this lay a trick played by both ancients and moderns, in twisting the meaning, casting dispersions on the validity of these documents.

The foreign professor looked out upon the listening crowd and paused a moment, letting some of this sink in. Then he asked them all, "So how do we approach these newly discovered texts, once considered apocryphal, nay, heretical, by the then burgeoning new Sect of Christianity?"

The group of Ecclesiastics near Gwydion audibly groaned at the speaker's word choice.

"As we near the 21$^{st}$ century, I feel it necessary that we maintain an historical outlook on these finds. That we begin to understand our religious traditions as historical development. They represent almost a thousand years of recorded intellectual workings of an ancient people. An ancient people that we have grown from, these, are our roots, all of us." Near Gwydion the men in church robes were becoming visibly agitated.

"This find near the tiny ancient town of Nag Hammadi is tremendously important in the fields of Anthropology and Archaeology and linguistics. That many of these works predate the Christian era is astonishing. That they tell of a savior long before His birth, does this discredit their words? Or does it verify it as prophecy? Does it matter? Do we no longer believe in prophecy, when once it was crucial to the validity of the story? Does their actual age of over 2000 years old discredit their validity? Or does it verify their actual value? Traditionally their scholastic value versus their biblical validity may be exactly the difficult debate, still, for many."

Lots of nods and shifting in seats as the foreign professor's thickly accented words swept across the room full of listening crowd. And the professor swept his hand out toward them all, including everyone in the conclusion of his speech. "But I present to you that such a large gathering of intellectual minds such as yourselves, from all around the world, from all points of the globe, certainly would indicate the importance of this discovery, the sheer magnitude of this find, this latest Treasure of the Nile."

## Chapter 25
## The Alley

The Polish Professor replaced his hat on his head and turned to walk off stage. The audience erupted into applause and Gwydion sat and absorbed the stir and excitement that his introductory speech had brought. As another man walked up to the mic, Gwydion thought it was time to escape. But the doors to the auditorium were over by the stage. So he turned and ran into the doors in the back, which led him straight into the kitchen.

The space had grown quiet as the talks had begun on the stage, hungers slaked by the groaning boards of hors d' oeuvres. There were a couple workers sitting at a table, eating from full plates of appetizers, talking in hushed tones. They hardly looked at Gwydion as he slunk by.

There must be an alleyway door out back. And hopefully it doesn't drop off into some canal, thought Gwydion to himself.

He hurried between the shining silver cooking counters and found the dark door at the back. He pushed it open a crack and looked out. Not much light, but at least not the surface of water he half expected.

The smell of smoke on a slight breeze and the shimmer of festoons of lights over the inky black waters of the canal. Slick black shapes glided by, the boatmen upright in the slim shaft of black lacquered barca, two lovers holding closely together, lit by a small swinging lantern on the prow.

Gwydion stepped out into the alleyway, and let the door slowly slip closed behind him. There was little bowl laying on the door jam to keep the door from going all the way closed, and Gwydion thought maybe it was to give the small group of smokers huddled together in the almost dark a bit of light to take a cigarette break by. Then he thought just as he kicked the bowl and it slid out of the way of the closing door, maybe it was because the door would lock from the inside, thus locking everyone outside. Someone yelled an Italian invective at him from the smoking group. Then they mumbled amongst themselves and Gwydion slunk off to a darker corner. He didn't smoke, but that didn't mean he couldn't stand and enjoy the dark, warm breezes off the canal. He thought about Sophie back at the hotel alone, and wished she could be here right now and see the beauty of this place. Maybe she was out on the tiny balcony gazing up at the slender slice of moon rising between the two black towers of the apartment buildings on either side of the tiny narrow canal at the back of their hotel apartments.

I guess I better be getting back. He didn't even stop to think what his parents might think about him just disappearing like that. He always just showed up at home eventually. He heard a rustling down the alley just a ways, and turned to see a dark form coming slowly his way, a bright red cherry of a cigarette lit up as the smoker inhaled on it. Gwydion paid no attention and leaned back against the cool stones of the wall. Then he heard a low voice, just in his ear. He at first did not understand what it said, figuring it was Italian, which he had only just started to pick up. But his mind twisted around and he found himself understanding the speaker and was horrified to realize it was in Egyptian. In his years there, he had picked up the Coptic language almost as if he were a native speaker.

But how did this person know he understood Egyptian? This person must know me.

He leaned a little away from the dark figure next to him, and looked down to the side, to get a periphery view of the person in the dark. Perhaps this was someone from inside the hall, someone who knew him from convention group inside. Yes, that was it. One of his father's professor friends.

Then the voice spoke again, and Gwydion realized that the voice was younger than any of his grandfather's friends from the Institute. So he turned and looked into the face, and was mortified to see two dark eyes staring at him from the gloom, two eyes just slightly crossed.

He turned and ran.

## Chapter 25

# Escape

"Where's Gwydion?" Mags turned and looked at Will sitting next to her talking to her father. He turned slightly and said, "Huh?" He turned away and began talking to Antony as she turned toward her mother who was actually looking at her, and asked the question again. Bethany shrugged and gave a look of helplessness to her daughter, and they both started hunting with their eyes for their wayward boy. Their eyes found nothing but mostly strangers milling around.

"I'm feeling a little nervous about that, why don't we head back home?" she said to her mother.

"I think we're done here, the boys are through with us, so , ya, let's head back. Maybe we will find him on the way or back at the apartment. I'm tired of all this smoozing anyway," laughed Bethany. The two women stood up and kissed their respective men on their cheek, barely rousing them from their engrossed conversation with some brightly dressed men from over seas. "Well, I think he's asking for trouble, being to bold as to suggest..." said one of the strangers. "Yes, we've been there, done that. But we cant let that deter us from doing the translations in the most sincere...." Antony continued, and the two women walked away toward the from entrance. They found their way through the lobby and out into the moist Venetian air.

So he ran. He ran down the dark alley past some people standing there smoking cigarettes. He kept running, the dark water on one side and tall apartment walls and locked doors on the other. He ran until he turned a corner and found himself in an even darker alleyway. He stopped and tried to catch his breath. He doubled over at the middle and rested his hands on his knees and breathed in and out, the black spots soon fading from his vision. He looked up and ventured a peep around the stone corner at the way he had just fled.

Nothing. Just some dark figures silhouetted by the dimly lit canal.

He looked around and got his bearings and continued down the very dark alley toward a more populated place along one of the larger canals. He stepped over an arched bridge and entered a small courtyard ringed by some tiny restaurants and patrons talking laughing and sipping drinks and eating dinners by the late night lights strung between and on the trees. He breathed a sigh of relief. He would not be attacked in this area. The presence of these people comforted him somewhat.

He picked out an empty table and plopped himself down on the chair. His breath labored and his heart pounded in his ears. That boy again! He thought to himself. After these years of peace, that boy again!.

Why didn't I see him inside the hall? Was he hiding? I didn't see him at all. I felt like I had actually gotten some rest and maybe it was over. But Gwydion was so wrong. He couldn't know how wrong.


That boy! There he is, thought the older boy. After these few years apart, there he is again. He's come back to take this part of my life over again. I thought he was gone for good. I have been praying and keeping to myself and doing what the priests want me too. And see how I am rewarded? Sometimes I hate you, he glanced up. Then felt a shiver of guilt. Sorry, I didn't mean that.

Then he thought maybe there is a reason for this boy to come back into his life. Maybe there is unfinished business. He hated that man on the stage for the awful things he was saying about the work they were doing. How can those intellectuals get it all so twisted around? We are here to make sure these documents are translated correctly, not find a new truth in them to spread around like a plague. And at every turn, they thwart us. Like some new disease, these so called scientists tell us what is in these ancient books. As if we cannot know. As if we cannot read Latin and Greek ourselves. And they way they twist meanings? That cannot possibly mean those things. Our Lord would never write those things in books. The body's elimination processes, prostitutes. How dare they even talk about those filthy things.

His rage boiled up inside him from a festering wound deep inside him. He hadn't felt this boil break open in a long while Something about finding the younger boy at this meeting of minds brought back all the old pain.

So that was it. The boy was his sign that it was time to make a difference. Do something about the travesty brought on by all these so-called smart people being handed those precious documents. Documents that belonged only in the hands of who deserved to see them, even touch them. Not these heathens, but the Men of God. So that was it. Show them, make a difference. Sacrifice this boy and show them the power of God.

From the corner of his eye at the end of the first talk, he saw the boy slip out the back door through the kitchen. He got up and went out the front entrance and went around the building. And just as he turned the corner into the dark alley behind the place, he saw the boy emerge from the back kitchen door, stand and look around. When he drew in deep on his fresh cigarette, he saw the boy look his way and freeze. And when I walk up and try to talk to him? He bolts. What a waste of a cigarette, he thought, as he enjoyed it for a few more moments. I know where he is now. I know that he is here for his final slaughter. I can wait. He will be around.

And with that he threw down his almost finished cigarette, and started to saunter down the dark alleyway toward where his prey had flown.


Gwydion sat at his table alone for a few minutes until the waiter saw him and came over. "Would you care for something to drink?" the waiter said in his late night Italian voice. Gwydion did not look up at him, but he knew he had to order something or he was not allowed to stay seated, using the chair and table that a paying customer might use. So he said one word, "Coke." and the waiter understood perfectly and whisked off to get him one. He was soon sailing back over and deposited a glass with no ice and a cracked open can of coke in front of Gwydion. "And will *sir* be dining tonight?" asked the waiter before he left. Gwydion shook his head in the negative without looking up at the waiter. So the waiter quoted him a price in Italian lire , which sounded like an awful lot to Gwydion, so Gwydion produced a pile of change from his pocket with the waiter sorted through and took what he needed. He also picked out a couple of the larger coins and tossed them on the table as a tip for himself to be left when the young boy left. Gwydion sipped his simple beverage after the waiter had taken his leave, not even bothering with the glass, even tho he had paid for it's use.

    He was realizing a few things as he sat there sipping, after seeing that boy, the one with the slightly crossed eyes. He realized he didn't even know his name. That kid that attacked him in Egypt and then again in the stone Temple. How can his luck be that bad? Thought Gwydion. How can he keep running into the creep time and time again?

    And what is his problem? Why does he keep following me and showing up and scaring the crap out of me? What is with that guy? Why cant he just leave me alone?

    But I have a table here in broad day light, well its night time which maybe makes me harder to see, Gwydion thought as he sat there for a while. He tried not to look around himself as he sat there listening to the sounds of people around him. Was he listening for that voice again in Egyptian? It sounded so strange to hear that here in Italy, isolated Venice. What a shock that was! He was getting used to hearing the Italian being spoken around him and then that voice! That voice sounding in his ear in that language he had hoped he'd forgot.

But he remembered it perfectly well it seemed. He hung his head and wished he could forget.

Now what do I do? Thought Gwydion to himself. He was almost done with his drink and he would have to leave.

I guess I have to get back anyway. They will be wondering where I am, as usual.

Just then a figure slink around his chair and plunked down into the chair opposite him at his table.

Gwydion froze in place. He never suspected the guy to have the nerve to just plunk down in front of him like that.

He was trapped. Trapped and frozen in his chair, staring at his can of fizzing drink. He couldn't just get up and walk away. The guy had him.

"What are you doing here, young boy?" asked the older boy across from Gwydion. "I didn't expect an idiot like you to be here with all these smart people."

Gwydion studied his sweating can still in his hand and he wondered what he was going to do. I cant toss this can at him; that's a crime. I cant just get up and walk away; that's rude.

He sat there and stewed in his fear and confusion, trying not to look up.

His tormentor saw his torment. "What are you going to do now, boy?"

Gwydion squirmed a little in his chair and he made a small animal sound and the young man smiled and made a derisive sound in his throat.

This boy had him trapped just by his boldness. A boldness that was new when Gwydion had remembered him being kinda clumsy and rash. And Gwydion wondered what this boy had been through since the last time he saw him about a year ago. He had grown. He seemed more of a man than back at the college in Egypt. He smelled like a man too. Like a predator, Gwydion noticed.

What am I going to do.

The unexpected, he decided.

He cant just keep me here just by sitting over there. I haven't even looked at him and yet he is talking to me like we are having a conversation. I haven't acknowledged him so he doesn't exist for me. I will simply stand up and leave.

Stand up and leave.

Let go of the can, slide the chair back, and stand up and leave.

He sat there and felt the sweat start to grow around his neck. He felt his face getting red, his finger tips were getting numb. He began to hear the roaring in his ears. He stood up. Knocked the wooden chair back onto the flag stones, and his can of almost finished drink flipped off the table and onto the ground bubbling.

He keep his eyes down as he walked past the other boy and quickly walked out of the lighted restaurant area as several waiters came hustling over and surrounded the table to clean up the mess and right the chair. And the other boy was momentarily held back sitting in his chair with concerned people milling around him.

Gwydion knew he had only a few seconds lead. And as soon as he was free of the lighted barricaded area of the restaurant, he sprinted. He knew the other boy would be right behind him as usual. But he didn't look back to check. He ran.

Ahead was a dark hole of another alley between three story apartment buildings so classic for Venice. He bolted for the dark.

He ran. And he ran some more until his lungs were screaming at him, so he stopped and leaned against a damp wall to catch his breath.

When his breathing calmed down and the roaring in his ears began to subside, he began to hear the soft sounds around him. He could hear the soft rustling of the wind in the laundry drying over head on wires between the two buildings.

He could hear the gentle lapping of the water in the narrow canal that ran along side the narrow walkway he was on. And he was relieved to hear that there were no other footsteps on the stones of the walkway. He had gotten away.

"That little creep!" thought the older boy as Gwydion simply stood up and ran. "He just ran away from me. I was talking to him and he just got up and ran off!" He struggled to stand up with all of the people standing around him trying to clean up the mess and pick up the chair and ask questions and apologize. Someone there said the word police, so the young man thought he'd better get out of there.

He apologized several times and made his way out of the crowd, out of the restaurant and in the direction of which the young boy ran.

"I cant believe he just got up and ran. And when we were having such a nice conversation. I was just going to try to explain to him why I disagreed with what they all are doing at this conference." He walked strongly toward the next alley opening, although he did not really know where the boy went, only his general direction.

"If only he would let me explain, I could make him understand how important it is," he thought to himself as he left the lit area where the restaurants were. "I'm never going to find him now," he lamented to himself as he began down a darker alleyway.

"He always seems to run away. He never talks, he never looks at me, is there something wrong with me? Maybe he thinks there is something wrong with me? I just try to do what is right, and do what I'm told. It's him that there's something wrong with. I am not the one that is weird and following around in the dark, and running away when someone tries to have a conversation." He stomped his way down the half lit alley, where there was no one and nothing. Just the tall black apartment walls, and those silly canals everywhere.

"If I could just get him to sit down and hold still, I could explain to him what this is all about. If I could just explain it to him he would understand. He is not that much younger than me. He's grown too. In just a year, he is getting tall." The older boy thought to himself as he strode through the semi darkness in the late night breeze.

"If I could just get him to look at me and talk to me, but he must think I am awful or something. How dare he think that? When I am just trying to be friendly. And he just wont hold still! I'll show him some day.. I will make him sit down and hold still and listen to me. I will. Someday."

Gwydion felt exhausted with exertion and fear. He slumped down and leaned against the damp wall. There were few sounds around him and he felt his body relax from sheer exhaustion.

If I just sit here a moment, then I can find my way back.

He was so strung out that he really had no idea where he was in this labyrinth of canals and alleyways. He figured he could follow the light and get back to a courtyard where there were some people, and then ask somebody directions back to the hotel. Venice was small; people knew where things were. If you could speak the language correctly, comprehensibly to them. although it seemed many of the locals wanted you to speak English. But Gwydion was not sure he could speak anything right now, his mind was such a jumble.

So, I'll just sit and be quiet for a minute.

He knew not how long, but he was awoken by a noise. Grogginess filled his head and sand paper had covered his eyes, so he figured he must have fallen asleep for a moment. Or two. Some people were walking down the alley way, talking and giggling. They came up to him, and quieted, their pace slowed. Then one of the girls giggled and pointed at him slouched on the ground and called him a silly old drunk. The boys giggled in amusement, and the group ambled on it's way.

Gwydion shook his head and rubbed his face. One of the group broke off and stepped back to Gwydion, leaned down into his face, and grabbed him by the collar.

"There you are," the voice hissed at him. And Gwydion was horrified to realize it was spoken in the Egyptian language.

"You asshole!" it hissed again spraying Gwydion's face with spit. "Who do you think you are? Can just walk away from me!" The eyes of a demon started into Gwydion's face as the older boy yanked on his collar, lifting Gwydion of his feet. Gwydion was too shocked and exhausted to struggle. "Oh, God save me," Gwydion's mind said inside himself. "Help me, please, someone," he thought quietly, unable to move his lips for exhaustion and terror. Then he thought of Sophie, home safe and quiet resting with a slight head cold. "Oh Sophie, I wish you were here," then he thought, "No, maybe I don't. This guy is crazy and I don't want him hurting you too."

"What are you saying, Freak?" the bigger boy snarled into Gwydion's face. He must have been mumbling. "Speak up! You never say anything, you freak!"

Gwydion blew a puff of air into the older boy's face, and the boy jerked back. "You are nothing, you don't even fight. Why do I even bother." Gwydion tried to swing up and hit the older boy in the face. It was rather ineffectual except to piss the older boy off, and he shook Gwydion harder by the neck. "You listen to me, you freak. You stay away from my people. All of you, stay away from us. In fact you should all die!" The older boy lost himself in his rage while he spoke incomprehensibly to Gwydion there in the late dark of the alleyway. He was ranting now in a language that Gwydion did not comprehend, but he understood it's intent if only by its violence. His native tongue, from the country where he was born, Gwydion thought. Some where else where his hatred and violence was born when this young man was a child.

Deep in the darkness of his mind, before there was even real memory available to him as a child, vague sensations of abuse and pain had buried themselves and festered.

And now this festered wrath was breaking over Gwydion, anonymously in the dark of a foreign alleyway.

He was shaking the younger boy so hard and with such fury that Gwydion's legs spasmed and shot out and caught the other boy in the groin, and a shriek of rage erupted from the older boy's gaping mouth. "You foul demon!" he raged at his captured prey. "I will kill you! Kill you!" All of his rage poured out over poor silent Gwydion struggling to maintain consciousness from exhaustion and stark raving fear.

"Oh, god save me," escaped Gwydion's lips.

"How dare you speak of God, you heathen filth!" the older boy frothed. But Gwydion was thrashing now, mumbling incomprehensibly. "God." "Sophie".

"Call for help, but no one will save you now. I have you," threatened the spent older boy, his face hot and wet with exhaustion and spent rage.

There was a commotion behind them, and suddenly they both fell to the cold stones at their feet. The sound of the water lapping at the sidewalk was heard and some rustling of clothes as a dark form leaned over Gwydion. "Are you alright?" a soft voice asked. "Gwydion? Are you alive?" it asked again, gently putting a hand on his shoulder. She looked at her white hand in the darkness and there was a dark stain on it. He was bleeding somehow. She didn't see a knife or gun, but she looked around just in case. No, just the slumped black form of his assailant and the stone she had slugged him with. She shoved him over and he rolled out of the way toward the canal. "Gwydion? Wake up," she said into his face.

His eyes opened slightly and he peered through the swollen slits, "Sophie," he said. "You came for me." Behind them they heard his attacker struggle to get up, let out a gasp, and run down the alleyway grunting and groaning.

"Coward!" said Sophie, as the other boy bolted away into the darkness. She turned her attention to Gwydion laying prone on the cold flagstones.

"Yes," she cradled his head in her hand and her lap. "We were worried. So I found you."

He breathed a sigh of relief and slumped into her arms. They breathed together for a moment. "Ok, lets get you going. Do you need a hospital?"

"No. I'm just banged up."

"But you are bleeding."

"Just from where he split my lip. He didn't shoot me or anything."

"Then let's get you back to the hotel. Your family must be worried sick."

Suddenly there was another commotion at the end of the dark alleyway. Sophie jumped up with fear, trying to drag Gwydion along with her. "Get going!" she hissed. "OK, OK," he said as he was struggling to his feet. He was having a hard time coordinating his movements he was so groggy. She sped off down the alleyway, expecting Gwydion, who was usually so agile and quick to come racing after her. He could not quite manage it and she disappeared around a corner as he turned to look at the small group of people coming down the alley. One of them in front broke into a jog and came running up to Gwydion. He looked at the scene, a boy on the pavement, bloody and struggling, and the large stone with a bloody mark on it and said in surprised Italian, "What happened? Are you alright?"

"Oh, my head," was all he could get out.

"Oh, English," answered the stranger in heavily accented Italian. "It looks like you were clocked pretty good," pointing the rock with a blood mark on it. "Did you see who it was?"

Gwydion could only shake his head at the boy's misunderstanding of the situation. He held his head and shook it some more.

"Do you need to go hospital?" Gwydion continued to

shake his head.

'The rest of the crew came up to him and one of the girls looked at him and cooed like a mamma bird. "You poor baby," she said in Italian. "Let's get you some cognac!" They laughed and said it sounded like a good idea. They hoisted him to his feet and led him down the darkened alleyway into an area where there were people quietly having drinks and talking at a couple small restaurants still open this late at night. They hosted a small party for him as they sat around a small table, bought a few drinks and tried to make Gwydion drink a bit of some sweet liquor while one of the girls cleaned up the blood on his face and neck.

As she leaned into his space to wipe his nose off, she said, "I'm Nikka. What's your name?"

Gwydion hummed his name as she wiped his nose and lip, which had just stopped bleeding.

"There!" she said sitting back and admiring her work, Gwydion's face now somewhat free of blood. "Here." She moved the snifter of cognac right in front of him. "Now drink some more of 'dis and you will be zhust fine."

Gwydion smiled as a thank you and pretended to sip the drink. It stung his lip too much. Then he wrinkled his brow as he turned and listened to what the others were heatedly discussing. Most of it was in Italian, but he recognized the words doctor and sanitarium and electric drill and he wondered what they could be talking about. Nikka noticed Gwydion's questioning look and said loudly, "Oh, they are talking about the haunted island again."

Gwydion made an even more questioning look. And one of the boys said, "Out in the lagoon, just out there," and he pointed south over St marks Square. "Poveglio, the haunted Island. You can see it right from the edge of St. Mark's Square, about a quarter mile out. although no one is allowed to go there. No tourists. Too haunted, too dangerous." He wagged his finger in the air in front of Gwydion.

The oldest boy, the one who seemed in charge said,

"We are selling it to help clear up some of our national debt, no thanks to......" He said some words that must have been some current events political stuff here in Venice that were completely incomprehensible to Gwydion.

"Ya, but it's haunted. They will never get people to buy that retched place." This boy looked at Gwydion and said, "Dead Plague victims from the dark ages. They were burned alive there!"

"Not alive! Edvard. They were dead."

"But they say the ground there is 50 % human remains ashes. Brrr!" Edvard added as he looked at Gwydion. Gwydion smiled.

"Ya, but the real thing is," added the first boy, who seemed to be a little older and more in charge, "Just until recently it was a sanatorium, you know, insane asylum. And the doctor was crazed. He used to give illegal lobotomies to his patients..."

"Victims!" interjected one of the girls quickly.

"... with an electric power drill."

"Madre de Deus," said one of the younger boys.

"But," added Edvard, "he got *his*. He fell off the highest tower to his death. But they say, no. He did not fall. He was chased by the ghosts of the people he tortured to death, and *they* threw him off the tower."

Gwydion thought, that's just great. Middle of the night and I have to walk home with that on my mind. My family is going to just love the fact I'm bleeding and being walked home by a band of drunk Italian kids.

Nikka looked in his face, and saw what was going on in his mind, and smiled. "Don't worry, my young friend. I will walk you home."

"Say, where are you staying?" asked the boy in charge.

Gwydion stated the name of the apartment hotel they were at and the kids knew right where it was. "Finish up and we shall deliver you." There was clapping from the small group as they began to stand up from their tiny table.

They lifted him up out of his chair, and the small group of guardian angels escorted Gwydion back to his hotel, much to the celebrating relief of his family.

## Chapter 26
## Guardian Angels

His mother was yelling. He was trying not to look.

"I'm sure it's not his fault," Will was saying to her. "Do you think he went out looking for a fight? Gwydion?" He was exasperated at Mag's reaction to Gwydion coming home in the middle of the night, early morning really, looking literally like the cat had dragged him in.

"And those kids he chose to take up with!" she yelled some more. "Drunk local Venetians. I've heard stories about this city and now I see they're all true." She threw her hands in the air and dropped them with a flap at her sides. Will rolled his eyes at Antony, who was standing spectating the playoffs between Mags his daughter, and Will his associate.

"They said they saved him," Will continued to try to explain, "but from what, we may never know." He looked at Gwydion huddled in the corner. "He's never going to give us the story. Look at him. He's terrified."

"YA, terrified I might smack him and knock some sense into him!" Mags said with a red face turned toward Gwydion, who huddled tighter. "I am soooo done! I am so done raising kids. He's 16, he's on his own now."

"Why are you acting like this?" Will said to her.

"I am so tired of caring. And worrying. And wondering where the hell he is all the time."

"I thought we agreed it was pretty harmless, when he went and did stuff on his own," Will said.

Antony interjected wisdom, "Well, not now. Seems like

someone beat him up this time. And we may not know who or why." He turned and glanced at the shaken and battered boy. "I think we should discuss this another time when we've all calmed down."

There was no way Gwydion could explain. The darkness surrounding him and being followed by someone who by all accounts could not be here overseas from the last trip in Central America. And then the attack and chase, and then Sophie showing up? Oh, his mother would go into a rage about her. Probably tell her to go home now, fun and games were over. Sophie was already hiding as if her life depended on it. Hadn't seen her since she fled when the strangers came running up to help Gwydion. Didn't seem like she was adapting very well to foreign people and places.

And those nice kids that found him and nursed him back to consciousness. That was pretty darn friendly really. He wondered if he could go find them again and hang out later. Then he thought he was probably was going to be grounded for the rest of his life anyway. They were going to be here for another six days of conferences and lectures and stuff, which at this point he had absolutely no wish to attend. I wish they hadn't made me go last night, he said to himself.

"He's not going anywhere," stated Mags to the family. "He is not allowed out at all, not till we leave this island."

"That's a little harsh," said grandma Bethany, knowing the little scoundrel would probably find a way around it anyway. "Maybe he could just stay here and not go to anymore meetings. And not go out at night." She looked at Gwydion who glanced quickly up and then away. They had a secret bond, his grandmother and him, and he liked her as an honest friend. He used to think that of his mother. But not since that Will Smithershins had come around. It had all changed then.

"Right!' said Mags. "Like he would really agree to it."

"Of course he will," said Bethany. "He's a good boy who got caught in some one else's trouble last night, that's all."

She looked at Gwydion, who was still too withdrawn to say anything. "Right, honey?" She spoke to him even though she knew he would be unable to answer right now. Maybe they would have a little talk later, when people cooled off and they could be alone for a few minutes. But it was hard to be alone in this tiny cramped apartment hotel room in this tiny cramped miniature city. Not like that huge old mansion in San Francisco where they could go hide and study in other rooms all over the house when they wanted privacy. Sometimes Bethany thought that huge old place had actually divided the family a little, because everyone could withdraw to his own space. She had noticed her daughter drawing away from her grandson since they had lived there. But maybe that was something else, she pondered. Gwydion's father had been gone for many years, and maybe it was time for her daughter Mags to have some male company her own age. And funny Will had shown up just at the right time. But then again, Gwydion was in his teens, and typically time for a youngster to start cutting those old apron strings, even if the boy seemed immature from anybody else his age. Strangely infantile really. Sometimes his withdrawn silence bothered Bethany. But she had grown accustomed to it. And in fact she understood his moods and thoughts maybe better because he didn't communicate by yelling and screaming like she had seen other teenagers do. He was introspective, and she suspected smarted than your average bear, which made her love him all the more. And she thought, against her will, that maybe all this fighting might actually get him moving in his own direction.

But looking at him now, slinking in the corner, she wasn't so sure. And she feared that he might have just gone further into his burrow. And looking at his swollen eyes, busted lip and tear streaks on his cheeks, she feared maybe for good.

**Chapter 27**

## Capture

He wasn't all that broken up about not being allowed to go to anymore of the meetings or seminars. He felt he'd had enough of that stuff anyway. He could read the translations and papers here with his grand father anyway. And study things on his own time, with the tedious lectures and talks and hand shaking that went on at those things anyway.

He was going to miss going out on his own and doing stuff. Especially at night. He seemed to relish the night, hiding in the shadows, watching the lights play on the waters of the canals, the quiet swish of the piccilo barca sliding among the waves and the inky waters.

But he would find things to do. He learned the back way out of the hotel and would sit at t the water's edge and read. Sometimes Sophi would join him in his quiet time, and they would speak infrequently. His family said it was for his safety. And he felt safe. Maybe a little insulated.

But the memory of that boy coming after him that night lay hidden away and he never talked about it with them. It sat in a dark place in there where he healed like a scab over it.

He didn't let them see him go outside. So when they were home he would slip into the closet with its hidden doorway into the cellar. And there Sophi would join him, and they would read to each other quietly, or talk about home.

"I don't really want to go back," he said to her one afternoon in the dank dark. "All those kids just hate me anyway."

"They don't hate you Gwydion," she would say in comfort. "They are a little afraid of you. You are just a little different." And he would curl a half smile and look at his hands, his big hands he was yet to grow into. "I like you though."

And he would look for just a second into her golden eyes and wonder at how she was here with him now. He would get embarrassed and look down. Today he pulled out a folded piece of paper from his back pocket.

"Look at this."

She bent around and looked at the typed page he was unfolding on his lap.

"You will like this one. Its about a woman. It kinda goes on and on. Its beautiful. "

"Thunder," she read out loud. "The Perfect Mind. How strange."

"I was sent from the Grand Place above,
to be among those who contemplate me.
Do not turn away, do not be ignorant of me.
 Am Alpha and Omega, I am wife and daughter,
I am whore and I'm holy.
I am the incomprehensible silence, I am insight, whose depths are dark.
I am found in the utterance of my own name.
You who speak of me in truth, tell lies of me instead.
You who know me, can not know me,
and those who don't, then know me well."

She looked up into Gwydion's eyes. "How strange."

"I like it."

"Strange."  She continued reading over Gwydion's shoulder, him drinking in the soft sound of her words, the soft air of her warm breath on his ear.

"See the words of this verse;
study the texts of old.
Pay attention you people;
listen well, too, of angels told.
All who have been sent,
and spirits risen from the dead.
I alone exist with none to judge me,
you should feel no dread, while,
seductive sins abound, and deeds without restraint,
disgraceful desires and fleeting pleasures,
followed and embraced.
Until sated and rejected,
all can become sober and rise up to their resting place,
there they will me find, and enter into grace.
And live and not die again."

He quietly folded the piece of copy paper and slipped it back into his back pocket. And the two of them sat in quiet silence for some time. Until they heard noise overhead and Gwydion knew he would make waves if he wasn't there in time to have dinner with the rest of them.

"What do you do in that closet, anyway?" asked his mother. He just shrugged his shoulders and sat quietly at the table. His mother and grandmother shared a look but said nothing and began serving some dinner.

After some time, Antony said, "We are going out for a while. There is a reception for one of the dignitaries that just showed up. Late contingent from Buenes Aries." He looked at Gwydion, somehow thinking he would want to go. But got no reaction."Well, OK, then we get ready in a few minutes. Take care of yourself. We wont be gone long. It's already late."

Which left Gwydion alone for the evening to find something to do. Out back by the canal was his usual haunt these evenings if he could sneak away. It was quiet and dark, and perfect for him to get away and be outside. And besides he was not really breaking the rules, was he?

He took a book and a tiny torch with him, blocked the door open with a tiny rock and sat out in the gloom against the stones of the ancient apartment wall and read his novel with the soft shushing of the water and the thumping of the small boat as background music.

Once he was deep into concentration of his book, he did not notice the dark form rise slowly out of the boat. The shadow jumped to the sidewalk edging the canal and begin to walk toward Gwydion. He looked up just in time to see the dark shape jump at him. And then all went dark.

## Chapter 28
## the Island

Stop moving!" said the quiet voice in Egyptian.

Gwydion felt muffled by something over his face and he felt the rocking of the small craft under him. He felt dizzy and disoriented. But he knew he was not on land anymore.

He must have moaned because the other voice said, "Shut up, complainer!" and a foot kicked him in the side. "We will get to where we are going soon enough, little man."

Gwydion relaxed a little, and tried to not draw attention to himself. What was that smell? And that horrid taste in his mouth? Maybe he threw up. Or the other boy had drugged him with something. And the back of his head hurt. And when he tried to touch it, he realized his hands were bound.

Then he realized with terror that if they were to capsize, he would be unable to swim. And would drown with out a chance.

# Chapter 29
## the island

The boat clunked against something hard and jolted Gwydion awake. He must have been sleeping for a while and crust had formed on his face inside the stinky burlap bag. His hands were raw from the rough ropes and his feet. Well, he couldn't feel his feet. And the air had gotten cold. He could feel it on his wrists and his neck and his back where his coat and shirt and coat had ridden up. There was a little water at the bottom of the small boat and it had soaked into his clothes and he was shivering.

His captor let out a sigh of relief as the reached the shores of what ever destination this was. He grunted as he secured some ropes and bent over to hoist his prisoner up off the bottom of the boat.

"Come on sleepy bastard. We go meet your maker now." he said gruffly. He pulled off the tape around Gwydion's ankles and hoisted him to his feet in the rocking boat. Being moored by a rope only helped a little to keep it steady and Gwydion lost his footing several times before his captor was able to maneuver him off the boat onto shore. Gwydion fell flat on his face when his feet touched the tarmac, his cheek landed in some gravel and dirt there and he could feel his skin [peel away.

"Get up," was the rejoinder to this move, and a swift kick to his kidneys. He scrambled to his feet, and wobbled to stay upright.

"This way," and a yank on his tethered arms, sending jolts of fresh pain into his wrists and up his arms.

The two of them scrambled up a slight incline of gravel with hard tarmac underneath, and Gwydion got the impression of a place out of use, of untidiness and disarray. Weeds clutched at his bare ankles and the cuffs of his wet pants. Good god where are we, he thought to himself. He could hear soft toots of ships out on the water and the sound of the lapping of waves against what ever they had disembarked upon which grew softer and more quiet as they ventured further up the incline.

There was a grunt and a slight decrease in speed of his captor and the sound changed, echoed off a hard surface in front of them, and Gwydion knew they had reached some sort of building. He's taking me in there. It is silent; there are no people here. Not sure if that was a good or a bad thing. Alone with this creature, this hunter. This sick man who had been hunting me for years now. God, he's finally captured me, all that I was running away from for years. It has finally visited me with ropes and sticky plaster. And a really rotten attitude. What did I ever do to deserve this? I don't even talk to people. I don't even look at people. And yet somehow I have engendered his wrath.

H was shuffled through a doorway with no door and into the interior of some kind of building that echoed mightily every tiny sound. No furniture or upholstery, Gwydion thought. In fact this floor doesn't feel like a floor at all. It feel s the same as outside. Like the floor of a barn or dirt yard. And yet I'm inside a hard dwelling. What is this place.

"Right over here, creep," said his captor, "and have a seat right here."

He was spun around and forced into a sitting position and pushed down. And Gwydion felt himself for just a moment flinging backward into space. And jarringly Gwydion's bottom landed on a chair. Quickly more sticky plaster was applied around his wrists and the chair arms. And before he could react, Gwydion's ankles were re-attached with a sticky around the legs of the chair.

"That should hold you, brat."

Gwydion tried his ankles and wrists but they were tight, very tight and they were already hurting and going numb.

I suppose you are wondering why I haven't just killed you

yet. As I've been wondering the same thing to myself for a while now."

He rustled with some things that Gwydion could not see for the blindfold over his head. Then all went quiet and footsteps were heard retreating form the room, shoe soles crunching and scuffing on gravel and weeds. For an eternity Gwydion sat re-breathing his old air inside the hood on his head, and his mind raced with crazy plans for escape. But he was bound too tight, and each time he moved, it seemed the tape dug further into his already bleeding ankles and wrists.

He could hear the footsteps approaching again. Crunch crunch crunch. Then some shuffling and a thud on the ground. Then a zipping noise and some more shuffling. Then a short shuffling and the sharp sound of a match being struck. Then the acrid smell of a match head alight.

Oh God! He thought. He is going to burn me! The animal part of his brain flamed to life. And he began his struggles anew.

"Quit your mewling like some wild animal, you freak. I am not burning you. At least not yet!" and there was a snicker that chilled Gwydion's blood.

There was some shuffling around him, beside behind, beside than in front, and the light had changed, what little of it he could see through the burlap bag. A flickering, like candles. Yes, he had lit candles. In a circle around him.

"Now, I want you to pay attention, freak." His captor squatted in front of him, and breathed in and out noisily a couple times. "I am going to teach you some things. You need to learn to appreciate us. The Word. These ancient of the righteous. You have no respect, you pip squeak."

And Gwydion heard the other boy start to rustle around, kicking off his shoes, then a zipping noise and the sound of a heavy garment dropping to the floor. Then the unbuttoning of his shirt as his captor began to take his clothes off. Gwydion held his breath and prayed it wasn't going to have to be this way.

Then there was more rustling and it sounded to Gwydion like the other boy was wrapping a blanket around himself. Robes. Gwydion visualized black robes of a priest going on this boy in front of him in the candle lit dark. A clinking of chain as he put some type of necklace around his neck.

"Well, now I am ready," he said to the shaking Gwydion. "How about you?" And he laughed at his captive quaking in the chair.

Gwydion felt the other boy's hand on top of his head. And with a yank of the burlap sack and a good chunk of his hair, he whipped the stinking thing off the boy's head.

Gwydion was blinded for a moment, his eyes accustomed to the very dark of the blind fold and now watering in the cold of the night air.

Without preamble the older foreign boy in front of him shot his hands in the air and began to call into the night sky looking down on them from the broken through ceiling of what looked like an old cellar room.

"HEY VAH, HEY YODD!!" he screamed into the night sky above.

Gwydion looked around at the room, and noticed old rusted equipment. Not like a work station, but like old medical equipment, glass shattered, a few wires hanging frayed. This must be the old island village for the insane. There they burned plague victims 400 years ago and made a soil of human ash.

Then his captor began screaming again.

"I request from the original! The virginal spirits of Barbelos. Give me Fore-Knowledge!"

What was he blathering in Latin about? Thought Gwydion to himself. What nonsense was he saying? It sounds kinda like the stuff he had been reading from his grandfather's brief case. But it was just sort of off, not quite right. Like the boy had read it wrong or just made up parts.

The enraptured robed boy swung his gaze down at Gwydion tethered in the chair, and regarded him with is outstretched arms, his hands open to his captive. "Free this heathen from his chains of ignorance!" His spit was praying out in front of him, some of it hitting Gwydion who was disgusted and tried to struggle or tip his chair away from the barrage..

The wild priest's arms shot to the heavens again. "By Christ!! and the Divine Autogenies. I call thee!!"

Gwydion hung his head to keep free of the frothing spit of the impassioned young priest lost in his fantasy of his own religion.

"Relieve this pagan of his wrongful mind. Remove his deamon of ignorance. By the First Archon who used your flame of Luminous Fire to create this ignorous seed." He shouted to the starry sky.

The priest frothed at the corners of his mouth and Gwydion tried not to look. He didn't want to catch whatever this freaked-out person had. Look away; don't be a part of his nightmare.

The young priest in the wrinkled black robes shouted into the candle lit night air, rising motes of old dust into swirls in the candle light. He thrust his robed arms into the air again and shouted, "Hey Yod, Vey Hodd! Remove this deamon and unveil his eyes! Great Yaltobaoth! COME!"

And with that, both boys screamed in agony. A blood curdling scream that filled the chamber and echoed in the dirty crumbling halls of the old asylum for the deranged. The screams echoed and found comfort in these old halls, where prisoners had lain and rotted in their own filth and personal nightmares. The priest in robes slumped to the dirty floor and continued to scream, his torture mingling with the pain of the ranks of tortured ghosts still haunting these broken halls with their ignominious deaths.

Gwydion slumped in his chair and tried to keep his eyes shut tight and his face away from the sight in front of him: his captor writhed in pain and screamed his bloody screams into the silent night, for none could save him.

And Gwydion heard above him the sound of a thousand wings fluttering in the rafters, as gray doves chose the cool night sky to this chamber of horrors below.

And the wind shook his jacket still after the birds had departed, and the wind came down and surrounded him in a cooling embrace, showering his with dirt and feathers and bird droppings, and dousing the candle flames that surrounded him. The soft flapping continued around them as the air settled and they heard the wing beats and the thump of two feet landing onto the floor, a different kind of bird of prey altogether.

The boy priest twisted and squirmed on the filthy floor in his smoking robes, moaning in pain and bewilderment, as the light of the Deamon's fury poured out of his eyes like liquid amber.

Gwydion fought the urge to look up. He would not regard the torture that was taking place. No, and risk it seeing his innocent gaze and entering his soul. He squinted as tight as he could and dug his chin into his chest to hide his face from the amber fury of the demon torturing his prey; captor now captive.

The boy on the floor was moaning in agony and Gwydion heard, no he felt a clarion bell peacefully chime in his mind. And then light hands rested on his shoulders, and a soft cooling sensation moved down his arms to his bloody bonds. And a sweet sound spoke into his ears, a voice he had maybe heard before but he wasn't sure.

"I have come in my Cherubim of Fire of four corners, with each of the eight shapes of stars within. We are only part of the Ekklasia of Angels of the $8^{th}$ heaven. You call us here to your plane in your foolishness and your impotent rage."

The cool touch moved to his wrists and touched the bonds away.

"I take you now. For our dotage as you have desired it so. And as you age, the seven angels will join and create suffering, lamentation, and bitter weeping, so as your mind will flay from its moors until you are ripe for our harvest at your meager life's end. "

The boy priest on the floor spasmed and flipped flat on his back, ridged with terror and pain. His mouth and eyes unnaturally open to the sky pouring out an amber force of liquid fear and horror, an unearthly roar emitting now from his tormented chest.

Gwydion wrenched his gaze from that horror and his hid face against his shoulder. A cool hand caressed each side of his smooth cheeks. "And you, young chosen boy. You have chosen the unenvious Androgyne, and follow a path in dappled sunlight to the hallows of truth, love and the face of Pistis Sophia. And you will not know it is so, that is was a blessed journey, until the end of your days, in the volition of the arena of testing in this world."

And with a mighty clap of great hands. And the fierce gust of winds from it's mighty dark wings, it was gone.

Gwydion's face hung down to his chest, and sweat dripped from his nose. He knew not for how long he had sat there, in a daze, not asleep, not awake.

The boy priest in his soiled and tattered robes lay in the dirt on the floor in front of him, not moving at all.

He heard a rustling behind him and tried to turn to look, but the pain from his dug-in bonds kept him from moving. The pain was everywhere in his body.

The robes in front of him seemed barely enough to cover a body underneath. But surely his captor must still be there, exhausted by his tormented wake performed on Gwydion, a ritual that seemed to have turned instead on himself.

There was another rustling behind him, and Gwydion thought he surely he was not just imagining it. The rustling came closer and then a soft step. Then another.

"Gwydion?" the soft voice he knew he recognized. From where he couldn't recall right now in his exhausted mind.

"Gwydion?" it repeated softly.

He grunted in response.

A soft hand lit on his shoulder, and he winced from pain and terror of his experience at the hands of this mad man on the floor in front of him.

"I think he might me dead," suggested Gwydion.

"No," said the voice thoughtfully. "Not quite. But deathly, for sure. A very sick boy, for now and forever, I should think."

Gwydion moved away from the touch on his shoulder. "Are you hurt, dear?" she asked.

Her hands moved softly down to his hands and lifted them up. She came around in front of him and moved his feet and pulled the sticky plaster tape off them and threw it to the side.

"We've got to go," said Sophie urgently but quietly. "They are coming!" she whispered harshly.

"Who?" he asked. "Who is coming now?"

"Well, I suppose the police." She paused. "And the others," she added cryptically.

She found his shoes that had come off some how during the ritual and she pushed them back on his feet. "We have to go. Now."

Slowly, and with support from his friend, he rose from the chair and stood up, wobbling just a little. He breathed in hard a couple times to anchor himself back in his body on this earth. Then avoiding the prone bleeding form at their feet, the two of them made their way outside and back down to the shore to the little boat he had been kidnapped and brought here in.

They could see lights and hear a siren coming from the direction of town, of Saint Mark's Square. They quickly embarked the tiny water craft and Sophie started its tiny motor. The motored away just as the other craft were coming around the jetty of rocks that was the circular 'driveway' of this little island of horror.

## Chapter 30
## Rescue

After they had cleared the small harbor of the tiny prison island, had left the lights and the siren of the police boat hitting the island shore, she found a dark quiet spot in the canal where there were no other boats. Sophie cut the engines and let the boat drift to a shifting halt. She was deathly concerned for Gwydion's injuries. He was just laying there at the bottom of the boat, in a small dark pool of water not moving or making a sound.

Se found the small on-board red cross knapsack that was attached under the rail, and dug around and found a small battery torch. She flicked it on and thanked the stars the owner of the boat kept the batteries recharged. She held the beam of light up so she could see Gwydion laying there in the water. She reached out her hand and touched his shoulder, on a part that didn't have any blood on it.

"Gwydion?" she said quietly. He did not stir.

She spoke his name softly again, "Gwydion, are you alright?"

He awoke and moaned a little, and his body stirred just a bit. Inwardly she sighed a bit of relief that he was not dead laying there in the wet.

"Are you OK?" she asked.

He moaned and turned his messed up face toward her. He was a mess, she thought. One eye was closed again, and scrapes and dirt and some blood everywhere. She might not have recognized his if she hadn't known who he was.

"Are you gonna be alright?"

He nodded his head slightly and groaned, "I think so."

"I am going to take you home now. Just sit tight." And with that she started up the motor and began their slow thread through the chop and other lit up boats towards the shore and the canal where his family was staying. It would take some time and the sun was coming. She needed to get out of the shipping channel as fast as this little boat would let her.

Gwydion only felt himself be dragged on his feet and out of that dank building, the gravel crumbling and popping under their feet. When they were clear of the walls, he could hear the clear sound of the water in the deep canal and a couple big boats hoot in the shipping canal.

Then he felt himself be lifted into the air a bit and he felt the bottom of a boat on his side, a little bit of cold water lapping at him. But it was cooling and refreshing after the candles and the wild incantations and the blows to his face and the kicks to his shins. He swore to himself that he was alive and felt a bit of gladness and relief that someone had come and gotten him.

The boat roared to life and sped forward. He heard another boat or two close by and even a siren of some sort. The police? What was happening.

The small boat rocked and bucked rhythmically as it fought the chop in the broad channel. The motion settled Gwydion into the bottom of the boat and he felt the cooling puddle of water start to soak into his clothes. It soothed his bruises and Gwydion felt the terror and fear fade away as he dropped into a slumber.

The motor noise lessened and the speed broke off and Gwydion was shifted so his face was facing the cool sky. He thought he saw some light but his eyes were partly swollen shut, so he was not sure. His vision was far too hazy to focus on anything. Everything, his whole body hurt and he could only half focus on what was going around him. A gentle hand pushed at his shoulder and he faced the light for just a moment. His rescuer. Another guardian angel. He knew he should recognize the voice, but his mind was a jumble. But it was a gentle girl's voice soothing and asking him gentle questions. He knew that voice, didn't he? He smiled and moaned in delirium.

The soft voice called him by his name, told him he was going to be fine. That she would take him home to be with his family now.

"Oh, no, my child," it said quietly. "Do not fight me. I am here to help, but only for a moment."

He struggled to understand the comforting voice. He was reliving the violence of the black robed boy priest of an hour ago and struggled in his delirium against these voices tormenting him over and over.

"No, you will not accept me yet. I know that," the sweet voice said into his delirious mind. "But I will be there to help you pass, when many years to come, it is time for you to join us."

He struggled against these words in his mind. "Nooo," he said quietly, squeezing his eyes tight.

"You have some work to do however. We struggle against forces that would change and destroy what is truth and sacred to all. This is the force we saw tonight. They struggle still, for 2 thousand years they struggle against what was once known, in your innocent entry into this world, as truth from the gods."

He was comforted for a moment, then he mind went back to his torture at the hands of the black robed fiend. "Who is that crazy man?" he said to his rescuer.

"He is just a man. A boy. But in his ignorance and desire, he has led these forces into himself. And dragged you into his horror."

Gwydion moaned. She held his head up and said into his face, "The God called to himself is even older than your world. "

Gwydion thought in his mind about the incantation the boy priest had said, "And what was the thing he called down?

Black wings and a stench. He used some weird words, not just the Latin and Greek bits."

The soft voice made a small laughing sound and Gwydion felt a sweet breeze lightly scented with a perfume of flowers.

"Oh, yes. In his ignorance he used the word incorrectly, and in reciting it backwards, drew down upon himself an evil demon. An all-pain-giving angel.

And Gwydion realized what she was saying, and the word letters he had used. Yod Heh Vod Yey, he had said it backwards. Hebrew is read right to left! The realization made him smile and it hurt his face.

"These scriptures from long ago are finally ready to be found by your race of mortals. But they must be understood. For 2 thousand years I lay in that bottle with the dreams and wishes of the old carriers of truth. And when it was broken I was released."

Gwydion thought, Scriptures? Broken bottle? The poems in his grandfather's suitcase?

"Who are you?" he thought inside his head, and he tried to open his eyes. But the light was too bright, and there began a humming increasing inside his skull.

"I am the arch Angel SophieL, and I have knowledge of the vining things in the rocks of the hills, and the wind that breathes life into it. And I've come to ask you to help us."

"You must be strong, and not worry yourself of your pursuer. For I say unto your pursuer, let him be confounded who persecute you, Gwydion. And be you not confounded, for he follows his false ideas. Let him fear, and not you. For I am here to take your pain, and register it to he who is more worthy. And he now carries the memory of the torturing angel within."

She held his head up and her light shone into his face. "And that ignorant fool used our truths unwisely, twisting them into a plan of his own torment. And in doing so rightly pulled into himself a thing that will bring him only pain."

And with that, the light left, the engines roared back to life and the little boat sped quickly through the waning night, into the morning in the ancient city just awakening from a close call with evil.

## Chapter 31
## Homeward

The heavy drone of the airplane engines rumbled around inside Gwydion's head. He slumped over in his seat and tried to sleep, keeping his eyes closed.

He didn't need anymore guff from anyone about that night.

As if it was his fault.

His mother had blamed him for going out into the night and getting beat up. That accusation had shut him up completely. He wasn't about to explain what happened. Not with that kind of accusation.

Will had actually stood up for him. Trying to explain to his mother that it might not be his fault he got beat up. He has a right to walk around and have people leave him alone.

But his mom would have none of it. Too many things have happened and he should just know better.

So, no way was he going to try to explain what happened that night.

Sophie had navigated their way back to the hotel ramp behind the building, unloaded herself and Gwydion onto the walkway and then set the boat adrift to find its way back to its rightful owners. Someone would find it and figure out if it had registration and get it back to the right place. She wasn't about to report it or try to figure out where it was supposed to go, by herself. She did not want to get blamed for any of it.

She had got them home, she explained to Gwydion. And that was good enough.

Then Will had argued that they should report the incident to the police. Gwydion fortunately didn't need medical help, but he looked pretty bad; this was obviously assault.

But Antony had argued, against his good judgment, that they needed to let it drop, and just get home. Their plane left the next day, as it was the end of the convention. And if they reported it to the police, they would have to stick around longer and file reports and give statements, and on and on.

They all opted to just go home and call it an experience. And everyone ignored that it was Gwydion was bearing more than a little bit of pain silently. But inside Gwydion knew that his guardian angel that had taken away most of it with her rescue that night. And he felt perversely strong in his silence among his family.

They had scanned the newspapers the next day to see if there was anything there about a fight or accident that Gwydion might have been involved in. But the only thing they saw was a small piece about a police raid on what was thought to be a Satanic group performing a ritual on the abandoned Island of Poveglia. But there were no arrests mentioned.

"I've heard of that place," said Will Smithershins to the Jacobs family. "Its an old insane asylum on the 7 acre island way out in the lagoon. Hasn't been used in like 20 years. And its said the dirt there is made up of 50% ash from the bubonic plague victims that were burned there 4, 500 years ago. And the Doctor of the asylum was said to have been killed in revenge by the ghosts of the inmates that died there, tortured by his illegal use of a power drill for lobotomies. Its all hear-say. But that's the story. And they want to keep it hush because they are trying to sell the island for a resort site."

"Perfect," quipped Mags. "If it weren't for the ghosts."

"Oh, no," said Bethany. "That sounds perfect for some American interest. The fact it's haunted will be a public draw."

"*The Haunted Hotel*," said Mags in a foolish spooky voice. And Antony and Will laughed.

But Bethany just folded her arms across her chest. She was thinking about the haunted Island, and the Satanic Rite, and Gwydion coming home early the next morning looking worse than being dragged in by the cat.

But all through their day of packing up, his mother still simmered. And Gwydion found himself avoiding interaction with anyone.

So when they boarded the plane the next morning, they happy to be going home, but they acted somber at their mixed experiences abroad. Once on the plane, when they were finally aloft, he had gone and found a quiet seat somewhere else on the plane alone. He was embarrassed and didn't want to talk to anyone.

So he plugged in his ear buds, got out a book, and shut everything else out for the duration of the flight.

Somewhere in the middle of the Atlantic, "Where's Gwydion?" asked Mags of her mother.

"He's parked himself somewhere else on the plane," his grandmother answered.

"I guess that's just as well. I don't even want to talk to him. He is so resistant," Mags shifted with discomfort in her seat. "And all that stuff he was saying the other night? When he came in all beat up. What kinda nonsense lies was all that?"

"You know he has a great imagination," answered Bethany. "Maybe he thought he was the hero of some story. But those cuts and bruises weren't make-believe. They're undeniably real."

"What do you think happened?" asked Mags.

"He obviously got beat up. But I don't know. Maybe that wrong crowd of drinking kids like the other night before," speculated Bethany. She was not going to discuss her irrational fears about a haunted island and that silly report of a Satanic cult ritual. There coulnd't be any possible connection to her grandson's brutal attack. Could there? He'd obviously just gotten in a fight.

"He's always avoided trouble before," Mags groaned. Then added, "But what was that stuff about a girl? Somebody rescued him?"

"He called those kids that night his 'guardian angels'," answered Bethany.

"No, last night. He said something about a girl named Sophia? You didn't catch that?" asked Gwydion's mother.

As far as Bethany was concerned, that stuff about a guardian angel and a girl named Sophie was just a made-up story. *That* was not going to be discussed. Her little grandson was going to safe and sound once they got him back to the states.

"There's no girl named Sophia that I know of," she answered. "Back home or here in Italy." She patted her daughter's knee and added, "He'll be fine. It's just a story. You know what a great imagination he has."

## Chapter 32
## Imprisoned

They had not been able to return by aeroplane from Europe; they had had to take a slow cargo ship back to Buenes Aries. This trip had not been comfortable for any of them. Slow and cold. But was worst for him for sure, nailed up in that crate and labeled as exotic animal so people would keep a safe distance.

But he was alive. And with time they would dig into the old texts the boy had been translating to try to find the ceremony to reverse what had been done. To try to free his tortured soul from what ever deamon had been summoned from the depths of some flaming hell.

Father Micheal hated coming down here, but someone had to feed and clean the poor wretch.

Deep in the dank crypts of an old church, an old stone church built 500 years before, on the bloody backs of enslaved natives, in the sepulchral darkness grown thick with time and imprisoned pain, a twisted figure screamed in the dark, his eyes crossed, tortured, burning from within, the fires from hell.

Chapter 1
Wildlands


The sun was high and burned in the sky like a rogue star. The soft sounds of the horses hooves crunching on the rocks underfoot had lulled the boy to sleep. And he awoke to the sound of Sheridan's voice riding next to him.

"Are you even awake, Rocky?" She asked.

"Hmmm..." He mumbled as he lifted his chin off his chest from the sleeping position and looked ahead at the trail. He looked ahead at the red rocks poking out of the ground, like the only thing that could grow there. And in most places around here it was. This landscape looked most definitely like the surface of the moon. But he thought it was beautiful, desolate, lonely, and pretty much devoid of people. Which suited him just fine. And Sheridan here riding beside him thrown into the mix wasn't such a bad deal either.

But the sun beat down and the top of his hat must've been 200degrees. Thankfully he kept it firmly strapped onto his head whenever he went outside. The sun was brutal, the sky mostly cloudless on most days. And he felt that living out here in the wildlands, your hat could become your best friend.

"Do you think will find them?"She asked him.

"Hmmm..." He just said again, his shoulders and hips swaying to the movement of the horse picking his way across the rocks.

"They said they was out here," she said dubiously. "But I don't see nothing but rocks and sagebrush."

He chuckled under his breath.

They rode some time in quiet, birds flitting from underfoot in the rocks. Soon she said, "We have a few hours before sunset. So let's ride a little further around past the outside watering hole, and will still have enough time to circle back around the ranch."

Again, he just said, "Hmmm..."

And they continued on down the trail side-by-side riding in the old worn jeep tracks that could possibly have been hundred and 50 years old. Still visible in the rocks from the time when the first settlers ventured westward from Utah and Colorado towards the promise of the gold and silver mines in California. And took a chance to cross the wasteland of Nevada, where many of them lost their lives, their dreams floating away in a burst of hot Nevada wind and moon dust.

As they approached a climb up a black hill, the shale dirt sliding downhill behind each step of the horse's hooves, Rocky lifted his arm slightly and pointed with his index finger and a tilt of his chin, and Sheridan saw it too. Just a hint of dust rising up from just beyond the hilltop.

"Wonder what that could be? Might be them."

"Maybe," was all he said.

The horses' ears flicked forward, maybe they knew something more than the riders did. Perhaps it was their sixth sense, knowing where others of their kind were hiding. They were herd animals after all. Or maybe their ears were better and sharper than their riders' kind, and could pick up the sounds they were so familiar with. But as the two riders crested the black hill they could see the small band of horses stomp at flies and kick up dust and dipping their muzzles in a big tank shimmering blue water.

Rocky pulled up his horse with a quiet 'whoa', and Sheridan's horse did the same without her asking. "Well, look'ee that!" She said dryly. Rocky grunted in agreement.

"I just hope Cinnamon is there with them."

They stood and watched a small band of feral horses kicking up dust in the canyon below. They hadn't seen the riders yet and hadn't smelled them yet either because fortunately the humans had been approaching from downwind. Otherwise the wild animals would flee from just the smell'a humans. They needed to get down among them and try to cut free from the herd their domestic mare that had gotten loose the day before. She was missing, probably coming into season, and smelled the wild horses and broke free of her corral. Nothing new for living out here. Just another of the many chores, the occasional problem that cropped up.

"Well, let's do it," was all he said. They loosened their lariat's from the saddle, untying the latigo straps on the right side in front of the pommel, and nudged their horses forward on down the black hill, towards the small band. Far down below, the lead mare picked up the sound, raised her head, pricked her ears and spotted the moving objects up on the black hillside. And she let out a whistle to chill the bones any man, and set that band to running. The two mounted horses immediately set chase. They knew what their job was, they had done this before and they were soon eating the dust of a band wild horses as they fled across the Silver Range.

In the noise and dust Sheridan pointed, and Rocky saw Cinnamon galloping with the rest. And they edged their horses over closer to where she was. Cinnamon must've known ; she saw them in hot pursuit behind her and her pace slowed. She knew personally the horses Jet and Tommy, and nickered softly and slowed her pace down to join the other two domestic houses. Perhaps she'd had her fun, and perhaps she needed a good night's sleep in a barn and domestic hay and grain fed her. And so Cinnamon turned with the other two horses as the three horses and two riders turned towards home. They slowed to a walk as the feral horses fled in a cloud of dust over the further rise of the rocky hills.

"Now Cinnamon," said Sheridan to her mare. "Where have you been, girl?"

They heard a shrill cry behind them and they turned in

their saddles to see where the wild horses had fled. And as the dust was settling they could see the silhouette at the top of the rise of one horse that hadn't followed the others. Mane and tail streaming in the wind, this black silhouette let out a shrill scream that Cinnamon answered with her own knicker. Rocky smiled and chuckled and gave Cinnamon the little swap on the rump with his coiled riatta, and Sheridan said, laughing, "yeah, he's handsome, but let's get on home old girl."

They rode in companionable silence for quite some time, heading into the setting sun west towards the ranch. "Mark your calendar," said Rocky.

Sheridan laughed. "You gonna give us little Mustang colt next year, huh Cinnamon?" Cinnamon shook her mane and snorted a half-whinny and started cantering down the hill towards home.

Chapter 2
Morning

Big chunks of fur were coming out in the comb. "I guess it must be spring time, Cinnamon," said Sheridan softly to her horse, and the mare nickered softly. She stroked the multi-colored fur that up close looked like lots of different colors of hair, but far away the mare looked pink, hence her name Cinnamon. She stroked her slick neck and the mare turned her head and nuzzled Sheridan's arm, wiping some dirt and horse snot on it. It seemed to Sheridan that Cinnamon always knew what she was talking about. Almost like the horse knew English.

"What do you want to do today, 'ol girl?" she asked her. Cinnamon flipped her mane back and looked Sheridan in the eye. What was the old mare trying to tell her. Her adventures over the last few days? Who was that handsome stallion they had seen on the ridge? Obviously a wild horse, but I haven't seen him around before, she thought to herself. The feral horses roamed far and wide, always on the look out for patches of edible grass here and there. It grew sparsely so they were always on the move. And the bands were usually small, and the stallions seemed to change frequently, with the younger ones that survived the battles amongst themselves, going and fighting the older stallions to the death, stealing the bands of mares and foals from them.

But Sheridan was glad to have her mare back. It was an awful feeling to come and find an empty paddock. The horses were often allowed to roam during the day, but they always came back in the evenings for some hay and grain and a safe place to sleep, away from the rattlesnakes and coyotes at night. Cinnamon must have smelled or heard the other horses out there.

Just then a knock and she heard a tap near her on the barn wall, and Sheridan looked up from combing her mare's mane. And just then Rocky rounded the corner with a smile.

"My girls," he said sweetly. "Cinnamon has had her grain, but I wonder if my other girl would like some coffee?" He held up a plastic and aluminum can-like glass with a plastic lid on it. The only way to bring coffee out to the barn. Otherwise it got cold in a minute. And coffee had to be hot.

They sat down on the plastic chairs in the shade against the wall that faced out into the desert canyon. As usual it was already getting hot out here. This was a desert, and the temperatures would swing wildly from morning to night, as much as 50 or 60 degrees sometimes. There simply was not enough moisture in the air to hold the warmth of the day when the sun finally went down.

"I trust you slept well," he said.

"Ya, I'd been so worried about Cinnamon that I had to come out and see her. Her fur is shedding like crazy."

"Well, that's to be expected," answered Rocky. They sipped coffee in silence for a few minutes, listening to the dusty bird song in the morning air.

"I had this dream last night, maybe that woke me up this morning, thinking about that," said Sheridan. They often talked about dreams in the morning, even tho neither of them were really morning people. But on a ranch, early was usually the name of the day. Sleeping in was just sometimes impossible with the ducks and the birds and often the horses going off just before sunrise.

He turned and looked at her. "Really? What about?"

"The skeleton of a friend. Why do I have to dream about an old friend being a skeleton?"

'Someone you know?"

"Used to know. Haven't seen in a while."

"Maybe you should call. See if she's OK." he suggested.

"Naw. No interest. Really don't care. Which is why its weird I dreamed about him."

"Hostile feelings?"

"Ya, maybe that's it. He was always trying to make something that wasn't there. And then this other guy, sort of an ex-boyfriend, told me I should just go have this man's love-child, he called it."

"Oh, so you were an item?' he asked.

"Not as far as I was concerned. But this guy has fantasies I guess. And I told him I didn't even want children. It felt like some kind of slave scam." She tuned and looked at Rocky. "I just don't get the presumptions of people. I mean, why push this having a child thing on me? But I know that's not it. They were just in their own weird head space, which had nothing to do with me."

"They both wanted you and neither of them could, so they made up stories between themselves to entertain themselves and try to confound you," Rocky said, turning toward her again and smiling.

It was a compliment, and yet probably just perfect. Untangling her from other people's nonsense. She smiled at him and said, "Probably that."

"Then there was this other thing, this sheep thing." she

said after a minute. "I've worked here for Mr. Mac Gruder for all my life, my dad used to live here. But for a couple summers, I went away to live with friends. Up to Oregon on a small sheep ranch. I lived in a camper out in the barn which was just fine with me. But the lady had lots of animals and this little flock of sheep, beautiful sheep with colored fur, I mean fleece, that she sheered from the animals and sold for good money."

He just looked at her and sipped his coffee. "I was working on making some furniture pieces in the barn, and one day I decided to go for a hike and check out the sheep pasture. It was rather neglected, I could tell, and the thistles were growing deep and thick. The pasture you could tell had been hacked out of the wilderness of the forest, and when I hiked to the far side of the paddock, it ended in a fenced off forest so thick I couldn't have climbed through it anyway. There was a nice little old barn in the middle, and I went inside. It was sectioned off in areas of pens I could tell for holding the sheep, sheering them and what not, like cattle. But the fences were so short, and I realized how small sheep were in comparison to cows. I walked around in there and one pen had a big pile of fleeces. They wrap and tie them, each one in a bundle." She stopped and sipped her coffee. "Now I remember this because it was vivid and maybe because I've thought about it a lot later, because of what the lady said to me later. I went into a little paddock, and turned and shut the tiny gate behind me. Then I left and went back to work. A couple days later the lady confronted me and asked me if I had gone out into the barn. Sure I had, but I felt guilty, like maybe I wasn't supposed to be doing that. I was a good kid and the youngest in my family, and I think I always got blamed for stuff. Maybe I did stuff wrong, but every kid does. But its that my older brother and sister tattled on me all the time. But this lady said the sheep got out and into all the fleece and kicked it around and made a mess. I swear I shut that gate, but I was too afraid at the time to defend myself so

I think I got blamed for it."

"Oh well," said Rocky. "If all that expensive fleece was just sitting out there, maybe she wasn't taking very good care of her business."

Sheridan just looked at him. "You know you are right. She said later that she should get out of the business. Her sheep had gotten eaten by predators, and she said, if she cant take care of her flock, maybe she shouldn't have one. Some biblical reference I think." Rocky smiled at that.

"But, you know, after all these years, I think I figured something out. She had 3 daughters. And now I see that they were jealous of me, of the attention their mother gave to me while I was there. And I wonder, I just wonder, is it possible one of the girls saw me go out there and then she went out later and open the gate and put some food in to get the sheep to go in a stomp the fleece around, and then blame it on me. Like I am a ranch girl; always always shut the gates. Those girls never had anything to do with the sheep, hated them. Is it possible that someone could think that way, be destructive enough to set that up, willfully destroy their mother's property to get me in trouble, because of their jealousy? "

Rocky looked over into her eyes and saw her pain there.

"Is it even possible, how can people think that way?"

"I don't know," he said and sat back and sipped his coffee from his travel mug.

"The last time I tried to call her, they never answered or called me back. I was actually thinking of getting sheep. But it just kinda cooled my jets thinking about that. The 3 girls are all fancy people now, a lawyer, a doctor and a teacher. That time shows the psychosis of the family: the eldest became a lawyer to get revenge and justice; the next became a doctor, still very important but more on a healthy help-people campaign; the youngest just a lowly teacher: the family has lost their supreme drive to excel and prove themselves." She sat back and sipped her coffee and listened to her mare stomp some flies just waking up in the morning warmth, soon to be relegated to the deep shade during the heat of the day. "Thing is, the father was kicked out of the house soon after I was there. The mom said that I told her to get rid of him. He went a lived with a mistress whom he soon married up in the fancy city. He was a doctor. I don't remember ever saying a thing. I was just a kid. How can she blame her choices on me? But I can imagine the daughters did." Rocky just shook his head a little and gazed out at the barren pasture of sage grass.

"Some things are happening up at the other house today." He turned to her and added, putting his hand on her knee, "Feel like taking another ride today?"

She smiled and said, "We ride almost everyday, silly."

"Just thought I'd make it feel like a choice."

"What's happening up there?"

"Some calves and stuff."

"Sounds like fun."

Chapter 3
branding

The acrid smell of burning hair hung in the smoke as the small group working in the sun. Not even the tiniest breeze stirred the air this morning on this desert land of rock and lizards.

They had gotten up early, saddled the horses and ridden over to Eldred's ranch. Doc Branson was there, and work had already commenced by the time the young couple had reached the holding pen. Black shadows reached across the sand westward as the sun struggled over the tops of the black peaks. There was no hollering or yelling, just a few grants from man and the animals alike as the lowly work took place in a crowded area inside the holding pen. A couple of people were on their horses, saddled with the big saddle, with the ropes stretching out in front of them connected to their quarry between. The calf mewled plaintively, and the hissing of the branding iron could be heard and the plaintive cry turned into a bellow of terror and pain.

Rocky hated this part. He had been helping on the ranches for a few years now. But never would he get used to this part of processing these animals in order for them to be allowed to graze the wild range lands. They had to be branded and ear tagged; it's just what had to happen in order for them to be safe from rustlers. It had been done this way for 150 years out here on this desert graze land, and probably for thousands of years previous in order to mark these animals with their rightful ownership.

But Rocky would never get used to this process of working cattle. He would help; but he was never going to like it.

Sheridan was an old hand. Her father had owned the ranch they were now living on and she had inherited it when he had finally succumbed to cancer, just a few years after his wife, Sheridan's mother, had died in a car accident, when the drunk had broadsided her downtown after he'd left the saloon midday with too many drinks on his tab. And her father didn't last much longer after that. So Sheridan had inherited the place and kept it on as a helping hand with the neighboring ranches, earning some badly needed cash to pay for modern expenses of living in the wilderness. There was no line electricity out to the house, and the water was pumped when the generator was started, and held in a large holding tank on the rise. Eldred's ranch, and Dr. Branson's too, were closer into town than the main highway, and both sported the fine new conveniences of local electricity wiring, and well pump that ran on the same, and it was rumored that Dr. Branson's house even had cable from the city. But that may have been just a myth.

Sheridan took the coiled rope off the side of her saddle, stepped her horse up to the gate, pulled the lever and cantilevered her horse's body through the opening. He did have to spin on a fore-hoof, shut the gate and pushed the lever back in place, never getting off her horse, and locked the gate. Rocky watched with admiration and said to himself, "Yup, old hand, she is." He admired her ease with handling that big bay quarter horse Mustang gelding of hers. She seemed more comfortable in the saddle than she did on foot.

As he watched, she walked old Jimmy around the perimeter of that old black corral, and joined another leather clad Caballero on the other side. They walked their horses to a cluster of doggies, pointed and picked one out, she threw her lariat at the hind end of the calf, and he threw his at the other end and they secured him between the two horses. It always amazed Rocky how the two horses faced each other, and gently backed up until the ropes were taught. The calf then loses his balance and drops to the ground, bellowing something terrible. The riders would then dismount their horses, and one of them, the heeler usually, would walk towards the calf and hogtie 3 feet together, the ones that didn't have a rope around it, and secured with a clove hitch with a loop that could be untied quickly when the job was done. One of the hands would walk over with an ear tag, bend down and snap it through the calf's flap of an ear, and turn to the secretary keeping notes, who would enter the number and the calf description, male or female, bull calf or heifer. The branding hand would then race over with red-hot branding iron with the ranches logo in cast-iron on one end and a handle on the other, and press this instrument of torture against the calf in the proper position on his flank or ribs. And the calf would scream, and Rocky hated it.

But for that little calf, if it was a male, the worst was yet to come. Yet another ranch hand would come with his pocket knife, sharpened ultra sharp just for that day, reach between them poor little critters back legs, pinch the scrotum between forefinger and thumb, and slice through clean about an inch. Then with that same hand he would squeeze out the two small underdeveloped testicles and slice them off with a clean slice and jerk. And toss them over the fence to the dogs happily waiting.

Rocky had seen it all before. But never was he going to get used to that. He preferred to spend his time with the horses. His life here was about the horses. He knew he had a gift for that. It was why he stayed on these years. He had not grown up in the mountains, working animals in the dust. But since his time in that program, the one where they sent young boys who had gotten in trouble, to work hard, and learn some skills, and perhaps be tempered through injury and hardship, he had decided civilization was no longer for him. So he stayed on.

And when he met Sheridan, that time at the grocery store, when he was trusted to run errands, it was instant, that they liked each other. Instant. And he decided when he got out from his term of service, he would find her and see if they could make something of it. She was in complete agreement and they fell in together into an easy partnership. Two young people, alone, following a hardship in each of their lives. And they fell into a fairly quiet companionship out in the mountains, where Rocky could continue to practice the skills that he'd been learning in the program, where he had found that he had an aptitude for the handling of wild horses.

The calf screamed and he was jerked back to the moment and watched as Sheridan pulled the loop and the two lariats loose , and the calf laid there in daze for a moment, till she patted it on it's belly and it jumped up and wobbled off. She shot him a glance, and she could see that he was pale and disapproving, but holding it in. She knew he would help with Roundup and run back, but never with this messy part. She smiled at him the tiniest of smiles, she knew what he was feeling, and appreciated his distaste for this process, but she couldn't know that there was more to it than just that.

She walked back her rope, coiling it with the dust falling off it, back to Jimmy and mounted on the wrong side, and undallied the lariat from the big horn of her saddle. She smiled at him again, wheeled her big gelding. Then her and the other big cowboy rode over to select another calf. This went on for quite some time, there were 27 little calves, all about three or four weeks old, for them to do and finish. Rocky helped walk a small batch of the finished calves out the big gate into a smaller holding pen while the hand shut the gate behind him and his horse. Then another hand opened the outer gate and Rocky walked the handful of calves out into the open where their mothers were waiting, and crying, for their babies. The Calves quickly found their mothers and began whacking their fore heads on the milk bags for attention and a snack of reassurance.

Chapter 4
wakeful

Later that night she found him in the barn quietly stroking his mare's neck. This was a wild animal he had caught off the range and was taming for his own. Not many people could do that, and Sheridan stood and watched in wonder at his quiet movements that were being accepted by the wild horse standing in the stall.

He seemed to sense her and looked up at her down the lane of the dark barn. "I think I can probably ride her soon," he said to her, even though she hadn't asked.

She watched him as he stroked her fur , his hands running smoothly down the direction of the hair laying against the mares smooth flanks. He spoke quietly and even hummed a little bit of a tune now and then. She said nothing, just backed up a step and took in his methods.

He seemed to pause in his progress, and he turned and untied the rope around the metal loop attached to the barn pole. He began to lead the horse out of the barn in the back, to the first catch pen. Sheridan followed after a few moments.

When they entered the sunshine out the back of the barn, she had to pause for a moment to get her bearings and let her eyes adjust. Rocky shut the gate behind him and the mare and Sheridan stopped at it and leaned on the rails of the gate, and watched him unsnap the lead. He coiled the rope and held it up in the air, which startled the young mare just a little and she trotted to the rails of the round pen. Rocky walked to the middle and held the rope in the air, all the time facing the young mare, who was trotting at the rails and looking back and forth around her. When the mare was not looking at him, Rocky would step a step closer to her. When she looked over at him, he slowed and stepped back. Every few minutes he would close the space and the horse would look at him and stop, and then change directions.

Finally after about 20 minutes of this dance, the horse

looked at Rocky and turned her shoulder, and Rocky stepped back and the mare slid to a stop and turned toward him to face him directly on. They both paused for a second, then Rocky murmured under his breath and stepped back one step, and the young mare walked up to him, her ears pricked and her eyes bright.

Sheridan watched in wonder at this non-verbal communication, as she stepped back out of the way and let them come through the gate again.

After Rocky had brushed the horse again, and put her back in her cool stall, finally Sheridan ventured to ask a question. She had been unwilling to break the magical silence before, while he was working with the wild animal. But now she asked, "How did you learn to do that?"

Rocky turned to her and asked, "What?"

"That with the wild horse. Like it was eating out of your hand."

"I don't know. It just comes naturally."

"No way that is all natural. You must have learned that somewhere."

"AT the boy's ranch. You know that. I was there a year and a half."

"Well, ya. But did they teach that there?"

"We rounded up the wild horses for the BLM. Bureau Land management. We did tons of ranch work, and some of us even got to break horses. Some of the boys loved bucking out the wildest ones. They liked getting thrown in the dirt. It was some kind of macho thing." They walked for a moment down the dark alley way of the pole barn. "But I hated that part. It felt like violence to me. They used to make fun of me how I could go and catch the wildest of them. I would talk to the babies and they would come up and sniff me. And those guys used to make fun of me. Call me Rock Head and stuff. But I learned from those colts. They taught me something everyday. I cant really describe it, but every day working with those wild animals, I learned something about myself that I would never have learned in the society of men. I stayed away from those guys. And the teachers gave me things to do sometimes. We got a few of the wild horses and we trained them up and sold them to people. Not ranches; they broke their own wild horses. They just come in and get caught sometimes. But sometimes I think those aren't wild horses at all. But somebody's escaped horses gone feral, and they decide to go back to civilization."

Sheridan just nodded her head and hummed assent, and watched her dusty boots on the hard packed ground of the barn. He continued, "I got this one horse I named Sugar Pop. Such a sweet little mare, colored like sugar on toast, brown and white. She was a wild little baby that came in and I tamed her. She even smelled like sugar." His voice caught and she looked into her face. "She had an accident. She didn't make it." His face closed down and she wondered at that, what the story must be behind there.

"What happened?" she looked him in the face.

"The other boys got jealous and they tired her up out in the pasture on a hot day. She fell on the rope and strangled. I wanted to...I wanted to...kill those guys. That was it for me."

"That's awful, Rocky. People can be so cruel."

"Ya, well, they got theirs too."

"Huh?"

"There were accidents among the boys too. The place got shut down because of it. Sad really, because it did a lot of good, both wild horses and the boys. I think they were helped by such a hardship program. But the state thought that boys dying was not good public relations. although those 2 guys did deserve to die, the way they treated horses. I think some people are just created mean and cruel."

"Ya, Maybe," she said. "But you aren't. You are amazing sweet to that mare. "

"Ya, well, I don't know about that."

Chapter 5
Convicted

They were making dinner later that night, and the steam was building up in the kitchen.

Ah, the weekend. There was always things to do on the weekend. But it seemed to Rocky that the weekends were just mellower for some reason. Maybe the rest of humanity was not so stressed out, and he could simply feel it in the air waves. He bent over the stove and looked at the water in the kettle. Almost boiling. Make some mint tea, cool off after a hot day and read a book. Sheridan was in the living room fluffing some pillows, making herself comfortable on the couch. He came in with two steaming mugs of homegrown mint tea and set them on the knee-breaker coffee table.

As he bent down and set the mugs on the short table, he clipped his little toe on the short curved leg of it. "I hate that coffee table," he said.

"I know you do, honey," Sheridan said. "That's why we keep it around. No really, it is nice to have in front of the couch, isn't it?"

"Ya, right, until I crack my knee on it again, then it goes in the wood pile."

"Or attack it with a hammer again." She laughed.

"I did not!"

"Yes, you did! Right there!" she pointed to a perfect hammer-head shaped hole in the frame.

"Ya, well it shouldn't have jumped out and bruised my knee!" he said in defense.

"Stupid coffee table, getting in your way!"

He sat down with a moan next to her on the couch.

"Watcha' readin'?" he asked.

"Just some crappy murder mystery. It's fun."

"Ya, me too. This one is a supernatural thriller."

"Oh, really? Maybe we could switch when we're done?"

"OK," he said. "No biggie. I just picked it up at the library last time. They have the free books outside."

"They aren't free," she said. "You have to put money in the drop box."

"Oh, I do," he said. "It's like 50 cents for paper backs, and a dollar for a hard back. Almost free. Pretty good deal."

"Ya, it is. I think it's cool that they just have the books sitting out there all the time and no one does anything to them. Not like people are going to steal books, tho."

"Well, and its like, if they want to steal a book, well, maybe we should let them, if they are hard up enough. Not the worse thing you could be stealing."

Rocky laughed. "That's for sure."

"So you never have told me why you were in that boys camp anyway. I am curious, but you've never told me."

"Its hard to talk about. It was a long time ago. I still don't understand what happened myself."

"Maybe talking it out might help."

"You're not going to criticize me?"

"What? Criticize you? I live with you here don't I? Let you into my house? I think you are wonderful. And after watching you work with that poor little terrified filly today, I think you are the most kind person I know. Such a beautiful heart, you have."

Well, that's comforting. Because I killed a man."

Sheridan let that hang there. And just looked at him while his face contorted and went through a set of emotions before settling on fear when he finally looked into her face.

And they just looked at each other for a few moments until she said, "why don't you just tell me about it.."

Chapter 6
My enemy

"I was at school back in California. That was a few years ago. I was in high school and things had settled down and seemed to kind of be going normally for once." He looked at her sitting on the couch next to him. "You know how it is. You went to high school, didn't you?"

She looked away from his face for a moment. "Yeah," she paused and swallowed heavily, "I hated it too."

"Ya, I pretty much hated it, every minute of it. Except for this one friend I had..." He didn't finish the sentence. But continued, "but after we came back from a trip abroad, people kind of left me alone. My mom said that I had grown a couple inches that summer, and I did gain about 30 pounds. So maybe people were kind of afraid of me. Or maybe they didn't recognize me from the year before. I don't know all I know is things were kind of calm, and then this thing happened."

She looked at him with a concerned look on her face. "What happened to you, Rocky?"

"He found me. I thought it was over, but no. After all that time, somehow he found me. Again."

The boy was waiting outside at the edge of the track and field yard. He felt like he had been waiting forever. He had been waiting for his final opportunity to take back what was his. To take back his dignity and his strength from this little creep that had stolen it from him years before. He couldn't recall exactly what it was, but he could feel the pain burning in his heart, in his mind and in his groin, the centers where all passions started.

Chains clanged in the dark dank air. A hinge squeaked as a heavy iron door swung just slightly open. "I've come to give you your evening ablutions, my boy. I know you don't understand what is happening. This daemon has possession of your soul and I feel that with the cleansing from God you can be restored, and it can be driven from your body."

The priest bent over the prone figure on the wet floor and touched his shoulder. "Josiah?" he said giving the clamming shoulder a slight shake. "Are you alright?"

An arm swung up and just missed smacking the priest in the face. And the pale body dressed in ripped rags twisted as if in agony and pushed itself into the corner and sat up against the dripping wall. From a pale face tormented with demons peered a young man with dark brown eyes, bearing the mark of Satan, slightly crossed eyes, now blood shot through with red. These wild eyes regarded father Michael with first hatred, then suspicion. And slowly this was replaced with the more civilized emotions of curiosity and understanding

The Father stood watching as his charge changed just slightly into a somewhat human being. He had been watching this gradual transformation grow ever so slightly more pronounced with each session with his prisoner he now called Josiah for lack of a better name. This ragged boy had shown up at the door of the monastery several years ago with just the clothes on his back and a new map of the town clutched in his hand. He had seemed disoriented but harmless and this kind father Micheal had taken him into the monastery and had given him tasks around the place. With time this young man had proven his intelligence and had learned the language that had once been totally foreign to him. Very quickly too, in father Micheal's opinion.

So he had begun tutoring him in religious studies. This was after all a monastery and the boy seemed to have no training in that regard at all. Father Micheal had no idea if the boy had been raised a Catholic or a Christian or what not. But the young man had never given any information in that regard. So father Micheal did what he does best, and gently brought this young man into the fold.


It was after school and I was just hanging out on the track and field. I didn't do sports or band or anything. I just liked being up there and watching all my friends playing ball and stuff. Well, they weren't really my friends, but at least I kinda felt like I belonged. But then *he* was there again. He was always just showing up when I totally did not expect it. Like the year before in Italy."

"You were in Italy?"

"Ya, with my family. They do archaeology and teach and stuff."

"GO on," she said.

"So anyway, he was there. Just standing on the field and this time I saw him right away. I could tell by how he was standing, it was him. Smoking his cigarette. And when he turned and looked right at me, I ran. I ran for the buildings, I figured I could find some people and be protected." He looked away and breathed audibly for a moment, and Sheridan said nothing. "It was like he had been waiting for me and watching me for a long time. It always seemed that way. Just watching me, with the hair on my neck prickling, and I just couldn't believe it was happening again."

He took a sip of cola and set it down with a slop on the pool of condensation of the table top. "I ran into the math building and there was no one there. So I ran down into the science building and there was no one there. So I kept going and went into the main building, the new one with the second story and ran down the long hall way and there was absolutely no one there. I couldn't find anyone. Maybe they were all up at the field. It was getting dark and the game was hanging over time. So I stopped in the foyer and listened. I couldn't hear anything but the distant noise of the crowd cheering. And my heart beating in my ears."

His eyes were bloodshot when he looked into hers for just a moment. "Then I heard him in the hall. He was right behind me, he must have flown. He knew right where I was. I hate him."

The tea pot let out a shrill whistle from the kitchen stove and they both jumped. Sheridan hustled to go turn it off and make them some tea. But by the time she got back, the terrified boy was curled in a fetal position on the couch, clutching pillows, sound asleep.

"OH, I really hate that kid. He is the worst," thought the older boy about his nemesis. "I thought for sure I had finished him last time. But he had help! Where did that come from? Out from the sky flew help for this punk kid that just needs to end. So cute and pretty with his curls and the love of his nauseating family. Well, we'll see about them too. Those kind of lies can only last so long in this rotten world anyway. He'll see that all fall away and then where will he be? In a grave because I'm putting him there! His smug looks and his comfort with those kids in Italy, them helping him get away from me and get back to his family, disgusting. How can he be so lucky?"

He stormed and fumed in his black heart, the boiling rage that had been festering for years, and had lodged on this one young boy. It was a rage from somewhere else, from long ago, from abuse and isolation suffered at the hands and filthy ingrown minds of his family in the outback of northern Greater Persia, a place where the new age of technology and internet had not even been imagined yet. A place where hardship and disease would destroy a young man's heart before it even had the chance to know love.

The priest captor had finally let him out of his cell. He had lost the moorings of his last vestiges of sanity after the attack on the island. He had felt his body become inhabited by a dark spirit from somewhere else, someplace infernal and dark, glowing with the red hot flames of hatred. He felt them burning in his chest now, but he had to control them; he had to keep them down. Just for a while just long enough. Enough to get out of here and finish his mission. That boy cannot be allowed to complete his translations. He held the key, and he could not be allowed to continue.

But he was out now. He had fooled this silly old priest. He had actually convinced him that he was going to be OK, going to be a normal boy again. Let me out and I'll show you just how good a boy I can be. And the lowly priest had believed him. With practice and concentration he had buried his torment deep into his soul, where it smothered and writhed. But he had soothed it with promises of revenge and of fulfilling his mission of snuffing out the boy. But he had to get out of these chains. He had to get away from this simpering priest and get back to where the boy was now languishing in his American comfortable home, with its air conditioning and refrigerators, and television sets and headphones. He knew right where to go too. The dumb kid's wallet had fallen out of his pocket when he escaped the island, and in it had been his student card. His high school library card. So easy to track him down and find him And show him. Oh! He would show him. He would teach them all just how strong he was and just how dedicated he was to the cause. That boy could not be allowed to finish his translations and send his blasphemous ideas back out into the world. The scriptures that had been safely buried for two thousand years, that had been safely locked away with the memories and their own guardian angel for two thousand safe quiet years, while the real religion held sway, with its successful controlling of the minds of these rotten animal aboriginals through the fear and persecutions they deserved.

And now there he was. Just standing there across the field looking at me. He's spotted me. Of course he knows. All victims know they deserve what they get. Why else would they stand there and take it?

The priest had just stood there and taken it too. He thought in his hubris that he was fixing me. He was going to fix his little boy all better, because he was the big strong smart priest who thought he had god behind him. What did he know of god? Silly simpering human. With his vestments, and his pomp and his chants and smoking incense. And that smug loving look on his face. What a fool. I fooled him. And when I stood up over him, after all the humiliations he had subjected my body to, his huffing and puffing and grunting and sweating on me, telling me those sick simpering love poems of god and little boys, when I pressed my thumbs into the soft flesh of his flabby neck, what did he do? He reached out and asked for forgiveness? He said Please? Please what, Old man? Am I your deliverer of your grace? Finally you get to go meet your maker? After all these years of wishing to but not having the strength to do it your self? Just starve yourself or shoot yourself, and end your body's tyranny over your immortal soul. Finally I am the one to release this from the earthly bounds for you. And yes, you say please to me because I am doing it for you. And you think because you call it murder that you will go to heaven and me to hell. Like a last minute's recanting and confessing changes anything. They read from the entire book of your life, weak mortal, the entire book of your choices and misdeeds and you think the minions of judging angels will give you rest because of a moments recanting and regretting your sins?. I know not! I know now for sure you do not get off that easily, old man. So here you are your deliverance.

And I had pressed and held him, while he struggled against me and what he surely wanted, release from these mortal bounds but was too afraid to do for himself. And he struggled against my strength, and he fouled himself in the most vile and animal kinds of ways, even the way he spilled his seed, as he had done to my mortal body during times of corporeal ecstasy, he fouled himself that way too, and disgusted all the angels and their minions of justice and revenge in the divine firmament.


Chapter 7
Damages

The next morning Rocky had to go into town for supplies. It was a hot morning, promising to be a hot day. A very hot day.

So he left as early as he could, to catch as much of the early morning coolness that was left after the sun actually rose above the mountain.

Which wasn't much. It was probably already almost 90 degrees at 8 in the morning and the steering wheel of the old truck was hot to the touch. He loaded the dogs in the back and started up the old jalopy. It coughed and sputtered to life and Rocky pushed in the clutch, shook the stick into gear, and eased on the gas, and the old truck started to move forward.

He liked this old truck. Simple technology. Hand-crank windows for air-conditioning. And he didn't have to worry about the dogs ruining the interior. The seat could always just be duct taped again. And the gray back window? Well, the windows came pre-slobbered on. He wasn't even sure if they would even clean off at this point.

So they clattered and chuffed on down the road. And really that old dodge ran pretty good once it got warmed up.

He felt he was in no hurry. He rarely was. It was mid-summer, and early in the morning, so that meant animals in the road, and Rocky went along slowly. Why hurry, was his motto anyway. Enjoy the sun coming over the rocks and pines, and listen to the air whistle around the wind wing of the old truck door. They just don't make them like that anymore.

The dogs hung out each side of the pickup bed, one on each side like ornaments, drooling like gargoyles over the side and onto the metal walls of the truck bed. Their tongues hung down and their ears and lips flapped in the wind as he drove. Some said it was a smorgasbord of smells for a dog to drive along in the wind like that.

Whatever. But to Rocky, it sure looked like they were smiling.

Just as he came out of the sun and around a shaded corner he caught movement just off the side of the road, just as a deer jumped the fence to get out of his way. He slowed almost to a stop. Because where there was one deer, there was usually another to follow. And right now at this time of year, the mommies were having their babies. Some mommies were heavy and sluggish with carrying their loads of a soon-to-be-born babes, and some others of them were going slow, waiting for their babies to catch up and figure it all out. They had to all learn about the road, and to stay away or hurry off.

So Rocky sped up after he passed what seemed to be the game trail, the area where the female deer had just crossed. And the dogs ran around the bed of the truck looking for some game quarry to bark at. Mostly they found and ran into one another and then resumed their slobber positions just behind the windows of the cab.

In town he parked in front of the small store and slapped the dogs on the sides of their wet jowls and told them to "Stay Here!". They usually did. They weren't that protective of the truck. But woe to anyone who got too close to them. For they would be treated to a faceful of slobbery dog kisses.

When Rocky came back out, those old fool dogs were waiting for him in the back of the truck, just a-slobbering and a panting away. But it was getting hot and it was time to get back with out further ado. The hardware store downstairs below the country grocery store was enough to supply the fence nails Rocky had needed to put back up the wire that the mustangs had pulled off the last time they visited and went through the gate.

Rocky popped a can top and settled in the drive home. It sure was heating up fast today. He was glad he had gotten some work done earlier this morning but maybe wasn't going to feel like it later today, not till later that night.

He turned the corner just as a truck sped past the other way going way too fast, and Rocky cursed fast drivers. As he entered the shade, he saw something up ahead on the road. Some kind of road kill.

"I guess I should stop and drag it off the road." He usually did this, and today alone he had already seen a dead wild turkey and a flattened skunk in the road. He usually stopped and dragged them off the road onto the shoulder or out into the grass. He didn't always stop. Not if they were too hamburgered or dry and flat. But a fresh carcass was bait for the carrion birds and the thing he hated most was when there would be a carcass and a dead bird there too, a big bird who had landed for lunch and then gotten hit by a car for his efforts. Just nature doing its thing. But people didn't care. They just kept on driving. And hoped their car didn't get any blood on it.

Kind of made Rocky sick. So he usually pulled over got out and quick-like pulled the dead animal off the road.

There wasn't much traffic this early, so he drove carefully over the dead thing, not letting his tire run on it again, and stopped just off the road. He quickly got out and walked back to the animal in the road. It wasn't very big and he wasn't sure what it was. A light brown jackrabbit with those big ears.?

But as he approached, to his horror he saw one long leg reach up into the air as if it was trying to get up. But the back end of it he could see was mangled. And then he saw its white spots. As he looked into its tiny face with the huge soft ears, its one eye rolled a little and looked at him, through the just-forming milky veil of death, and it seemed to breathe its last breath and go slack.

He cursed out loud and grabbed the little fawn by the back legs and pulled it off the road onto the gravel. Just as he turned to get back in the truck, a car drove by with some kids in it, going way too fast, and they shouted at him, "Slow down asshole, for killing animals!" Rocky just shook his head sickened by the irony, and made a split second decision. He hoisted the young fawn up into the truck bed with the dogs and clambered back in the drivers side and sped home.

Others might not have understood. But to him it seemed it was an honor to the useless, careless death of the week old baby fawn, to not let it go to waste, rotting on the side of the road, to feed his working cattle dogs.

Chapter 8
revelation

"I just don't know," he shouted at her. "I cant remember so stop trying to get me to talk about it."

"I just want to help you," she answered, sounding just a little too plaintive. She turned away and swore to herself she wouldn't sound whining to him. But she continued quietly, something was lurking in his mind sometimes, like a black shadow would pass over him and he wouldn't speak for hours, days sometimes. "What is it?" She sat down with a thump and a puff of dust onto the couch, folded her arms over her cotton button up shirt. Something to do with those dang calves. That's been eating you for months now, and just wont let go."

He turned his body facing away from her, and looked out at the sun setting behind the Sierra range. The sky was a flame red with the fires that had burned around the state today, now that summer was in full swing, there were always a handful of fires burning somewhere.

"I cant shake this feeling that it had something to do with my time in South America."

"But you were just a baby, weren't you?"

"I was a baby there, but we stayed for a while, until I was in like 4th grade, when we went back for a time to Kansas."

"So like 9 years old...?"

He was silent and sat down on the barcalounger across from her. It squeaked in protest and launched a little cloud of dust all its own. Summer on a ranch.

"Why don't you just start and see where it goes," she said quietly.

He sat back and closed his eyes. "My mom was really young. I don't want to blame it on her but sometimes I just really hate her guts for what she did. She and my dad ran away from home during high school. My grandfather warned him, they didn't listen. They ran away to Mexico and I was born a few months later. And we lived near the ocean beach just a short walk from the cabin we lived in. It wasn't much of the cabin but I remember it pretty well. I had my own room

"But sometimes it night I heard things. There were sounds that came from the jungle that didn't sound like wild animals. It sounded like drums and yelling, and I was often very afraid. Dogs would howl and screeching sounds I'm not sure where birds. And I would shut myself in the room and hide under my covers."

"Where were your mom and dad?"

"Thing as, I don't know. They just weren't there. And then when my dad left for good, my mom was there even less."

"What do you mean," she asked. "She just left you there alone?"

"Ya, pretty much," he answered ruefully. "So then I learned to escape. I remember being really afraid, like I was going to get in trouble, but then I realized that she wouldn't, well, no one was around to know if I went off." He stood up and moved away from the window, as if someone was watching him make this confession. "I guess I learned how to take care of myself that way. And I would just wander off into the jungle."

She just chuckled and shook her head. "But then they found me missing one time, and that freaked her out. She must'a yelled at me for days. She was worried. She left me there alone and she was worried."

"Oh, she was feeling guilt and trans placing it off onto you," said Sheridan with a laugh.

"Ya, you are probably right. But she was really mad. She started by locking the doors and the windows. But I managed to get through those anyway. Figured out the latches, and just climbed out into the night." He looked at her during his pause for breath. "Then when she found out I could still get out, she tied me down. At first it was a joke, but then she kept doing it. Tied me to the bed so she could go out catting around. No way was that going to stop me. I learned to chew through one. And once you have a hand free, I discovered you can untie yourself.'

"I cant believe she did that!" she said to him.

"Its true!"

"No, I mean its just wrong. I think its illegal to do that."

"Well, welcome to my weird world and my weird mom." He said shaking his head.

"So where did you go? What did you do once you got free?"

"I think I thought that once I was free, why stick around. I really left and went off to play. But then one time, I followed them. I got out fast and followed the noises. I figured they were having a bash-out party and wanted to see what it was all about."

"You went to the party, and you were how old?"

"I was seven. The first time I followed her, I was seven. It was the last time too."

"Why? What happened?"

"I don't know. It was just adults doing weird things."

"Like what weird things?"

"I don't know. Just weird adult things. I don't want to talk about it." He got up and went into the kitchen and got a glass of tea. She followed him in there, and got something to drink too.

"You aren't getting off that easy, Rocky. My interest is all picked now."

"I don't even remember. Maybe I have blocked it."

"Why don't you just start describing what they were doing and see if we get anything?"she said encouraging him, sitting him down at the table.

He took a big drink of tea and then started. "At first they were all sitting around a big table and I was watching through the window. Remember these are not much more than huts down there. Nothing really like the houses we live here in the states. Most of those places don't even have windows. Never snows or anything. So I could see. They were bending over the table and sniffing at stuff. There was a pile of white stuff in the middle of the table. And bottles of beer. Just a party."

"Drugs," she said.

"Huh? My mom doesn't do drugs!"

"Really. Well, maybe she wasn't partaking in the white stuff. Or maybe she was."

"What are you talking about, Sheridan?"

"Cocaine, ding-dong. That would have been the late 50's right? They were just starting to make that stuff down there, that's where it comes from, right? You said Central America? Right?"

He let out a loud exhale and did not acknowledge her theories. But just continued in a monotone. "Then they all got up and went outside. They were carrying things, musical instruments and drums, and they walked off down the trail into the jungle, and that was it."

"Oh, bull. You followed them."

His face started to get red and his breathing was speeding up. "No, I don't remember anything else."

"By the looks of your face, you are remembering, or starting to remember. You need to let this out. This is bothering you."

"There's nothing more!"He shouted top of his lungs. "Leave me alone!" He stood up and his chair flew out, and he stomped back into the living room and sat down on the couch. She felt he was just willing her to come out and join him, that the subject was not really closed. So she stood up from the kitchen chair and went and joined him out there. She turned sideways and looked at him on the couch. "And then what happened?"

"They walked way into the forest, and I was totally freaked out. I mean I was just a little kid so I had to follow now. I would have gotten lost if I had tried to go back. So they walked and walked. Middle of the night, a little moon, and they came to a temple. You know one of those pyramid things they show in science magazines."

"Oh, ya, you mean the ones with the steep steps up one side. The south American pyramids thingies."

"Ya it was one of those. And they all walked up the steps, and there was light coming from inside the door at the top. So they all hiked up there and I watched them go up and inside. They disappeared inside the thing. So I wasn't about to stand there watching so I had to go up too. I went up the steps and went inside the door. There was a set of steps back down and there was music and voices and light and smoke coming from down there. I was freaky curious now. Like the cat whose curiosity gets the better of him. I climbed down to the bottom and saw what they were doing. I fucking saw what they were doing." He said as tears squeezed out of his eyes. Sheridan was too shocked to even say anything. She just stared at him, until he continued.

"There was this boy, a dark boy, one of the local kids, and they had him tied up onto the rock slab that was there. He was screaming and moaning, but I think they must have drugged him because it wasn't normal screaming, like he was only half awake." Sheridan just stared at him. "Tied and there with ropes. And he was...he was..."

"Yes?"

"He was naked. I mean totally. And there was a guy at his feet, reaching between the kids legs, you know, his, you know, privates?" He looked into her eyes beseeching that he didn't have to tell this story, knowing that he had to, he needed to.

"And the kid let out a terrible scream, like what the priest was doing down there woke him up in an instant. The priest held up a shining knife, and then reached in and swiped with it, and his hands came up red, holding something, dripping, and the screaming stopped, like the boy had passed out."

There was silence for a few moments. "That's all I

remember until I woke up back at home. I don't remember anything more." He looked at her with tears in his eyes. There were tears in hers too. She simply reached forward and held him in her arms.

Chapter 9
mother on the couch


"Well, doc, I was really hoping to get a little help with my son."

"Oh, well, what has he done?"

"Well, nothing really. He just wont visit us anymore."

"Oh, I see. And how long has this been going on?"

She shrugged and moved around in the deep chair facing the doctor's desk. "He moved out a few years ago. He had some trouble in school, and he went somewhere for a while."

"So, he didn't come back to live with you after that?"

"Right. He just stayed away. It's like he found another life or something. We were so close before. But then we started to grow apart and there seemed like there was nothing I could do. I tried to be friendly, you know, get to know my own son. He was going through that awful teen age period and just grew away. He had trouble. He always had trouble."

She sniffled and looked up at the doc. "And I was hoping you could help him."

"Well, let's just start with you since you are here," he said as he looked up from his notes to look at this mother estranged from her teenage son.

"I want to help him, but he wont listen anymore." She sniffled, "Well, he never really listened. He was such a strange boy. Right from the start."

The Doctor said, "Hmmm..."

This was an appointment paid by the institute, along with her working wages there, teaching in the large classroom with all ages, she might not have gone to a psychologist if it hadn't have been paid for by her work.

No, really quite frankly she definitely would never had taken this kind of an appointment if it hadn't been paid for by her work. Her boyfriend was kinda out of the picture, and since her father's death, she was really having a hard time with any of it. Slog to work in the morning, slog back to the house in the evenings and have a meal with her mother. But the boys were gone.

All the men were gone. What was it about her that she always drove her men off. She had often wondered that, and of course had never found an answer, but vaguely slipped a little further into a sinking feeling in her heart with each time.

If I could just have one of them back, she would tell herself.

No, I cant have any of them back. I am just going to have to learn to accept it.

"You can never accept these things if you don't talk about them. The human mind doesn't just stuff things to the back and they are gone. "Accepting" takes a kind of inner dialog with ones self, to talk about your life story to yourself and learn about what changes are taking place. Sometimes talking about things that have happened to you bring to light new things that are bothering you and then you might be able to let them go finally. So why don't we start there."

"Start where?" she asked.

"Start anywhere."

I ran away from my home when I was barely in high school I couldn't stand my parents, they were so...so... smart. They knew everything. They always knew everything and always made me feel stupid. So I showed them and moved out on my own and left the country with a guy.

"Oh, you moved away from your family young, kind of like your son?"

Huh?" She looked at him stunned. With anyone else she would have yelled at him. But you cant do that with a doctor , can you?

"No, actually I was younger than him when I left. And I went further. I went to central America.

The doctor just looked at her. "Alone? No , with your boyfriend. And how long did that last?"

"Last? Right up until the baby was born. Then he was outta there."

"And he was American?"

"Ya, he left and went back stateside. We sort of picked up again after I came back to the states, and then the whole family traveled abroad." She twisted a handkerchief. "Then he left again. Haven't seen him in years."

"The father of your boy?"

"Yah. A real dead beat. Doesn't give us support. Well, didn't. I've lived with my parents since then. Until my father died last year. Now it's just mom and me. Broke his heart you know. His grandson getting arrested and all."

"Arrested? Sounds serious."

"It was. Very scary. But they let him go to a boy's school instead of jail. He was too young to go to real jail."

"So, tell me about Central America, where the boy grew up."

"Not much to tell. We lived simply, I worked during the day doing fruit and shipping. And the landlord watched over my boy. I think it was a nice life. So simple and clean. The ocean was right there, and we used to go for walks on the sand. And he would pick up shells and crabs and fill his pockets, and I would make him put back the live things."

The doctor watched as tears grew in her eyes as she wistfully recalled her first years with her baby boy.

"No sign of trouble yet for him?"

She looked at him with haunted eyes and shook her head almost imperceptibly. "He was strange. I loved him. But he was strange."

"Strange in what way?"

She looked away and wrung her hands. This doctor was new to the institute, brought in just recently. So he didn't know anything about his patient here, before him nor her son. She couldn't know that he was brought in specifically to help this woman and perhaps help her win back her son.

But the doctor couldn't know, not just yet anyway, what strange alley of human consciousness he had just wandered into.


Chapter 10
haunted past

Oh, ya, your mom called."

"What did she want?"

"She said she had some stuff from your grandfather she wanted to give you."

"Did she say what it was?"

"Nope," she answered. "She just said it was wrapped up for you from him."

"Huh," was his cryptic answer. "Did you give her our address?"

"Yup. Again." she looked at her young boyfriend. "I don't think she likes me."

"Oh, you know, don't take it to heart. She is kind of a looper. Really don't worry about it." he said. "besides its none of her business."

"She said that your sister misses you." She looked straight at him and put her hands on her hips. He avoided her stare. "You did not tell me you had a little sister. How old is she?"

"She is just two."

"She's, two and she misses you?"

"She's uh, different."

"What does that mean?"

"Precocious. That might be the word. Like I was, weird, but she had
   s the gift of gab. She talks all the time, since before she could walk."

"Well, so what's her name?"

"They call her Cindy. But I call her Shalome."

"Well, I hope I get to meet her."

"Maybe some day."

"Your mom also said there is a thing coming up that you should go to."

He let out an animal groan from deep in his chest.

"Something in New Mexico. I think we should go."

"WE?" he said looking up at her.

"You are not going with out me."

"What about the animals?"

"Doc Branson always has young students that need a place to stay and practice running a ranch. Easy-peasy."

He exhaled sharply. "And when is this thing we have to go to in New Mexico?"

"Later this summer. Whoohoo a trip!" and she began dancing around the room. "Oh ya. And they want you to work on some of this stuff your grandfather left unfinished, whatever that means."

His eyes lit up just a little, "Is she sending some stuff?"

"Ya, with the box of the other stuff from your grandfather." She stopped and looked at him, and asked, "Do you think she will bring the baby? I mean your sister?"

He just shrugged like it was inevitable, and he was uninterested, and Sheridan started dancing again.

He just looked at her and said under his breath, "Ya you're happy now. Just wait till you meet these creatures!"

Chapter 11
Old stuff

He had been so bold as to make copies and take them with him when he went off to the school for boys. He had them in his books and they allowed him some certain freedom with these things. There were two boys to a room and his room mate even had taken an interest in them. Simon had been fascinated by the pages of ancient letters, and had once commented on how it looked like what his grandfather had often read during Passover.

From the original Hebrew of some ancient scroll, he had told Rocky one night. And from then on the two of them had a secret friendship and bond like no other.

But they were teased, two nerdy boys doing weird non-boy kinds of things. But the wardens had encouraged reading and studying, after all they were skipping out on high school and he figured if the boys took to studying on their own, then great, encourage it and keep them safe from some of the more bullying of older boys.

But Rocky had started telling some of his ghost stories when he had the chance, especially at night, they seemed to be effective, and the other boys granted him a bit of respect and showed him some deference. His friend Simon had suggested that it might also be because it had been spread around really quickly that Rocky was in here because he had killed a man.

So what are you in here for, Simon?" he had asked his roommate finally after some of the newness had worn off and little mutual respect had been shown.

"I got in a fight," was the reply.

"Must have been quite a fight, to land you in this place."

"My family was livid. They didn't exactly stand up for me. Some things just didn't get said and so I get persecuted."

"Oh, religious persecution. I get it. So you stood up for your religion."

"Well, actually no. I stood up for my friend's. He was catholic. And they were taunting him about going to church every Sunday. So I stood up for him and the boys attacked me. I smashed some heads, that's all."

Rocky smiled at his friend. A bar room brawl was one kind of thing. But this was another, and he smiled and nodded his head at his new friend.

"So, what is that stuff you are reading?" Simon asked him one night.

"Some stuff my grandfather gave me. Well, I stole it from his briefcase and copied it. But I don't think he would mind. He used to read this stuff to me at night when everyone else was in bed. Old stuff from his work. He translated ancient manuscripts from Egypt."

"And you can read this stuff?"

"I cut my teeth on it when I was 5. We were traveling and I didn't really go to school, and just picked this stuff up looking over my grandfather's shoulder. "

"Let me see that." Simon grabbed the sheets and looked at the letters on it. "This is Greek."

"Some of it is Greek. You read Greek letters?"

"I know some of it," said Simon. "Some of our books are in Greek. The old Torah and some of the things we read at holiday. I cant really read it, but I recognize it. Will you teach me?"

"Well, you can follow along and maybe you will catch on."

Simon got a pencil and some paper from the office the next time he was there with the warden and used those to write and copy down the letters to learn them. Next was translating the lettered out words into English meanings. They had a dictionary, but of course the art of translating was not an exact thing.

"What is it that you are working on now?" Simon asked his room mate about the folded up papers he had under the small light at their shared desk. He pulled up beside him and read along with what he had been translating.

"It's called the Origin of the World, kinda like the Genesis in the bible."

"That's old testament, actually from the ancient Jewish bible." Obviously this boy knew exactly what he was talking about. How could he? It must be something about his religion. How many secrets could they have, If only I could pick his brain, thought rocky.

"It's called the "Origin of the world" from the Nag Hammadi scriptures," said Rocky.

"Oh, ya. Its one of the apocryphal gospels."

"The what?" said rocky looking at his diminutive friend in the upper bunk. You know about that?"

"Sure. The apocrypha are the stories left out of the bible when it was finally formed in the year 362 ade Domini, something like that. which was when the Christian church was formed."

"You know about this stuff?"

"Sure. Normal stuff we learned at Shule for boys. I know. Not regular reading."

Rocky was astonished. What a friend he had found.

So he read out loud for Simon what he had translated so far. It wasn't that much.

In the beginning, in chaos actually comes from shadow, and the shadow is sometimes called darkness. But a shadow comes from something that had existed before, so chaos came after what was in the beginning..

Sofia or knowledge flowed from Pistis, or wisdom and faith. Sofia served as the veil separating humans from those beyond.

When this shadow sensed that the Sophia was stronger than it, it became jealous, and became pregnant from this powerful thought. And it swiftly gave birth to envy. But this envy was an aborted fetus at and therefore had no spirit in it and it came into being and existed as a shadow on the surface of a watery substance. Bitter wrath formed from the shadow and was sent to exist in the region of chaos.

When Sophia saw this darkness and deep water she wanted it made into a define image, and an arch on appeared like a lion in face androgynous with great authority but ignorance of his own origin. She named him Yaltobaoth, or Ariel, because he looked like a lion. And here the faculty of speech came, and it pertains to the gods, angels, and people. Things come to be made by the power of words.

But here it left off, and there was no more translations of this particular document. He really hoped he could find the rest of it. he knew there had to be more, and it was probably in the latest translations of his grandfather, the ones he made right before he died. But where would they be? Most likely, hopefully, locked up in those boxes his mother had for him at the old house in San Francisco.

"Oh, I like that. where did you get it?" asked Simon of his friend.

"This is part of a translation my grandfather was working on. and I stole this and copied it from his briefcase. But that's all there was. I know there is more somewhere."

"Ya, there is much more. I recognize that as the old beginning of Genesis. And it gets to the part about the fall from Eden. Paradise."

"I hope I can find the rest. Maybe when I get outta here Al can look for either the originals or more of what my grandfather had translated."

"Then you come find me and we'll read it together. Now let's get some sleep." And the two boys tucked in their bunks for sleep.

Chapter 12
stuff from Grandpapa

So what kind of stuff is coming from your mom?"

"I really don't know. Could be some books and stuff. I'm hoping its some of the old stories we used to read together."

"Your grandfather used to read to you a lot?'

"He was an anthropologist-turned-linguistic scholar. He could translate old documents." He got up and left the room, and she just looked at him, like what the heck was he up to now? She could hear him banging around and then some rustlings and some exasperated exhaling on his part.

And then he reentered the room carrying a small pile of papers, old, worn and heavily dogeared and annotated with scribblings.

"See here's one of my favorites. The Gospel According to Mary."

"What? Mary had a gospel? I didn't think people could ever read or write back then."

"That's what people think. But these stories were printed in books that people carried around and read. The society at the time was Greek and they published novels. I mean paperbacks that people read. In fact Plato was widely read at the time. Maybe they didn't have machines and air planes and stuff, but I think they might have even had a higher literacy rate back then than now. Like we are now in the dark ages in comparison."

"So strange," she said. "And Mary? Wasn't she a prostitute?"

"There is no evidence she was a prostitute. Or his wife. None of it anywhere. In fact, in this gospel it is understood by the other disciples that she is another disciple and probably closer to the savior than any of them. And in this story in fact, he reveals himself to her in a vision after his resurrection, something the other guys cant brag about."

"So what is this Gospel of Mary about?"

"She says some really strange things about the laws of heaven and earth. And the meaning of death."

"Like what?"

"Well let me read this."

""As the soul of a body was leaving the body for its journey upward to the kingdom of heaven, it encountered the first authority on the road to heaven and freedom, Darkness, and it was not afraid. She knew all of matter and spirit dissolved and found its way eventually to its roots, cool stable place in the void.

And as the soul ascended, the body of desire, the second gate keeper toward the heavens, asked the soul, "I didn't see you come down into me, but now I see you going up. Why are you deceiving me? You belong to me."

"And the soul answered its body it was vacating, "You did not see me and you did not recognize me when I was there, inside, inhabiting you. You possessed me as you would a garment, and wore me as you wished, but never did you try to get to know me." And the soul felt joy at having revealed this to the body she once inhabited, and happily and unencumbered lifted toward heaven."

The ascending soul encountered the third authority, Ignorance, and it didn't know what was happening. But the soul could not now enlighten it, it accused the soul of wickedness. And the ascending soul replied, "How can you judge me when I have not judged. I was rules with ruling. I was not known by my possessors, but I myself have come to know that all will be dissolved, all in heaven and earth."

There she encountered the fourth authority of ascent, Wrath. And it took the seven forms of Power: Darkness; Desire; Ignorance; Envy of Death (Divine knowledge); Kingdom of Flesh; Foolish Wisdom of the Flesh (pursuit of pleasure); and the seventh, Wrathful Wisdom. These are the 7 powers of Wrath, the fourth authority of ascendance.

And these powers all confronted the ascending soul, with questions. "Where do you think you are going? You kill humans and you destroy their worlds?"

And the soul replied to all, "What has been my prison

and keeper has been slain. The earthly bonds of ignorance was temporary and I have remembered, and am now going home. And may I rest now in Quietude."

Rocky folded the papers back over and looked up at Sheridan. She was just staring at him, then she slightly shook her head. "Weird. Really weird. I sort of understand it tho. It sounds Eastern. Like Mysticism."

"It is, really. It's Gnostic, which was around before the birth of Christ. And I think it migrated there as a philosophy from the east, Tibet and India, which I think have even older religions than anything in the west. "

"Except for maybe the Celts."

"Well, I think the Celts came from the East too. They were all over Europe before Romans took over. And the Romans pushed them Westward from Italy."

"Really? I never heard that before."

"There are religious similarities."

"Well, I really like that Mary has a gospel. I like that. Maybe Jesus was the first feminist." she said.

I think He didn't really care that she was male or female. Just that she was smart and listened to him and remembered what he said to her. And then she preached it. The other disciples got all afraid and had to be reminded that they were supposed to, were told to by Jesus, to go preach and spread the word. And Mary had to remind them, and this Gospel tells us that."

Chapter 13
Preferred Basement

They decided instead of having the box shipped, the two of them would simply drive to San Francisco and visit his family.

But as they arrived, he was startled to find that his little sister was no where to be seen.

"Mom, where is Shalome?"
"She's down in the basement."
"What?"
"She is downstairs. She likes it down there."

So he found the door to the basement was locked with a small hook up high on the upstairs side. He unlatched it and went down the 14 stairs into the gloom of the basement. It had a cement floor and one tiny window looking out at the feet of people passing by. But it was covered with a thick layer of grime.

"Why are you down here?" he asked his baby sister.
"I like it down here. And *she's* not down here."
"But this is the basement." he said
"Now, don't worry about me. I like it down here, Rocky."

He just looked at her for a moment. "I like that you call me that."
"Its your name."
"Not really. I think it makes mom mad."

She smiled and said, "Ya, I think it does. Just like when you call me Shalome. She hates it I think. Shalome Shalome hello hello." she sang in her baby voice.

He looked around and saw that she had the dank place decorated just so. There were shelves on all the walls filled with books. And on the shelf over the desk there were rows of small pots with plants on them. And feeding them from above was a narrow row of florescent grow lights beaming the strange black light color onto the leaves. And they seemed to be flourishing. She saw him staring at her plants and said,

"There are now 32 of them. And you know I didn't buy a single one. I picked and plucked baby plants off of big plants where no one would notice. I pulled a tiny spider plant baby from one in the administration office. And a tiny strawberry plant baby off of a plant on the library desk. And I even got the tiny nub from the huge schephlera from inside the mall. It didn't have roots or anything. And it is growing. I wonder how huge that thing is going to get, though?"

He smiled at his baby sister and said, "You are amazing."

"Thanks big brother."

"Why don't we go upstairs and get some lunch. You can meet my friend Sheridan."

Is she your girl friend?"

"I think it qualifies as that. We live together on her ranch. It was her parents ranch and they just passed away a few years ago." He smiled and said, "We have horses."

And baby Shalome lit up at that. "I have to come see them sometime."

"Yes, you really should. Now some lunch."

She set down what she was working on and the two of them went back upstairs to find the others and have some lunch.

After a few days it was time for the two of them to head home. He had picked up a couple of boxes that his grand papa has sealed just for him. He was glad they had driven down there, not just because they got to see everybody for a while, and that they all got to meet Sheridan. But that these boxes were bulky and he had a feeling that his mother would not have sent all of it. And chances are she would have gone through it and thrown out most of it. Towards the end of his living there, he had gotten the distinct feeling that she did not approve of him having all of these old documents from his grand father. She didn't approve of someone so young and without a proper degree being able to translate this stuff by himself. The institute had told him they wanted him to continue to translate and work on the things his grandfather had been delving into, even tho he had had the run -in with the law. They didn't seem to blame him for that. In fact they continued to respect what he had written, what little he had written , on the documents that his grandfather had been studying. They kept telling him that his time at the boys school was really just a mistake of the law, and that it probably actually did him some good to get him away from his family. His mother was getting a little smothering.

But he couldn't wait to get home and dig through some of this stuff. He had to hold himself back from opening boxes while Sheridan drove. But he controlled himself and provided small talk all the way home so she could stay awake for the 10 hour drive.

But when they got home he dug through and found the fresh copy of what he had been remembering as one of the last things he had been reading. One that he thought Sheridan would find especially interesting.

"Here it is. I thought you would enjoy this one. I didn't have a copy of it, but its here.

"Well, here it is. This story was found in two of the great recent finds in Egypt, Dead Sea Commune and at the cliff of Jubal al Tarif."

"I've heard of those. Big stir up. But I didn't know that was in there."

"Wait," he said as he looked at the translations. "What is this thing. Looks like something my grandfather translated after I left home.

"Well, it just hasn't all been translated yet. Here listen to this." And he read from his translations.:

from The Pearl

"I was given a great task by my fore bearers.
They to me a garment of Yellow made fit.
And they wrote a covenant in my mind,
that in my journey I shall not forget.
'You shall to Egypt go,
and the white pearl to find,
it lay in the devouring serpent's lair,
under a garment you shall don,
your earthly appearance unbind.' "

"That's really beautiful, Rocky," Sheridan said. "I hope you will translate the rest of it and then read it to me. What a beautiful poem. "

He folded up the papers and began to put them away. When Sheridan asked, "What do you suppose it means?"

He again looked down at the poem fragment. "Well, yellow is the color of illumination, of wisdom to be gained. Egypt was then the land of sophistication and riches. The serpent means some sort of degradation of human character, in this case I think greed, earthly choices of value. And the pearl would be the greatest of riches, probably not money but wisdom and inner peace. And the garment? I think it is speaking of our body, our earthly bonds here as physical beings."

She just looked at him with something on her face, when he walked away and stowed the papers in a safe place in the bedroom. The look was something he did not see, and she was a little glad that he did not know just exactly how much she admired his amazing insight things most people don't get in a lifetime, let alone in just 20 years.

Chapter 14
old boxes

Responsibilities reigned and it was several days before Rocky found himself alone and able to dig into the boxes left for him by his grandfather.

There was a lot of stuff here. Pictures from their time in Egypt, and other places they had traveled. There was a folder entitled Palanque 1944. But rocky didn't remember anything about that; he thought if he remembered correctly that they were there in Yucatan in1965. And when he was a child in 1955, there abouts. He remembered hearing that they had all been there once before, when his grandfather was a student at the university. But not much more did he recall from that era before he was born. He held the old golden envelope, sealed with yellowed crackling old tape, and the gold paper worn soft through the years, and he thought he would keep that little secret for later. He wondered what things he would find in that envelope containing memorabilia from that time wrapped in secrecy and trepidation held by his family.

He kept digging into the box and stacking the sheaves of paper to the side. All kinds of copied documents, most of it in ancient foreign languages. When he came to the bottom of the box, he found another golden envelope, this one looking not as old as the first one with the old Palanque files in it. This one was taped and then sealed on the back with a dab of melted wax stamped with a seal from the institute. And it said on it in Greek letters: My grandson. And Rocky sat there with it in his hands until the sun set and the room got dark and he began to get cold.

He set that aside and as if in a trance he stacked it down below some other folders and decided to head off to sleep. But as he was shuffling folders one popped out and caught his attention. On the front was written: "The Origin of the World: NHL  97, 24-98, 11".

No way! There it was. But his eyes were tearing up and he couldn't see for his big yawns, so it would have to wait for some sleep.

And he went to sleep with anticipation on his mind. And his dreams danced of pack-laden camels, swaying girls on worn carpets, moving to quiet strange drums, with the smells of the caravansary wafting around his thoughts.


Chapter 15
The Couch

So how many times were you there?"

She turned to the doctor with haunted, tired eyes and said, "What?"

"How many times. You said the second time. So you have been there two times."

"The Temple? Ya, just two times."

"Do you think you would be open to hypnosis?" the doctor asked the woman on the couch.

"What's that?" she asked.

"Hypnosis is a new form of therapy that allows the patient to relax and recall his or her memories and recall experiences more clearly," began the doctor slowly. "It's a technique that's been around for a while, but became in greater use and practice by Dr. Freud. It's perfectly safe, I assure you. I think you might even find it relaxing and comforting."

"Okay," said the woman on the couch quietly. She was just beginning to relax and had begun to find the doctor's voice soothing, after a dozen or so meetings here in his office.

"So let's begin. Close your eyes and feel the fingers of your hands against the cool of the couch. Then imagine your hands growing light like a balloon and floating just above the surface of the couch. Now as you begin to relax you can feel yourself growing drowsy, and by the time I count five you will be in a deep sleep."

And after a few moments she wasn't aware of anything.

"Now let's go back to what you were saying about the Stone Temple that you visited when you were younger. So now you have visited there to that particular place, the Stone Temple on the Yucatan, and that was the second time."

"Yes," she said drowsily, "that was the second time, when my boy was very small."

"But I thought you said that the second time was later when he was a teenager, just recently when he was in high school. So when was the first time?" He asked putting it together now that the story was longer than she had recalled, with way more history, substantiating his suspicions that there was far more to the story and she was letting on, then her memories would allow her to expose.

"Ya, yeah the very first time I was there, I was just a child myself. I had gone there with my parents, my father was a just graduated anthropologist, and mom and I went there with him on a school dig. Do you know when a dig is, Dr.?"

"And what happened there on this school dig, as you call it?"

"There were lots of other people there. It was very busy. And I was a little overwhelmed as a little child. And I really didn't know what was going on, except that I loved the forest and the trees, and the wild bird screaming overhead. And I enjoyed climbing on the monuments, the ancient stone monuments there, in the jungle, that all these people seem to be so excited about. But there was something about this monument in particular that everyone was very interested in. They were clustered around the front of it with machinery and lights and he wrote barricade to keep people away. And there were people watching at first. And then their work on this and they ran the locals off. They scared them with their guns in their attitudes and their uniforms. Military uniforms. They were gray and green, and they had metals and bars and things on them and I recall one symbol now that still evokes fear in me: it was a four spoke wheel gray and red. And at the time I didn't know what it meant, other than fear and control. Here she stopped and the doctor noticed that her breathing had become heavy and more quick.

The doctor noticed this and he said to her, "it's going to be just fine. Everything is just fine, and you are safe. And how did you feel about these people there controlling things? Did they harm your family?"

"At first, when we first got there those people weren't there. And my father and my mother were allowed to climb the monument and we went inside and there was a photographer with a tripod taking pictures. And my mother and my father worked making drawings of what they were seeing. And as a child I didn't see anything interesting at all. It was just a long stone hallway with stairs in a small room with kind of a stone table on it and not much else. Now that I think about it there weren't any inscriptions or drawings or carvings on the wall, like were so common in Egypt, all over inside monuments and outside on the pillars and everywhere in the Egyptian monuments. But not here, it was very plain and I thought it rather boring and I ran out and played elsewhere. But then those men came with their machines and their guns and eventually everyone had to leave."

"Did you make any friends there, as a child? And how did that make you feel when these men came and made all of those people leave?"

"I remember a couple of children there, they were younger than me, and they were foreign. I didn't know at the time, but I think they were Middle Eastern. And they were the children of an anthropologist that worked with my father. But something happened. They did something to the little boy. He was a lot younger than me I was maybe 12, and he was more of a toddler. But the men with the guns did something to the little boy in the Temple, I don't know, but there was yelling and there was blood and the little boy was taken away wrapped up in white sheets."

"And how did that make you feel?"The doctor seemed clinical, uninterested, as if this was a curious fiction she was making up in her mind.

"I was afraid. I was fascinated as a child, by the blood in the excitement, and I didn't understand, but it made me afraid. Stefanos. Stefanos. That was their name."

"Who is that now? Whose name is that?" The doctor asked, the information coming in disjointed chunks now "The family. Their name was Stephanos. I remember because my father was very very upset. And my mother was crying. And we left for home in the states as soon as possible. I think those people quit anthropology and we never saw them again. Even though we've done lots of activities with the world anthropology scene. I've never seen them again. They hurt their son Christos. His name was Chris, the little boy. They were from Afghanistan, Pakistan?."

The woman on the couch began to make animal noises, starting with a groan, the fidgeting in the hands, and she started to sob. And the doctor quickly interjected his safe word to bring her out of her trance. The woman stopped her feral behaviors, and quieted and stretched out on the couch comfortably. And the doctor began his backwards count to bring her out of hypnosis.

"Why is my face wet?", she said after a few moments.

"Oh, you're fine. Sometimes people's eyes leak when they go into hypnosis. It means nothing. How do you feel?"

" I feel fine," she said. "Except that my face is wet and my hands hurt a little. What did I say? "

"Oh", said the doctor nonchalantly." Not much you just described what you told me before about your experiences at the stone temple in the Yucatan."

"Oh, well I was only there twice", she said confidently.

"Okay then that's fine", said the doctor. "Let me know if you have any trouble sleeping or any other discomforts. And will meet again as usual next week.

Chapter 16
boxes

The next morning was hectic and he couldn't get away to read his treasures. A foal was born next door and there were a few complications and they needed his help. A couple more strong arms were needed for carrying and pulling, and fetching this or that. After a rough 24 hours of doctoring, the foal was fine and nursing happily on its contented mother. The humans were dead tired.

So it wasn't until the second day he was able to dig out and contemplate even opening the two files he, in his heart, so desperately wanted to read. In fact he had a hard time deciding which one to open first.

After some time of sitting there in a trance with the two sealed brown envelopes in his hands, he leaned over and switched on a light. He got up and sat in the easy chair, turned one of the envelopes over and popped open the wax seal. He pulled out a small stack of papers and began to read the letter written in his grandfather's hand, in the Greek letters, but written in the English words:

My dear grandson,

If you are reading this then I am gone. I have traveled to another world, like in one our pages we have so often read together explored in the ancient traditions of Gnosticism and other forms of philosophy. I do not know what it will be like. But I hope it to be an adventure to continue the ones we had together studying and reading and traveling. I would like to say I have gone to a better place, and will see you soon. But not too soon. I hope this letter and this folder find you safe and well.

I had hoped to help you avoid the problems of going away to the boys school. I know that the world of justice knows no gray. And that you have suffered for forces that none of us are able to control. Or even understand for that matter. I simply hope that it will serve you to be away from the ladies, your mother and your grandmother, my faithful wife of all these years, so that you can begin to become the young man that you are destined to be. See it as a time of growth and I am sorry to leave before you are free to join us here again.

I know that I am going; they say it was that blasted pipe I smoked all those years. It will be quick they say and I will not be able to talk to you and tell you the things you need to know. So many things I should have said but was afraid to drag you into it.

There are things I need to tell you. There are things happening in this world that will make great changes soon to come. Have you not wondered why those ancient documents were just so recently discovered, all within a few years of each other? And why the forces to conceal and obfuscate them were eventually thwarted? Though they still try and you need to be aware and careful out there. There are still ignorant men who wish to quell understanding and research. And I think that person who attacked you and dragged you down was one such force. I believe I know who that young man was. And possibly what force it was that possessed him to become so hateful. Perhaps it is too complicated, but I must try to explain. That boy was the son of one of my fellow archaeologists in Palanque. We all got swept up in that time and fervor of the 40's and the war effort, and some of us got swept away. We left that ancient cursed place in Mexico, your mother and us grandparents. Just in time. Others were not so lucky. This other family were not so lucky. There son apparently, very young at the time, was nabbed and used to test one of their hypothesis in the chamber. It should have gone innocently enough. But I think there were some of the, we'll say Europeans, who knew very well what was going to happen. It destroyed that little boy. And his family. And when they returned to the middle East, Afghanistan, I think it was, they were never heard from again. Then the boy surfaces several times in the melliue he knows best: archaeology, his mind warped and out of control. Was he the one who attacked you in Italy? I suspect it is so. And what he did to you was part of what the officials thought was a pagan death ritual. But it wasn't quite that was it? I think you know precisely what happened. The Gnostic gospels warn of dabbling where we are not welcome. The realm of angels and demons is not easily understood by mortal man. And so it shouldn't be. It is the stuff of the gods and not ours to know.

But I am rambling. I am writing to you, well, because I miss you here. And I love you so much, my grandson. Gwydion. I know you are using a different name now and I understand. Your sister is a strange one and I hope the two of you strange cookies can find each other and help each other in the near future. For a storm is coming. I have seen just glimpses, though I think your sister is a weather vane. Or a telegraph. Or a time machine, so strange she is and such strange adult prognostications she has whispered to me in the late night when we read together. That a child of 11 months can talk and read along is beyond my understanding. But it is not for me to know what, just to accept and wonder.

Inside this envelope are stories. Stories from the greater list of stories that have been found in the last few years, the great Nag Hammadi Library, Berlinishe Gnostica, and the Dead Sea library of scrolls. These, these few here have been suppressed. These were hard to get and I had to do some sleuthing, and felt I was in danger all the time. I copied them and began to translate them and received such a shock that I put them away. I hope that you are more prepared than my feeble self to take a look. To translate them honestly and know what to do with that knowledge.

For there are forces out there that do not want this known.

Back in Egypt, I was attacked. I didn't say anything, but it was why we left in such a hurry. You were just a young silent boy then. I was attacked in the basement by the man that later got his deserved end. And it seemed to point to me. But it was not me. And I suspect you know who it was. But "why" was always a question that was never answered. No one ever hinted at why the professor was killed. But I had a sense at the time. When I published my first translations, I was reviled and castigated for the truth of what I wrote. And there were some things in there that the ecclesiastics did not care for one bit, and they wished them suppressed. But I persevered, except for one facet I skipped. There was a passage at the end of one of the quatrains of the Gnostic rituals written in Greek that described a religious rite involving man -on -man. That part of the ancient scroll has since disappeared. Along with the passages about using mushrooms in their ritual ceremonies. These concepts are very uncomfortable for most people, not just religious people. And I felt uncomfortable publishing those particular bits. And I feared for my life and my livelihood. I did have a family to support, after-all.

So I thought when I was attacked that this was what it was about: suppressing an undercurrent of homosexual society to the church, the Christian church. And I think perhaps partially this is so, and it hints at what kind of thing was going on when Professor H was killed in his bed.

But now I am not so sure. What you are about to read has not been widely published, and is usually taken with a grain of salt as an old interpretation of a story that accompanied the original resurrection story. But the references are undeniable. With the recent announcement of the finding of a celestial craft in the desert of Roswell, New Mexico, it brings these ancient texts to light. If you find when you translate them, with the illumination I found, and if you publish them as they are, in the context of this discovery in the desert, be careful. This may be the most dangerous knowledge and proof that there is.

My dear grandson, I hope you find life as interesting as I

have. And that you find a way to fit and affect life in a way that pleases you and helps theirs. And I hope you write. And I hope you continue to translate what we have just found in the desert of the middle East and seemingly in our own continent of the US.  The ancient texts hint that god was not what we think, and ghosts may be closer to angels and demons and fit into the same category. Now, do all of these experiences of other being fit into the same realm? And what of the spirits of the ancient Natives of north and south America? Do they fit somewhere in the scheme? I am thinking of Palanque. And you see that it is a great wheel, and we have come full circle as the Mayans predicted to occur later in this century. And perhaps you, Gwydion, are the one to bring it to light.

Be well, my grandson. Take care of your sister. Or maybe she will be taking care of all of you. And try to be patient with your mother. She's the only one you got.

Your loving grand father,
Professor Antony Jacobs.


Chapter 17
confusing


Their trip had been long and exhausting. And they were lounging on the couch with the radio on with some sports game playing innocuously on the boob tube. He hadn't told her about any of the things he had found and read in the box yet. It was just too much to even explain.

But he was tired and in in kind of a trance when she started talking to him. Some doors had been opened by his letter from his grandfather, may he rest in peace. Which was maybe why he was able to recall the rest of the story to her. A kind of hypnosis on the highway.

"You never told me the rest of the story about the accident in the high school," she said the evening lunging wound the living room, papers and envelopes scattered around, and Rocky looking off into the distance like a caged animal imagining other freedoms not afforded here. "You spaced out and I couldn't make myself shake you from what seemed like a comfortable eye of a terrifying storm of a memory."

He looked at her, somewhat dazed and just getting what she had said a minute ago. "Huh? Oh, the high school mirror. It shattered and broke around me like shards of some hot sun." He looked around himself at the golden envelopes strewn across the living room floor around him on the rugs.

That boy. He seemed to appear out of nothing. He was just there, waiting for me. Staring at me again..."

The story he was telling himself stretched and bragged in his mind, "That priest died so smoothly and easily. And so too will this boy," he said to himself as he stood breathing in smoke as he watched the boy turn and run.

Run, run little rabbit. Soon for the slaughter and stew pot for you little weakling.

So his feet were light as feathers as he pursued the boy across the fields and into the hallowed hall of learning. And there the hunter found his prey crouched in the dark corner of the huge marble hallway.

"Stay away from me! What do you want from me!" said the young form in the corner.

He smiled smugly and said quietly into the silent air of the falling dusk. "Oh, nothing much, just your immortal soul, you fool!"

The younger boy made a feral sound from deep in his chest and he shoved himself off the marble floor and began jumping up steps. His pursuer leapt after him. He grabbed his coat by the back edge and the two of them fell on the stairs in a heap, the older boy gaining the upper hand by sheer size and strength. But not by much. The younger boy had grown, gained some pounds and strength in the last couple years at high school. A growing boy for sure, and his adversary was a little taken back by that change. He had known him first off years ago in Egypt and he was a skinny little kid, and the old boy much bigger stronger and wiser too.

But not now. The scales were actually pretty much even with them. Except that the pursuer had pure hatred on his side. And the boy, well, simple survival in the face of annihilation.

So they struggled against the cold stone of the marble steps. And just then the doves let loose from the ceiling rafters and flew down the stairwell at the two boys and burst against the windows, breaking one of them, where their dark gray forms all spilled through out into the gathering night.

The older boy looked up at the crashing sound, and the younger boy fled from him up the stairs. Up and up to the top floor he ran with the hot breath of his tormentor right behind him. He stopped and pushed the older boy right in the chest which stunned him for a moment and he stumbled back a couple steps and let out a roar of hatred. At the top of the stairs was hung a huge mirror, so that students running in the hall could see that there were students on the stairwell and wouldn't turn the corner and stumble on them as they began their descent. But tonight the two boys only saw themselves in it as they topped the stairs, the older boy hanging onto the younger boy's coat in the back. I got you, you whelp."

He turned to dislodge his attacker from his coat and in so tangled his legs and they fell in a heap below the mirror, their faces reflected in agony, each with their own objective: the pursuer, murder, and the younger, a rictus of fear to escape, once again, this crazed captor. He had him by the throat, the slightly larger boy had gained the upper hand, fueled on by rage and hatred. "You may not finish your work," a voice boiled up from inside the belly of hate. "You cannot be allowed to finish your work, I forbid you."

The younger boy just stared at the hatred in his face, drool dripping down from the foamy corners of his wild animal mouth. His teeth protruded like fangs of an animal, and the strangest of sensations took over the youngest boy. He felt a warmth and strength permeate his body and a determination over take his mind. He was no longer afraid, but he simply needed to finish this, to win and to survive. There was a fluttering and dark flapping over his head and the black coat of the older boy on top of him seemed to swing and lift in the wind and his weight was lifted for a moment, then the hunter crashed to the ground and he let out a shriek of frustration and pain. The younger boy piled on top of him and held him down. "I don't know who you are but you will stop. Stop tormenting me. You will be damned to hell if you do not stop, your life forfeit to all that is good and real here. I read that boys like you will fester for a life time and then be taken away by darkened angels to a place where for an eternity you will hang by your neck over a river of molten fire which burns but never consumes, your body as your immortal soul has another lifetime of eternities to think over and consider your life of evil deeds. You can change this now with the choice of always doing good and being humble to your fellow man. Or you can go with your dark angel into the pit forever, evil boy. What's it going to be?" the words spilled from him, from a boy who rarely spoke, he was filled with the things he had learned from all of the scriptures he had read, and a few he had even translated himself from the ancient Aramaic, and he for once found the words to describe what he was feeling about this mean evil boy that had tormented him for the last 10 years. He had been following him and torturing him and even tried to kill him, which now was obvious was his evil intent. And for why? He could not fathom why. He thought of himself as a kind person who did nothing much to anyone. And yet this evil kid pursued him and followed him and tried to kill him. So be it, it was time for him to go.

And the older boy twisted in pain and rage and the younger boy saw his face reflected in the mirror on the wall. And the edges of the mirror turned red and began to warp around the form of the older boy twisting in rage and fury. They came a whistling sound from the boy's throat and he jerked into a straight position on the floor as the archeon of some angel daemon took possession of his soul and wrenched it free right in front of the boys eyes. He let go of him and slid away, blood seeping from his hands and smearing on the floor. And just as the devil's howl reached a crescendo, the mirror shattered and showered the two of them with shards of hot glass, the older boy in the bloody black coat inert on the floor. And the younger boy crouched in a pile sobbing.

It was a little while before anyone found them. The night watchman came around and discovered the two prone figures and the mess of glass and blood. He surmised that the two boys had fought and broken the glass , and that the boy who was alive probably strangled the dead boy laying on the floor. And in his terror the younger boy had once again lost his powers of speech and was unable to tell the real story

"So you really didn't kill him," she said after a few moments of silence.

He turned and looked at her with haunted eyes. "What?"

"You didn't really kill him. Someone else did. Someone else was there. Why did you get blamed?"

"I didn't get blamed for it. They just didn't know. They showed up and there I was laying on the floor with this dead guy. They didn't know what to do."

"Why didn't you just tell them?"

"I couldn't talk."

"Why couldn't you talk?"

"I just couldn't talk."

"What does that mean?"

He was uncomfortably quiet for a few moments, then he said, "you don't know me that well."

She said, "What is that supposed to mean?"

"You just don't. Don't get mad at me. If you want to understand, stop yelling at me."

She grumbled a moment and then said, "Sorry, I just don't get it. You'll have to explain it to me."

"I was never good at talking. I could never explain anything to anybody. They called me names and stuff. But really I always felt that no one was really hearing what I was saying, so I just didn't talk. I stopped talking. They said I was autistic."

"What?" This startled her. What a strange thing to say about this person she was sharing her home and her bed with. "What does that mean?"

"I don't know. I was weird. And I was an only child living with my grandparents, and it just didn't matter. We traveled the world and I learned stuff on the move and it just didn't seem to make that much difference."

"But you are so smart. You translate stuff, like ancient Egyptian and stuff."

"Coptic and Aramaic. But ya." She laughed at him and he glared at her.

"I am laughing next to you not AT you. You are so funny and underestimate yourself."

He smiled and said, "Thanks."

"OK," she started again. "So they sent you to this home for boys because you ended up besides a dead person in the school hall."

"That's kinda it," he said and laughed a little. Kinda stupid but maybe I was glad to get out of that school. All those perfect people who act perfectly. And no one was listening to me again. My mother had gone off the deep end and my grand parents were kinda getting old."

"And you got to learn how to train horses."

"Ya. I loved the ranch work. The hard work, I think it turned a lot of those violent boys around. Then someone got killed riding a wild horse. They closed the school down after that. I was only in there for 6 months. But when I went home I couldn't tolerate my mother. She had flipped. That guy had left her, and she just flipped. And grand pop was sick. I think he was sad."

"That's really a lot, Rocky," she said as she put her arm around his shoulder. "That's too much for anyone, especially a teenager. "

"I just needed to get outta there."

"But you found me and here we are."   She smiled at him. "Good thing I walked into that bar that night. I would never had found you."

"Hey, what were you doing in that bar anyway? You were still a teenager?"

"This is Nevada. They don't care, as long as you aren't drinking. I can't drink. Makes my head swimmy."

"Oh, ya. I am just a couple years older than you. But that's OK. Everybody needs somebody. She grabbed him around the shoulders and dragged him down onto the couch, and kissed him solidly on the lips. And he smiled a contented smile, one fraught with a few demons and worries still hidden from this best friend.

Chapter 18
releif

He was happy he had told Sheridan the story of his torment. It relieved some of the congestion in his chest after enduring all that and no real friend to tell it to. He felt so relieved that he got out the brown envelope and decided to reward himself with the story he had waited a long time to read. He thought of Simon and how he would never be able to hear this story, as told from the original texts. and rocky wondered how the story was told in the original versions of the Talmud, which is where Simon would have read it, being a young Jewish boy studying in Schule, and wishing to be a Rabbi some day.  But if Rocky had learned anything from his studies, that Simon was probably in a better place.

And this was the story that his grandfather had hidden away. The one he felt so radical and threatening that it could not be a story told in this age. He had had part of it before. But the rest of it lay sealed up in this old golden folder with a wax seal from the institute on the back.

His grandfather's writing came into focus on the page, after he had ripped open the wax seal on the back of the large flat brown envelope. And it started back at the beginning, the part the Rocky had and had read to Simon.

In the beginning, in chaos actually comes from shadow, and the shadow is sometimes called darkness. But a shadow comes from something that had existed before, so chaos came after what was in the beginning..

Sofia or Knowledge flowed from Pistis, or Wisdom and Faith. Sofia served as the veil separating humans from Those beyond.

When this Shadow sensed that the Sophia was stronger than it, it became jealous, and became pregnant from this powerful thought. And it swiftly gave birth to envy. But this envy was an aborted fetus and therefore had no spirit in it and it came into being and existed as a shadow on the surface of a watery substance. Bitter wrath formed from the shadow and was sent to exist in the region of chaos.

When Sophia saw this darkness and deep water she wanted it made into a definite image, and an Archon appeared like a lion in face, androgynous with great authority but ignorance of his own origin. She named him Yaltobaoth, or Ariel, because he looked like a lion. And here the faculty of speech came, and it pertains to the gods, angels, and people. Things come to be made by the power of words.

And here is where it began to be new for Rocky. His grandfather had translated this in the interim, between Rocky last seeing him, his release from the boy's school, and when

his grand father, Professor Antony Jacobs had died.
And Rocky began reading it aloud to himself.

Then seven androgynous beings appeared in the chaos, and each has a masculine name and a feminine name. You may find the masculine names and their powers in the arch angelic book of Moses the profit. And the feminine names can be found in the first book of Noraia.

And Yaltobaoth believed he was the only God, and in saying this he sinned against all the immortals who watched him carefully. And Pistis called him Samael, meaning Blind God. Yaldobaoth had a son, Sabaoth, and Pistis Sophia gave him her daughter, Zoe, and he made himself a mansion with a large golden throne on a chariot with four faces called the charubim. And next to them were created the serpent-like angels called seraphim. Sabaoth created another being, Isreal, meaning one who sees god, and another, Jesus Christ, who is like the savior in the 8$^{th}$ heaven, to sit on one side of his throne, and another, the virgin of the holy spirit, on his left.

Yaltobaoth saw his son Sabaoth and his glory and became jealous and generated death from his own death and became the sixth of the Authorities of Chaos. Since Death was androgynous, he had sex with himself and produced seven more androgynous children. The males were named: envy, wrath, tears, sighs, grief, lament, and tearful groans. And the females: anger, pain, lust, sighs, curses, bitterness, and strife. These seven double-sided characters interbred and produced each seven children, so that there were 49 androgynous demons. You will find these names characteristics in the book of Solomon.

Zoe, who lives with Sabaoth, then created seven good androgynous powers. The male names are: the one not jealous, the Blessed, the joyful, the true, the one not envious, the beloved, and the faithful. And the female names are: peace, gladness, joyfulness, blessedness, truth, love, and faith. And you will find their characteristics in the book "Configurations of the fate of heaven beneath the 12."

Forethought fell in love with this messenger of light that passed out of the eighth heaven above and through all of the heavens of this earth, and he was called Adam of light or the enlightened person of blood, or holy water; (Adonis is another word for Adonais, Hebrew name for god, and he begot earthly love with his beauty.). Hence some androgynous arrows appeared, and all the Gods and their Angels fell in love with him. And thus the first sexual desire sprouted on earth. Trees sprouted from this earth, that came from the semen of the Authorities and their Angels in their love for Adam the first.

Justice created beautiful Paradise, and desire dwells in the middle of its trees. The Tree of Life is eternal, and north of Paradise, to give immortality to the souls of people. The Tree of Knowledge stands next to it, and is there to awaken our souls from our demonic stupor.

Psyche, who loved Eros, was the first soul born on earth. She poured her blood onto him and there bloomed a rose within a bramble, to bring beauty with the thorn.

Sophia created the heavenly lights, the stars and planets, that there would be seasons, chronological signs, years, months, days, etc. Adam of the Light had returned after just 2 days on earth, to his realm of light and there was darkness on the earth.

The authorities in high heaven saw Adam up there and asked themselves, "Is this not the one who will ruin our works?" The answer was 'yes' so they decided to make slaves in his form to work for them. But Zoe saw what they were doing, and laughed at them, because they created humanity in ignorance, born to work against their own interests. So she created one for herself, so he could instruct humanity how to escape the authorities. The Greeks called it Hermaphrodite, the Hebrews, Eve of life, or female teacher of life, and the child who is born to her is Lord. But later the authorities called this child The Beast, to lead humanity astray, when really he was the wisest of all, this female-form androgyny born from Zoe, the first of Humanity. This Eve gave birth to the first blood human, without the help of a man.

The souls that were going to enter the bodies shaped by the Authorities were told to "flourish and multiply,..." And these souls were then taken captive by the Authorities and enslaved and locked up in the prisons of the molded bodies made by these Authorities, to stay until the end of an age."

"Wait. Stop." said Sheridan, startling Gwydion out of his reading out loud.. "What did you just say? Eve was on the earth first and she gave birth to the first humans?"

"How long have you been standing there?"

"Almost all of it, I think. I love listening to your voice. "

But he showed no embarrassment at all. He was so engrossed in what he was reading. "I think she was the first born there, and she gives birth to one guy, the Lord who is the teacher, the emancipator of mankind."

"Ok, go on," she said.

"Then it seems the authorities get on with making their slave humanity from their semen, and this first one they call Adam, it is shaped after Adam of Light. But it is empty and has no soul like an aborted fetus. "

"That sounds like some kind of cloning to me," said Sheridan.

"It says in a note "seed" so maybe not 'semen' but more modern interpretation would be DNA." He continued, "Then Zoe, Daughter of Sophia felt sorry for this dead thing and blew life into him and he began to crawl around but could not walk. (Note: Symbology: ignorance). The Authorities asked him, this breath, this soul within the body, "Who are you?" And it answered, "Through the power of humanity I've come to destroy your work." But they reveled in his answer, because now they knew their foe, it gave them rest from their fear and concern and called this day, the 'day of rest'."

"I guess it was a Sunday," said Sheridan.    Rocky just

shook his head and laughed. Then said, "No wonder they took this stuff out. Its all upside down on its head."

He continued reading: "The Authorities were happy with this thing (human/Adam-of-Light simulacrum) and they took him up to paradise where nothing much happens, and they left him there and retired to their heavens."

"So they created this ghastly empty thing for a human and left him, wow," she said shaking her head and getting up for some hot tea.

"No, wait! Wait! Listen to this!" he read from the text, "Eve Gives Adam Life."

"What?" She stopped in mid step and just stared at him from the kitchen doorway.

"Right here. It says it right here. Listen." He began reading some more.

"Zoe, who had given birth to Eve as an instructor to Adam, saw him struggling on the ground with no soul. She said to him, "How can our children be vessels of light is you insist on laying there on the ground?"

"It does NOT say that!" she yelled from the kitchen.

"Ya, you are right, it doesn't quite say that. But close. So she actually commands him to stand up and come alive, and just because she says it, it happens, her word became a real occurrence. Weird, just like Jesus did in the old stories where he kills people with a word and then with another word brings them back to life. And he is not ungrateful and realizes what she has done and says to her, "You will be called the Mother of Life for what you have done for me today."

Sheridan was carrying some cups in to set them on the table for tea. "So, on Monday, Eve creates life by simply stating it. I like that. I really like that."

"That's what it says right here in Greek." He smiles up at her and she smiles back. Then she turns to the sound of the tea kettle whistling., and disappears into the kitchen. With her gone, Rock reads quietly ahead the next paragraph and is looking ashen by the time she comes back in, and sets the tea kettle of water on the Unicorn-shaped copper heat doily.

"What? What's wrong?" she says looking into his face.

"I can't believe it says this. I cant believe it. Listen," and he reads.

"The Authorities got word from the gossiping Angels that their creation had stood up and was talking, and they were greatly distressed. So they sent seven archangels down to see what had gone wrong. Then they saw Eve talking with Adam, and said she looked familiar but who is this enlightened woman? Quick! Let's grab her and inseminate her so that she is unclean and she wont be able to go Into Her Light anymore, and so that her children will serve us. But let's not tell Adam, in fact let's put him into a stupor so that he doesn't recall any of this, and we can convince him she actually was made from his rib so that he can control her and that she may serve him."

But Eve is smarter than the Authorities are and creates a simulacrum that looks like her, and she disappears into the Tree of Knowledge." He looked up from the papers. And looked at the startled Sheridan.

"It does NOT say that!"

"It says that, right there. It's a translation."

"This is some joke of your grandfather's right?"

"I seriously don't think he would think this a joke at all. He died protecting it. He packed it away and sealed it here in this envelope. It may in fact be why he died. Imagine being a believer all your life, even denying that you really were but in your heart, you know, its there from childhood. And you translate this from two thousand year old texts. And like, a thunderclap. Its all been a joke. A ruse. A deception." They stare at each other.

"Unbelievable," she said as if coming up from a trance.

He set the papers down on the coffee table. "I cant read that to the convention. I'm supposed to read something at the meeting of minds, archaeological thingy. Oh, I certainly cant read that."

Chapter 19
Indian rocks

From the journal of Gwydion:
"When we arrived in the south west, the lands seemed so strange. We visited nearby the Zuni Indian reservation. They are reported to be very quiet and secretive. But in the rocks of the desert lay many drawings and diagrams of all sorts. I've seen pictures, but I was curious about it.

We stopped on the way to the convention to meet my mother and grandmother, and when I walked into the local country store, it seemed to take on an inflated feeling and my ears began to ring and my fingers went numb. I shook my head to try to clear it, and when I looked up I saw a big tall dark man looking at me. He beckoned me with one finger. So I followed him through the store and out the back. Where we walked for some time out through the sage brush and the lizards and red rocks. He began to speak to me in a voice from deep in a well.

"The sky people came to us from the stars, and they tried to teach us how to live. You can see the pictures here carved in the rocks. This one here has a dome over its head and a square kind of coat. We can't see them. But they are here." He paused and pushed some sand from around his boots. "We cant see them because they are just out of phase from us. We call them Kachina. They brought humans through a birth hole in the sky, and they were brought forth into the world of light from out of the underworld. The world of dark. Up there. The world is on it's head."

"I have heard of the Kachina. But I never thought about why they look so strange."

"Yes. They have helmets and looks like a suit. These are our star people, who came to this planet and seeded our planet. And they flew in shining objects."

"This is not written down, is it?"

"No. The Zuni and the Hopi do not have written language."

They walked a while there in the sun, a shining that didn't feel like the sun. But felt like an electrical vibration of light. After a time they came to a dark wall of rock. And there was the dark entrance to a cave. The tall dark man stepped aside and motioned with his hand for the young man to enter the cave. Rocky could see within it a dim yellow light throbbing, throbbing, seeming to pulse with the beat of his heart. And as he stepped into the golden darkness, a hum penetrated him and shook him to his core. The pressure in his ears increased until he couldn't think or see anymore. And with a burst of light, he felt pain, the release and then thought no more.

Chapter 20
the Abduction

Thanks for coming to me, Gwydion," said a disconnected voice above him. He realized he was now lying down on a surface that was neither sand nor rock floor of the cave. He struggled to open his eyes, but the light seemed to penetrate his eyelids and make him shy to try. A cold silver light it was and seemed to reflect off of hard surfaces around him an a room that was no longer a cave of rock on the Earth. He reached up and felt nothing but air.

"I recognize your voice," he said quietly.

"I knew you would not be afraid, I am relieved. We lose a sense of human limitations sometimes when we become so wrapped up in our work. But you are different, so different, we are so happy we found you."

"Oh, ya. Thanks. Have you been watching me?"

"Why, of course. We try not to meddle. But your species is so fascinating it has become a millennial obsession with us." The disconnected face above him turned a little, and a huff of warm comfort blew gently over his face, as if an angel had just laughed at him.

"Ezra. What exactly are you, anyway?" he asked.

"Hmmmm," said the disembodied voice. "We are just like you. We are trapped spirits, angels if you will."

"I am no angel. I killed a man."

Another warm chuckle. "No, that was not you, my dear. That was your guardian, Sophia. That one would do anything to protect you, I think."

"But why? Why me?"

"Have you still not realized the meaning of the ancient words you translate? They are of very special importance. They are our words. Our gifts to you, long ago. And there are forces all around us that would wish to cover these words up, and destroy them so curious others will not read them and learn the truth. Become enlightened. And you are bringing them back to life.""

"Those are your words?" he asked, keeping his eyes closed still for the glare that seemed to pulse and flare.

"Well, not mine exactly. But our kind. We have visited here many times. Have you not noticed that in your kind's history there have been several, no, numerous periods of miracles? And then long periods of disbelief?"

He tried to open his eyes and look at his interrogator. "Miracles?"

"Yes. Impossible things that your species cannot do?" another puff of warm air of angel laughter. "Miracles like you have now: computers, space flight, TV? Imagine how those things would have looked a hundred years ago. Your own great great grand father would have thought you a god. Or worse."

"My grandfather was a great man."

"Yes. He was a visionary. Very open. We never met him exactly. But here you are."

"Miracles? Those magic things that happened in those old scriptures? Moses and the Pharaohs, and those obelisks."

"Now you are getting it. That first time, when we made too many changes, it was really by accident, we're sorry and we've been involved ever since. Their story is that their craft crashed many years ago and without their aubule to re-phase the memory of them, they cannot escape."

"What? Who? Those ancients who wrote these things?"

"Yes. They were here for a long time. They were prisoners of this skin you call the human body. You see, the mind is a spirit possession of a wet-ware brain that thinks it is something from this planet. an animal. You think you are from this planet, because, your wet ware over-comes your "knowledge" you possess as spirits when you are born. Actually the first few years of a humans life is actually the forgetting of that knowledge that the spirit possesses from life in its higher plane. Although "life" isn't quite right either. Because there is no time up there. Time is created by the confines of the wet ware brain, the limitations of corporeality. There is only memory of the past, and memory of the future is burned out of the child very young. That's why we liked you so much Gwydion. Something about your brain refused to burn all that old stuff out. You chose to be quiet because the world is so different than you perceive it to be, what you perceive to be reality. You still see the past present and the future. You see the shadows of the angels that are not corporeal. You see where it all goes and are fine with it all and you never really grew up; you have a bit of that multi-dimensionality of the higher spheres, that which the human mind is blocked out of seeing. Usually. You see the dimensions are not limited to 3, or really, you humans have four, and you see three passing through the fourth, that's time. But there are more. And there is a place were it can be all experienced simultaneously, higher up there. But here, its like a blind man experiencing the elephant, remember that Zen joke from grammar school? One blind man sees the tail and thinks the elephant is like a rope; the 2nd blind man feels his ears and thinks he's like paper; and the third blind man feels his leg and thinks the elephant is like a tree. Just as people see you as a child and think of you that way; and another person will know you only as an adult, and will see you only that way. But you are all those things. But your human mind can only comprehend just one bit of it at a time: your total self being dipped through the one dimensional screen of time, and you are you right at this instant.

"The higher planes are where all spirit lives. It is simultaneous, all things and possibilities at once. Our spirits come into this limited experiential sphere for a reason. This plane is not a mistake: It is for the education, and punishment, of the spirit. When a spirit is discontent or needs to learn some things, we send it here and trap him inside on of your bodies that you generate with your reproductive practices. Other animals have spirit, or animus, also, but their brains aren't as complex and so their spirit beings are less complex. But the real interesting ones are the rogue spirits. And we send them here to experience once again the pain and anguish of corporeal life; life in a body. They forget, you all forget, you're spirits when you enter this body, but these rogue spirits are especially mean, and they flaunt the rules and are cruel, and inevitably they learn the feelings of pain, again. And as they are passing through the painful frightening veil of death again, if they do remember and they always repent, but not until they are on that threshold again. Something about your human wet ware and bodies seduces the spirit into forgetting right and wrong of the universe, and they think they can outsmart it again. Think of your stories of the erroneous pacts with the devil that are always a scam, and he has you in the end, every time. Because where they go and what they go through then, after the shedding of the corporeal body, is even worse than death. It is the punishment that you all down here call hell. It is of your own doing and of your own free will. Ah, yes, free will. That's what you call it when you hominids use your brains to make a decision. You are changing your path when you do that. All paths exist, but you can choose, by free will, to change the path you are on. And it changes the paths of others too. That's why working for good will make good for others, too.

And that is our hope. You body-beings make good, and you can go home. Make the good choices and you can go home. Haven't you ever noticed that the truly sweet and innocent beings die first? They go home. And the terrible ones, the ones that wreak havoc, stay around and continue to punish each other for a long time. That's why we wonder at your medical practices, keeping people alive for so long, and in so much pain. We often wonder at why you don't want to leave. I think it is your fear of the pain of death. I don't think its that painful. Just frightening since you don't understand.

But these trapped beings here, they could not get back. they lost their Aubuel in the crash. It is the magno-electronic device that stores memories, it shuts off the brain for its memories, which is what the consciousness of you humans is. Without memories, you aren't you anymore, just a shell. And the spirit is released. We have released the spirits you have brought to us Gwydion, thank you. I think you just might be an angel hunter after all.

"So, what are demons?" he asked her.

"Demons come down with out permission. You can call them angels too if you want; not much difference. They inhabit a body sometimes with out the permission of its born owner, and often can run that one out, if they are strong enough and stay in long enough. They cant stand mirrors because their energy gets reflected back and causes a feed back that dis-attaches them from the mind wet ware. Then you break the mirror and they are released back to where they need to go to be punished again before they are given permission to inhabit a body. There are rules Gwydion, rules, lots of rules that I cant get into now. Things your philosophy and your physics are only beginning to describe.

"But why would they want to come down here to this prison planet of hard knocks?" he asked her.

"One word, pleasure. Pleasure of the flesh. The wet ware of your mind's bodies have this intensity that exists no where else. You never wondered why the young go on rampages for sex, violence and drugs? Pleasure, pure pleasure of the corporeal kind, something we don't have in the higher spheres of existence. Very low on the experiential scale, but new and refreshing after being with the one-mind for eternity. A demon breaks the rules and slides through just when someone is vulnerable or even asks for it, I've seen it, and then he's in. And it will destroy its host while it sucks all it can from this worlds and its new body's pleasures. Even human with a new spirit rightfully born into a body can do this too. That's a sliding scale. Each born being has a certain intensity of experience and strength and can chose to not indulge the destructive urges it feels so fresh just after its born. Some can resist; some destroy themselves with the first chance at free choice from his training procedures of the parents. Which is what some of these spirits actually want: to reunite with the great spirit above, the great void where they just were, where there was peace and not pain. No animal games. Lately during your time, parents are spending less time with their offspring and the offspring are learning less and set free sooner, to indulge. Hence the destruction of your current society. It will come around again, and after a session of serious privation your kind will lapse again into superstitious mumbo jumbo to try to appease the 'gods' and deserve to not have all that pain. Instead of learning. We are amazed at how your kind are unable to learn and better themselves so there is less pain in your world. Its a choice, one you aren't making. But we've seen it come and go; it happens in waves. Your societies happen in waves. You cant help it; you are weak and not in full control of your consciousness.

## Chapter 21

But we are very glad you are here, Gwydion. You heard your calling a long time ago. We came hare long ago. Not when your kind finally were able to travel by light speed; you have not even reached that ability yet. But we became interested in you when your kind became aware. More than aware, you, as your book says, ate from the tree of the knowledge of good and evil. Your brains acquired so much self-awareness that you became afraid and self destructive. You knew evil now, which the animals do not know, and you have the honor now of choosing between good and evil. And in your youth you are choosing evil, most of the time, your kind choose evil. It is more fun. You do not yet know why you should be choosing good. You do not know how. We came to help. You did and still do not want our help. Like children, you want to do it your self. You are destroying yourselves and you wont let us help. We suppose that you must hit rock bottom before you will grow out of that phase. But we can hardly help not wanting to help you change your path of self destruction. But when we hit your planets atmosphere, we crashed. We hit your Psyonisphere. Psyonisphere, the level which our craft could start to feel the aggression and carelessness that your brains are now giving off. Your dissonance that you are thinking in your youth exuberance and confusion and aggression. Because we have a very special purpose for you. Something we think only you can do."

"There are changes coming, changes to your world that you are not yet aware of. Things that will happen in the next 50 to 75 years, and want to be ready for them. I will try to explain.

"Already they are calling this era "Anthropocene"

meaning the age of humans. When humans have single-handedly changed the planet to the tipping point. Very soon there will begin to be seen very great changes. Changes even in the weather. The gases on this planet are in a very delicate balance. And this balance between oxygen making and the oxygen breathing will be tipped by your carbon dioxide breathing machines. And the pride of the human will not be able to see these changes nor make changes soon enough to make a difference.

Then the planet will begin to warm and the seas will boil, that is, the ice will melt and become part of the great seas, and the oceans will rise and inundate your coastal cities, that will be most of the population Gwydion, because that is where most of your cities will be centered. But as this ice melt, it will uncover things buried deep in the ice, deep in the layers of frozen waters and gases. Animals and microscopic flora that they harbor will become warm enough for them to once again escape, after a hundred thousand years or a million years of being safely stored in your great warehouses of ice and carbon gases and microbes, these remnants of your planets beginnings of life, the ancient RNA microbes will invade your planet ecosystems. And great plagues will reign. Millions upon millions will be wiped out as your weak and prideful medical systems in the huge mega cities that will form upon your free-wheeling use of petroleum energies are slow to respond. At first it is just your poor third world nations that are effected and your prideful leaders will ignore it for too long.

Ironically as your oceans rise some three hundred feet in just 100 years and overcome your great coastal cities, your inland water sources will dry up. Great weather cataclysms will occur and turn rivers backwards, and silt in lakes and pollute underground natural cisterns. And in some areas the storms will be dry, and fire will rage and clear out mountains of ancient forests in swift sweeping conflagrations. And many of your kind will flee underground.

You see Gwydion, we need to get off of your planet. We have been stuck here for many many generations but now will come the time, in about 75 years, your own home- made cataclysm will come and with one fell swoop of a shower of thermo -nuclear instruments of destruction, after the natural cataclysms have brought civilization to its knees, then those humans that remain, a few who have the keys to these destructive weapons in their ignorance and hate, will take care of the rest of your planet turning it into a glass covered orb, completed uninhabited nor ever again uninhabitable."

Azreal looked into Gwydion's soft brown eyes, which were now wide with wonder at all she was saying. And we need you to guide us out of here. Only you can do this for us. We have been watching you for so long. We have seen you in our future, riding over this time of total destruction and bringing us back to our rightful place among the stars. For we have lost the ability, being here on this alien planet for so long, we have lost the ability to navigate. We cannot visualize our way out of this gravity well, back into among the stars. And we are sure that you can. We have seen in our aubule that you can do it. And will do it."

He just looked at her and a fear began to grow. "And my family? What of them?"

"They may not come. They are born here and will stay for the duration. "

"Why cant my sister help? She is special too. I have seen her float things that cannot be lifted in the air by nothing. She has the power of speech over the animals only more so than me. Why cannot she come? She would be better help than stupid old me."

"No, Shalome is too young. We were hoping but she is not yet grown and her abilities are firmly rooted here on this planet. She is a female and she will have children and grow and die here on this planet. You must forget her, and remember your destiny . You are destined to save us Gwydion. Save us from the ruination of your planet by its own aborigines."

Gwydion looked down at his hands and stared at them for quite a while. All became quiet inside the ship and there were just a few of their kind milling around him doing import ship things he knew not what.

He looked up at the strange eyes regarding him. "I will not do it. I will not leave my family."


Chapter 22

Gwydion awoke again but in a different place. Still the sterile ship walls and that hum. That weird mechanical humm just below consciousness. He hated that sound. It was the sound of all that man, and these weird guys too, and all of their inventions of metal and science. The inventions that all of them were so caught up in they couldn't even see the birds outside. Couldn't here the hum of all life, and the uneven, gentle beating of natural hearts.

Only this hum. This steady cold hum of electrical energy on metal.

The door opened a crack and one of them looked in. It saw that he was awake and it said, "So, are you ready to resume your responsibilities?"

"I'm going home."

"Hmmmm...." it said without inflection.

"Let me see Azrazeal."

It turned and shut the door. In a few minutes, the one he knew and recognized as Azra entered the small room.

"So you are ready?"

"When did I say that?"

She hmmmed like the other, without inflection or meaning, as if what he said meant nothing to her, only a distraction.

"So, Azra," he said loudly to catch her attention. "This

climate change and wars and disease? I don't see any of that now. So that's in the future?"

"Yes, the future, about 50 to 75 years from now. You doubt our ability to see these things?"

"No," he said. "I'm just asking. Its in the future. So it hasn't happened yet. Why don't you do something. You have powers to do things. Why don't you just do something to stop them, er, us, the humans down there. "

"Well, we have done that. Many times before. And it just doesn't work. In fact some of us think that our meddling is what caused it all. We meddled in their genetics and gave the humans more brain power and ended up giving them the ability to manipulate each other. And we taught them civilization and just gave them enough experience to control each other. We gave them the ability to make incredible tools. And they went and built machines to kill each other, that eventually eat your biosphere and cause the big war that melts it all down. No, Gwydion we have tried and I think we just made it worse, there is nothing we can do."

"But they don't even know about you!"

"Yes, and that is for the better. We tried to mingle with your kind and we tried to tell them what we were. And your feeble minds made up all this religion and god stuff and then started persecuting and killing each other for it. Your crazy ideas about some god caused humankind to chop up and burn your geniuses and artists. When we tried to give you some written down rules, you threw them back in our faces with lies and manipulations the likes of we have never seen before in all our zeno-formation activities. We sent down half breed instructors to help with your directions. And you crucified and murdered them, creating more violence and ripples in your future. No, we stopped doing that Gwydion. We tried in recent years to make small changes to help your kind get through the growth spurts and cramps with a little shove here, a tweak there. With education institutions like the Happenstance Foundation and with supporting science foundations of all sorts, we tried to help give you the knowledge to help yourselves. But still your thinkers are ignored or persecuted. And your people in charge continue to make choices according to their own personal greedy plans, sending any efforts we make into the trash. No, I am sorry Gwydion. We have decided it is just best that we leave now. We have tried and we think it best we take this knowledge and you, and skedaddle. Find safety in the cold stars."

"But they don't even know you exist. They don't even think there is life anywhere else in the galaxy or the universe!"

"You know Gwydion. As a race we have traveled to many worlds. We hold this information in our storage banks in our ships and in our aubule which is time and space-less. And we will find other places to to explore and to learn from and to teach and help them into a new age of enlightenment. That has always been our goal. And we have found that we cannot make contact until the inhabitants are really ready. And your race is just not ready. They don't even have space travel yet. Oh you will very soon. But it will be smashed down by your power brokers and your religious people as too unimportant and a total waste of time."

"But I think if you just told them about yourselves, it might make a difference."

We have tried to expose ourselves, and look what happened. Just a few years ago, they bombed down one of our attempts to enter the atmosphere with one of our hidden ships and it was gunned down in the desert right here in Roswell. And look what they did. They killed the two flight crew, and the ship was hidden. They announced for one day they had found an extra-terrestrial ship. And then the next day they said it was a foil weather balloon. They became afraid and had to cover it up. They wanted total control of that information and didn't want the public to know. They say you all cant handle it and I think maybe they are right."

"I just think you should try. Do something . Try again."

"I understand, Gwydion. You are a kind person. You have a good heart and a beautiful kind soul. But it wont do any good. We simply need to save our selves and by taking you with us, because of your special mind, your more active and complicated brain connections, you will be helping us save a part of your kind with us. We just need your help to pilot this broken ship."

He shook his head, closed his eyes, and sat down on the hard floor with both his hands tucked under his bottom and began rocking and humming one of his secret tunes from childhood..

He awoke with a start to find himself laying on the sand in that cave again. Light was just dimming from the rock walls as if a great energy had just been extinguished by their cool surfaces.

He got up and walked out of the cave and followed his tracks back to the general store when he had first seen that Indian guy.

"Why in the world did I follow him anyway," he was thinking to himself, as he pushed open the screen door at the back of the store. He strode through and stepped through the front door.

And there was Sheridan, standing there with her hands on her hips.

"Where the hell have you been?"

He was thunder struck that she was just standing there, like he had never left.

Like maybe she had left and come back for him; it had been hours, maybe a day, since he had gone up. And he wasn't even going to try to explain where he went. He knew where he'd gone; he'd been there before. And he knew Azra and he knew the tricks they can play. The powers they had. But what was this? Like he'd never left?

He opened his mouth to speak, and she said, "I don't even want to hear it. Its been like 20, 30 minutes. Where the hell have you been? No! I don't want to hear it!" and she turned toward the car and just said, "let's go, they will be waiting for us."

They drove in frozen silence for quite a while until they arrived at their hotel, where they unpacked and got some good hot showers and a good night's rest. Tomorrow, Gwydion was supposed to speak. What was he going to say? After all that with Azra, what could he say?

Chapter 23

Gwydion's mind spun in a dream. And he felt himself lift and spin in the air. He could see the solid metal deck in the walls with touch sensitive surfaces that would help control the ship in flight. But his arms and his legs felt like lead. And he couldn't move. And he knew it was just a dream.

Shalome finds herself on board the shining container. She beseeches them to try again and she cries in front of them and it moves them to reconsider.

"No, not talk to the leaders. Talk to every one, on the lines. "

"Oh you mean the electronic communications in the future."

"Ya, just go on everyone's line and tell them about yourself."

And so they did. They hooked in with their comm devices on the ship and translated the short message.

"You are not alone here. We are above and have been for thousands of years. We are what you call god but we are beings like you. You will join our kind in the quest for knowledge and peace through out the universe."

And the message went out on all the wavelengths and all of the electrical lines and to all the computers and electronic devices. A few people fainted, a few had heart attacks. But the calamity was less than the one that was coming.

And a new awareness was born, and people saw the people next to them no longer as enemies, but as co- pilots on this planet. And a change was made, and hands were lifted off the control panels of the ICBM's and the nuclear subs. And we raised our eyes and saw the stars in a new light. Not as the black unknown void. But as the new frontier of possibility and wonder and friendship.

In his dream Gwydion asked them, when was that? You didn't just do that, right now?"

No, we sent it into your far future."

Frustrated he shook his head. "but then you will take it away, because its in the future and not written in our minds yet."

"Yes, we can change it. You may not be worth the risk.

"Ya but you made us the way we are. We don't fit on this planet. You have to do something." Gwydion's voice rose with emotion.

"No, you are mostly aboriginals. The animal part of you is replicating. You don't listen and learn, you are all afraid of asking the hard questions, you hide behind denials and excuses and we cant help you anymore." The face of the creature in the padded chair began to distort and deform, and Gwydion stared in wonder, trying to make out what was happening. He continued.

"But we are trying. We've come so far, such a long way from caves and wearing skins."

"Your technology does not define your race. There were civilizations more advanced, more literate and intelligent than yours now. Your kind now life in pampered homes with environmental controls and you have to look at the info-screen to find out the weather, so you can wear the right shoes and not ruin the good ones. Ridiculous; you barely merit living in your modern lives."

"We have the best schools and the most technological advances, we publish more books and music now than ever."

"Again, just technological advances that make these goodies available to everyone. And yet most of the population on your globe live in abject poverty, with out the slightest convenience, like shoes or running water, and the rich do nothing about it. In fact I think your affluent enjoy seeing someone else suffer. Makes them feel better about themselves. I would call your era, Gwydion, the era of entitlement."

"That's not everyone! There are many who care."

"A few. Not enough to sway our minds. We were perhaps too hasty in coming here. Too primitive for us to bother, Too ignorant to even know what is good for you. Too animal yet to accept our teachings. Indeed, even accept our existence. If we exposed our selves, your kind would just try to kill us and take out huge portions of your civilization just trying to deny our existence."

I don't understand what all these scriptures have to do with you? Are they real?" Gwydion asked Azra.

"Oh, we didn't write that stuff. We don't really know what most of it is about. Made up stuff by your people to try to understand what they cannot understand. Most of religion is to put the world around you humans into perspective for humans. The attributing of characteristics to animals and weather, that is made up. And then humans began to believe what they had made up. Anthropomorphism is what your scientists call it. Giving human attributes to non human things. Inanimate things even. Rocks don't have souls. The weather is not controlled by some god generally. Unless we want to make a change but Why? That would just make a mess and the repercussions would be endlessly harmful."

The face completed it change into something luminous, something beautiful, so beautiful as to be almost hard to look at.

"Who are you?" said Gwydion. He felt as if he had just shifted into a different dream.

"I am old. I am older than these beings you see before you. I am closer to the Authorities that once established this place. Although I do not always agree with what they do. I watch and care. I knew you grandmother when she was 120 generations ago, I knew her then as Zaphora, with all of the daughters of Eve. Each one is Eve and her royal blood, the first of our kind to have blood and raise man from ignorance and crawling on the ground like a slug. I knew and loved your people then. I tried to help. And have tired in the intervening years to help. But do not believe what this being is telling you. They are almost useless and make more waste than help. They are barely humans themselves. More like machines really. They don't reproduce, they don't have blood, not anymore than a car or robot might.

"You read the original creation story, Gwydion. You just translated the last of it. You know what it says. These beings here are lowly things, far below the range of your friend Sophia, and the archeons above her, I am one of them, the Arch Angels with the authorities above that. This is a world of ignorance and deception, it was created that way by these deceivers, so they could rule over these creations for work they molded from the earth. You. Humans. But Eve outsmarted them and tricked them into defiling themselves. And they have never forgiven her for that. And they continue to pour poison into the ears of your clergy so that their rule by ignorance will continue."

Gwydion looked at this shining visage and again asked his one question, somehow knowing what the answer would be. "Who are you?"

"I am the Angel Gabriel, Gwydion. I can only do so much. You and your kind must find a way to balance your numbers, and stop relying on war and pestilence to clean your world. Each time, over and over, you have suffered this cleansing when there are too many of you. And some of you will find your way out of your prison and be lifted. But beware. Some of these your mingle with are not what they seem. I doubt they will help you."

"How can I fix things?"

"You take too much onto yourself, young boy. You can only do what is right for you and hope others will see. You are special among your people, although they persecute you for it. You are a revenant of what you once were, Us. Your brain is more advanced, and those around you hate it, they diagnose you with mental diseases and do not benefit from your special abilities. A species like that will die, and they may never know it is their own fault. You cannot help them if they do not want to see. And if you tell them before they are ready, you will become like the Christ, and sacrificed wastefully. Write and think. Answer when asked. Otherwise, you must let go."

And the instant he said that, Gwydion let go. And he fell. And he fell. And he fell. Until falling was become his breath ad self, and he was free of gravity and worries and the weight of the world. Free.

"I chose to see, and I chose to let go." he thought to himself.

"You can chose to help us," said his little sister's voice from the bottom of a tube. "Its about choosing. Otherwise it is neglect."

"Ah, but we are above that, Gwydion and Shalome," said the pinched voice of the Being in front of them. It was no longer the inscrutable face of the Angel Gabriel. But once again Azra.

"Well, to know the difference, you would have to begin to work on it. And there in lay the conundrum."

Gwydion just looked at her for a minute or two. "You mean free-will."

"Choosing. Consciously choosing and changing the world." Azra tilted her head at the young boy. "And that is a strength your kind has chosen to neglect. In fact there is more effort going into making the wrong choices. Its strange, that evil force of destruction has a stronger force of will, of purpose. Hate is a very strong emotion in your kind. Where we rather lack it."

"You're confused," said Gywdion. "You've created us in your image and now you blame our lack on ourselves. You are playing both ends against the middle. You don't know what you want. And when it didn't work out all peachy for you, you want to bale."

Shalome looked at this strange being with her big brown eyes. "Seems like there are other things you lack. Like feelings."

"What do you mean, child?"

"Love; caring. You don't even reproduce do you? Haven't in what, a million years? You've lost your heart for anything. Just thinking and watching, always rejecting a feeling or caring."

"That's not true. We care."

"Oh, do you?" she said in her tiny voice. "Then why are you just leaving?"

"We have seen it. It will be the total destruction of your planet's surface. All life, virtually every living thing will die and anything left will be unable to survive in the planet left behind."

"But you wont even try!"

"Oh, we have tried. For thousands of years we have tried and are we tired."

"And now you're leaving. What about my mom and my grandmother? What about them? And my stuffy toys and my turtle? You don't care?" and with that outburst of a young person in the throes of a cataclysm of unbelievable proportions, Shalome burst into sobbing and shaking.

Azrael just crossed it's thin arms and looked away. In a cold voice it said, "We have learned not to care about your human outbursts. We are above loving and feeling anything you feel."

Gwydion glared at the wrinkled old being. "Kinda like my mother. Just *done* helping humans, are you?."

"It helps us do what has to be done. Like raising plants in a garden. Its simpler that way."

"Ya, like abandoning what you've started." Gwydion said into her face with a calm cold.

"We are more advanced and have learned not to get involved. So we can do what is needed."

"And everything you do is calculated..." said Gwydion.

And Shalome continued, "And every step turns evil, because there is then no understanding life with out the love for each one of us," said the sobbing child in a cold adult voice.. She then continued to sob and Gwydion stepped over to her bent down and held her in her arms. For a long time they remained locked together brother and sister caring for one another. Then they both looked up at each other and shared an unspoken idea. They let go of one another and walked toward Azrael, who was staring at them with mingled shock and disgust. Then the ancient person's eyes grew wide as the two human children walked up to her and put their arms around her.

"Stop it. What are you doing?" cried Azrael. The Being reacted with panic, thinking these two were attacking it.

They simply put their arms around it and held it. Shalome began to whimper again, caught up in the seriousness of loosing all of everything she had held dear.

"This is what my grandfather did to me when I had shut everyone out. He just held me." He whispered to them as he held on to Azreal's squirming. Then Gwydion began to softly sob too as he began to feel what Shalome was feeling. He had just lost his grandfather last year, and the hole still gaped where his grandfather's unconditional love had once been. He felt pity and care for this wretched Being that could not feel, could not care for the human kind, that they themselves had help create. Just create this world and then skip town, and pretend they were above feeling anything. How sad and pathetic.

But this hugging, what they were doing affected Azrael deeply, and the thin body began to shake. "I...I....don't know what to say. This is too much. I have been on this planet too long with you cold earthlings."

"Not us," said Shalome, "Humans are *too* emotional. We think that you are cold and calculating."

"No, " answered the off world-er. "You humans have become calculating animals trying to go back to the lush forest and simple pleasures. I have lost my world, too long here in this one. We are wise, yet in our space travels we have gained simplicity and we just wanted to help. But we did poorly. Maybe we stopped feeling, which was the wrong thing to do. We don't know your way here, we have only watched and in our innocence we have become like you and hardened our hearts to others, but we are not you. And we can feel, and we can use that feeling to guide us all, if we just let it back in. All of our attempts to become like you, innocent and loving like children, empathic, what we were like before I became twisted by my experiences here. This secrecy and fear your kind feels for ours. And you have just showed me this way back again."

Gwydion's face lit up, like something was just revealed to him. "And the Lord said, "Go as the little children." And how about, "The meek shall inherit the earth". It makes sense now. So much sense!"

And Shalome smiled a huge child's partly toothless grin, for she had all of this inside her, and she knew it, but she hardly had the words to express it, and her learn'ed strange brother, study-er of ancient languages and manuscripts had found ancient words to do it for them. Words, that perhaps the progenitors of this very small strange visitor in front of them had written as a gift to humankind several thousands, or more, years ago.

Gwydion was rubbing his chin, and thinking hard. Then he looked up and said to Azrael, "So what difference would it make?"

"What do you mean now?" The being was truly exhausted with all of the human cathartic sharing.

"Well, if the future is already written, and you have seen what's going to happen in the ancient recording of our future, and it will all be destroyed, what difference will but make if you announce yourselves? What are they going to do, annihilate the earth? Looks like they are already doing that in our near future so what difference will it make if you just try?"

"He's making sense," said the controller at the info panel

glowing green gray in the semi dark of the ship. "If there is the slightest chance it will change things and save the planet, why not just do it and try?"

What should I say? What is going to get through to anyone?"

"Just the mere blitzing of the info channels will make it known. Flood all of them, and bust through the secrecy. Let them know we are all one species with one small planet to live on."

"I, I don't know, young ones. I cannot do this with out consulting with the others."

Said the old one. "Maybe we can sit down with your leaders..."

"No, not talk to the leaders. Talk to every one, on the lines. "

"Oh, you mean the electronic communications in the future."

"Ya, just go on everyone's line and tell them about yourself."

And so they did. They hooked in with their comm devices on the ship and translated the short message. And sent it into the near future.

"You are not alone here. We are above and have been for thousands of years. We are what you call god but we are beings like you. You will join our kind in the quest for knowledge and peace through out the universe."

And the message went out on all the wavelengths and all of the electrical lines and to all the computers and electronic devices. A few people fainted, a few had heart attacks. But the calamity was less than the one that was coming. And in this small catharsis, maybe the future cataclysm would be lessened.

And a new awareness was born, and people saw the people next to them no longer as enemies, but as co- pilots on this planet. And a change was made, and hands were lifted off the control panels of annihilation. And we raised our eyes and saw the stars in a new light. Not as the black unknown void . As the birth of our race; the new frontier of possibility and wonder and friendship.

When Gwydion woke up he realized that this was just a dream They say dreams are just the subconscious living out wish fulfillment, fantasies of the deeper mind. And as Azrael had told them, they have sworn to not interfere, because the things it would cause, have been caused and harmed humans irreparably The last time they showed themselves and tried to help, humans were so overwhelmed that they either died of fright, become deranged at the thought of another human-type being of greater intelligence, or the humans became supplicants in the face of their terrifying superiority. So when the visitor returned again, at the call of the ancient beacon in the stone temple, their ship was shot down and it crashed and as the small gray beings were dying on the sands of the desert, they communicated, scionetically with their human discoverers and agreed that it would be best to cover up and deny their existence. Because the human mind was not yet ready to understand.

There was a shock of bright light and a boom that rattled the very bones of the building he was in and the bed he was on. And he wasn't so sure this was a dream anymore. He woke up in a tangle of damp sheets, with Sheridan no where in sight. His vision was blurry and he looked around at the room, and hoped it was made of real stuff, and not of hopes and dreams, nor of the intentions and constructs of others. As his vision screwed and adjusted, the phone rang, assuring him that he was awake and in a hotel room.

"Are you ready?" his mother's stern voice spoke over

the phone line.

He grumbled something nonsensical but his mother understood completely. "I will be over in a moment. Go get in the shower," she said over the line.

Again he mumbled something incoherent. "But Shalome?"

"Now", says his mother with no hesitation.

In a daze he stood before the crowd at the convention. He had promised to read from some of his grandfather's works, from some of the most recent translations he had been working on. Everyone was expecting that. More of Professors Antony Jacob's work.

But the latest translations from his grandfather, from the ancient Nag Hammadi, he just couldn't do it. He couldn't read it out loud. He had read one of them last night. And maybe it was the source of those weird ass dreams he had had all night long. The story was still in his mind, as follows.....

Chapter 24
Light Beings

"Pilot gave them soldiers to guard the cave where his body was stored. The slid a huge rock to the front of the entrance, and sealed it with seven layers of incantations and spells to keep it safe and closed. And there they pitched a tent for the night.

And when the sun rose in the morning, it was the Sabbath, a crowd came from the surrounding area and Jerusalem, to see the crypt. But during the night before this dawn as the soldiers stood two by two to guard the crypt, there came a voice from the sky. And then in the dark the sky opened and great light came and two figures descended to the surface. The went to the rock in front of the cave, and the huge rock was seen to roll away from the opening all by its self. And these two bright beings entered the cave."

This was the story he had considered speaking for the group. But after his illuminating dream the night before, it felt like he had traveled miles and miles, he could not be sure, but this story cut a little too close to home.
It was a small stack of papers, two sheets really, with the Greek lettering of the original gospel of Peter, who wrote about the events that occurred around the death of the savior. It was just a portion of the gospel of Peter, and his death. But this passage was short and was about the resurrection of the Savior. He had never read such a thing and it had obviously been taken out of the finished bible stories. He had always questioned the idea of the savior being resurrected, who can do that? A god that is strong enough over life and death? Or something else that had been misunderstood at the time?

"When the soldiers saw these things, they woke up the elders and Roman Centurions. As they were explaining what they had just seen, three figures emerged from the cave, the two bright ones supporting the third between them, and a bright cross followed behind them. The two bright ones were so tall their heads went up to the skies. But the third between them was even higher, far above the skies. And a voice came from the skies and asked, "Have you preached and taught the ones that are asleep?" And the cross, the one once holding the Christ, said in answer, "Yes."
While the guards were making their plans to go tell Pilate what they had just witnessed, the skies opened up again and a figure was seen to descend, and he too went into the cave. So the guards hurried to Pilate on this night, in the middle of the night to explain, and they told him, "'He truly is the son of God.", as he had come directly from the sky and had gone back up again with Shining Beings.

And Pilate replies, "I have nothing to do with this. You did this and left the tomb unguarded." And so he ordered them to be quiet and not say a thing, because this was an impossible thing that they described and would only incur the wrath of the people and get them stoned for allowing their savior to escape and be taken away by Impossible Beings.

Now Mary Of Magdalena came with some mourners and wished to mourn now, as they hadn't before, as they should have, as law and decency required. But they wondered who could roll the stone away, it was so large. But when they arrived there, the stone was already rolled aside. So they peered into the crypt and saw a shining bright man sitting peacefully in the middle of the cave. And he said to them. "If you have come for the one who was crucified, he has already left and been taken back to the place from which he was sent." And the women fled in fear of this strangeness. "

No, he could not read that to them either. Maybe it was too weird for them. Or maybe it was to near his heart right now, he wasn't sure. But either way he could not read that to them. No way.

Instead, he set aside the small stack of papers that he brought with them, and placed them on the shining podium there in front of him. He put out of his mind that there were a thousand eyes watching him, waiting with baited breath for the words he was about to say.

And he began to recite one of the poems that he'd been translating from the ancient texts. But as he began, the story itself changed and became a story of his own.

"When I was young, I ran away from home, from the shining comfortable home my parents had provided for me. They were as a king and Queen to me.

But I needed to learn many things and find my own way. So I left the comfort and love in the jeweled tower of my parents, and ran into the deep jungle.

But I knew in my heart, from the wisdom that my parents had given me, that I was setting on a journey to my heart. To the heart of the world, to gain access to the core of its meaning. And I would find in the center of the deep dark cave, that Pearl which lay in the grip of the shining cruel Dragon hiding in its lair. And as I neared the land where the serpent dwelt, it became apparent that I was different, and I stood out among the crowd of locals. And for that my parents had sent me a garment from the skies. It covered my true self and helped me to fit within this society new.

And as I dwelt there for more than a year, I became alike the others that surrounded me in this new place. And I had slowly forgotten my original toil, my original quest set about for me by my parents, in their tower of glittering wisdom, where once I dwelt.

I dressed as they did, I spoke as they did, so they would not recognize me as something different and turn their Dragon loose on me. I never once let anyone know of my true quest of heart, for that pearl that lay deep in me, in the cairn that they had hiding.

I ate of their new foods, I played new games, I had new pleasures, formerly unknown and un-experienced by me. And soon I no longer remembered that I was the son of the king and queen of great wisdom in a high tower.

I fell into a deep sleep and slumbered in my soul from the heaviness of what they provided me, they, here in this new land.

And my parents in their tower saw that I had strayed from my past. And they lamented it so.

So they sent me a message, a vision from high, in the form of a brother that I seemed to know although he was a stranger, and that spoke to my soul and reawakened me to my original purpose.

Awake and arise from your sleep, Simon had said. Remember who you are, and your once worn Golden raiment. Re-claim your star-like garment, and remember your quest for the Pearl at the heart, that lay wrapped within the coil of the serpent.

I found this Dragon, for I had always known where it lay. And with my father's voice I subdued its strength, snatched the Pearl from its loose claws, and turned to go back to my parents home.

I took off my old dirty clothes and found my clean self beneath. And there on the road east, I met a woman who would become my friend, my Oracle, who, with her gentle voice, would guide me into the light.

It had been so long before that I'd left my parents home, and I had forgotten my original beauty. But on this road my Oracle became the mirror, in which I saw myself and my golden raiment once again. And I saw the two selves, my old self and my new self, join and become one again.

And I am speaking here today, of the words of wisdom given us, so many centuries ago, by the parents of us, who we are. For it is they who are stronger than all of us; it was him, my grandfather, that was so much stronger than I, and my friend-brother Simon, both who attend now in spirit only, and for whose sake I am here today and will continue to study the knowledge and words of the ancient worlds.

I bow my head now, as the young son did in the old story of the Hymn of the Pearl from the third century acts of Thomas, which is thought to originate from a much older text before even the time of the Christ, to my grandfather and Simon's grandfather's that set me on this path of wisdom and light, so that I might with this Pearl and star-light raiment, appear before my king and queen once again."

With that, Gwydion picked up his thin stack of papers. And with un-shed tears in his eyes turned away from the podium. In dead silence he walked across the stage and made his way to the stairs that led down to floor level. As he did so a few claps were heard from the audience which started other claps, which crescendoed into a wall of applause.

And Gwydion realized in the dark of the side wings of the stage, that they were clapping for him. He found Sheridan and his mother in the wings and they pulled him out of the auditorium into the hall and they each gave him a hug.

"That was amazing, Gwydion" Sheridan said, with tears in her eyes.

"Come on, let's go," said his mother briskly and clasped them both by their hands and pulled them away from the wall of sound.

As they got to the auditorium door, they opened it and let themselves out into the brighter light of the atrium entrance way. Where people were standing around and clapping and pouring out of the auditorium to meet him there. There were claps on his shoulders and on his back and many people asking him questions and shoving their face at his to try to get his attention. And he heard such things as "when are you speaking next?" "Where you going now?" "Who wrote that?" "Will you come to our event? We're having an event we'd like you to speak!"

And so it happened that his speaking career was launched in such a humble beginning, to a boy who once could not speak. From a talk he did not want to give, and a paper that he did not write. But a story had made up as he was reciting it from memory of an old poem from the Nag Hammadi library from writings more than 2000 years old.


Chapter 25
Desert Shock

They headed home as quickly as possible. His mother returned to the old house that had been bequeathed to the family when Antony died and the Happenstance foundation was disbanded. Grandmother Bethany and little grandchild Shalome were there waiting for their return.

But Gwydion and Sheridan returned to the desert of Nevada. And they couldn't wait to get home back to normal life.

When the unlocked the front door and walked into the living room, they had a shock. There on the couch sat little Shalome reading a book.

"What are you doing here? You are supposed to be in San Francisco with mom and grandma?"

"Oh, I am," she smiled. "Oh, no, they wont miss me."

"How did you even get here?" She simply pointed at the ceiling. The sky. And then shrugged her shoulders.

"And what do you mean they wont miss you? Oh, wait. I don't even want to know." Rocky turned to go to the bathroom after the long journey.

"That's 'cause I'm there too." Said Shalome.

He just shook his head and went and did his business. When he returned, he was less agitated and sat down next to her. "They couldn't get the timing right after I visited them. I went on my own you know. So they deposited me here, just in case. I cant run into my other self now can I.?" She sat for a moment and wrung her hands. "I suppose when that one goes up to visit them I will just dissolve and then be in San Francisco again. It kind of tickles."

He reached over and grabbed his tiny little sister by the shoulders and pulled her into is lap and started tickling her. She erupted in peels of laughter and they squirmed a while laughing on the couch.

Rocky sat up a moment, caught his breath and said, "I think you should arrange it to come stay for a while if you can. Maybe you all should come live up here. Pretty peaceful, you know."

Rocky stepped into the kitchen to make some food. He heard a knock at the front door and looked out to see Shalome walk over to the door and open it. He heard her say,

"We don't want your religion! We don't want your alien program! Take your angel Maroni from the Plaidies and go away!" Rocky walked up in time to see two young men dressed in black suit and tie run back to their bicycles and pedal on down the highway.

She turned quickly away to slam the door, and said, "Or, is it the arch alien ruler Xenon and his Thetans?"

"Geez, Shalome. You sure know how to handle them!" They both had a laugh and some sandwiches. "Where is Sheridan, anyway?" he asked her.

Just then Sheridan burst through the back door, red in the face, "Quick Come quick! In the barn." and she grabbed a sandwich and peeled back out the door for the barn.

When Shalome and Rocky reached the barn, and rolled open the big wood barn doors, a warm soft sense wafted out toward them. They found Sheridan in the back stall, the one with the most light and air coming from the outside sunlight. And she was kneeling next to the big squirrel-colored mare, Cinnamon, and there across Sheridan's lap was the soft face and neck of a baby foal, snorting and shaking her head from the flies.

Shalome was just standing there in wonder, petting the young foal. She got up and had a strange staring look in her eyes. She backed up to the stall wall, and there, her form and image began to disintegrate before the eyes of her brother and her brother's girl friend.

"What's wrong, Shalome? You look strange?"

"I lied Gwydion. I lied to you. I am actually going away with them. I can show them how. I can make them leave. And maybe they will leave us alone."

And with that, Gwydion reached out and just felt his sister's baby hand disintegrate against the touch of his fingers. And Sheridan began to sniffle and cry softly. "Good bye Shalome!"

Terror gripped him at the sensation of his sister disintegrating before him.

Up to now it had maybe just been academic. Gwydion had spent most of his life in a pall of shock. Of his angelic self awakening into this cold hard world of sound and fury, of screaming demons by the millions. This corporeal world of convicts and prisoners, angelic trespassers held here by the laws of Yaldobaoth against their will for His sadistic pleasure. Gwydion's young sensitive soul had been for so many years twisted and tormented by their screeching torrents of intention. But he had persevered, despite being pummeled by continual shock waves of light and sound. Finally to land here in this desert oasis of love and acceptance with his little sister and wife, Sheridan. Only to be shocked again here by the sheer terrifying reality of the Visitors. These beings who were probably both their parents in the very real sense, and their zoo-keepers. For now their taking of his beloved little sister was an awakening and a pain beyond his very ken. It was beyond his ability to tolerate. And yet he must. Tolerate this apocalypse of thought and awareness. He must continue to live on and follow this road he did not choose. At times he wished for respite or even escape, which of course was not allowed, for suicide is a mortal sin.

Then another thought struck him like a bell. He might see her again. Another time. Another place.

"I will see you again, Shalome, my girl," he said to her fading shape.

And through the thin air, although he could no longer see her, he heard her thin child's voice say, "Gwydion, be careful. They are not what they seem."

**From the Journal of Gwydion Jacobs:**

When you realize
that was that agonising
moment of Apocalype,
grasping finally the psychosis-inducing depths
of the betrayal of your truth and reality.

"And a Great Trumpeting was heard.
Garbriel the Great one from the Heavens.
GOD is not dead. Nor does he sleep.
Let the Wrong fall;
and the Wronged Prevail.
Peace on Earth.
Goodwill to all human kind."

Henry Wadsworth Longfellow

**Continue reading with from the Authors:**
Glass Planet 2: Demon's Child
Glass Planet 3: Apocalypse
Glass Planet 4: Sky Door: Gabriel's Return

**On the subject nonfiction:**
The Original Origin Story of the ancient Bible
The Grail Was a Gift from the Gods
The Alien Hoax of Religion

## Author

"I first wrote this story The Clear Beings as a short story in 2008 in front of the fire place in January. The story has grown and changed.

"Gabriel's Objective" is the second in this series, "The Glass Planet". McCarthy Preston has been great influence in the chapter, The Cup, it was constructed by us together one morning over breakfast on the ranch. The two hour brainstorm resulted in much of The Cup story, and I feel it is an inspired one.

Book 3, The Silver Sarcophagus takes on a more science fiction-horror flavor, one that I had a great deal of fun with. I apologize if it gets too yucky; but you can just skip over the really icky parts if you want. The press release on the Stone Temple Pilot in book 3 was written by Mr. Preston (my husband).The poem by Charlotte Stetson Gilman (1860-1935) was given to me by my father for Christmas 2012, borrowed from womenshistory.about.com/library. I've made a couple small syntactical changes to make it flow smoother for reading, but it's appropriateness to this book was undeniable.

So much of my becoming a writer is due to my mother, who was an English major in college and a school teacher for 30 years, and my animal doctor father, who is so much more, a scientist, engineer, inventor and inspiration. I also want to credit a great deal to San Francisco State University, for their broad educational curriculum, and specifically their NEXA program that allowed two teachers in a class room, bringing the ideas of the sciences and the arts together with the resulting explosion of possibility in my young mind. And then of course, all of the thousands of other works of literature I have read over the years, including the Holy Bible.

**I hope you find my stories fascinating, and know that there are no answers to the puzzles that surround us, just more interesting questions, more journeys of exploration to take.**

# Fiction

This is a work of fiction, although I borrow all kinds of things from my life and learning. All good fiction takes factual ideas from life and turns them into a journey into new possibilities. Or at least into fun things to think about. Part of the job and fun for the reader is to sort through and separate the factual from the made-up.

The carved stone slab is fact, you can google it and see photos of the carving yourself. It sits in a South American stone temple on the Yucatan peninsula, called the Temple of Inscriptions or the Temple of Writings. The singing stone steps are on that temple, and have been measured to resonate with a frequency that sounds much like the beautiful, revered jungle bird, Quetzalcoatl, also the name of the local God. The possibility of a slumbering pilot beneath the carved slab is pure fiction, and was though up by Whitney Lee Preston, a man of great imagination. He will be exploring this idea in his forth-coming fictional work, "Stone Temple -Cryo Dreams".

If you haven't surmised I draw very heavily from the Holy Bible, the King James version, and there are words and phrases that I use very closely in the retelling of the Exodus story. At first I found the old English style very difficult. But with practice it took on a beautiful poetic quality that I couldn't help but adapting into the story.

The older Bible is a fascinating history of our ancient experience, the newer ones being largely made-up, and I have tried to put more humanity into the story than I find in the old version, without the proselytizing of the newer children's fables. I have always wanted to know what those people could have been thinking in doing the things they were. And of course my interpretation of how the miracles occurred is somewhat original. Aliens, and all. But I have been told that my version is "not right." But I must remind the reader that all subsequent stories from the bible are interpretations. 'Subsequent' because they were not first written in English. Or even Latin. And even if you go read it in Hebrew and ancient Greek, and I wish I could, but learning those languages would be another life-time's work, the story would still be an interpretation, a retelling of an even older story. For these are very old folk tales of the human race, and I believe they are somewhat factual, as factual as thousands of years old stories can be.

The Pharaoh-ic archaeological finds mentioned in the story are real, descriptions can be found in various digests, especially the periodical "Egypt", a publication of the Archaeological Institute of America, however the explanations of these archaeological artifacts are my own fictions. I had fun making them fit nicely with my idea of alien intervention in our past. Thousands of years ago religion was poly-deistic. In some lands there was a god for each natural occurrence: One for lightening, one for rain, one for love. Then we grew in our capacity to understand the connection of things and all the gods were joined into one god who was in charge of all these things. Now we are at the cusp of the next step in complexity. We are getting ready to join all of the disparate only-one-god -which-is-mine gods from all the cultures, and join all of the new-found influences and interrelationships of science and nature into one force that rules it all: The unified field theory perhaps. It is however in our minds. We have grown in understanding, perhaps even in literally brain size and complexity. We need to step into the age of Aquarius and move into a greater broader understanding of the forces around us, holding all of the workings of nature as one force, and not as a dude in a throne. The dude on a throne is a limited view. Not necessarily really wrong; just limited. It was a good, but now antiquated, attempt to explain the larger forces at work, and the need to obey the laws.

The laws of right and it's consequences from disobeying them is illustrated by our understanding of being struck by a thunderbolt when we disobey. What a wonderful combination of the old and new: the natural god of thunderbolt striking someone who has blasphemed against the newer idea of natural forces to be obeyed, God. Interesting that when the new one-god ideas came into fashion, poly-god , or 'pagan' belief was ridiculed, no  worse, persecuted, to force this new idea on people, when it really is an idea of evolution of awareness not dogma. Our awareness evolved and became more encompassing, our minds being able to hold more ideas and more complicated ideas at once. Ecology is also a good example: the complex inter-workings of many things in nature, not just one tiny aspect science can research and measure.

So as we move into an ecological understanding of our world, humans as part of the natural world, our emotional reactions as part of physical imperative and mathematical structure and biochemical mechanics, are we going to persecute the old mono-deistic forms? Persecute it's believers? How about education instead. That should open up new vistas of space for this information to seep in. We will stop using "faith" as the measuring tool of "truth" and understanding. Faith might have been the corner stone to the last wave of world understanding. I am not sure how much Jesus taught faith, or another kind of healing; that will be the subject of The Glass Planet 4. The churches and the priests preached faith because their sovereign reigns depended on faith. 'Obey without question' is not a better world view. Asking questions and listening will be the hallmark of the new understanding. Science based in human compassion. How can it be any other? If each of us is the product of a natural process of physics that created each one of us. If our minds are the complex fusion of biochemical reactions, atomic physics and electromagnetic interrelationships, and maybe something more spiritual and less measurable, yet absolutely undeniable, how can we do anything but keep asking questions and keep listening to one another's ideas.

It is in fact fascinating that during most of the Christian reign of the last 2000 years, nature has been subjugated and feared as an evil influence. Ironic that it is the gateway to understanding the true influences and forces that shape who we are and what we think now. Almost as if they saw the truth of natural forces and were afraid, and therefore persecuted it. I always assumed it was the rejection of the old pagan ideas. Maybe that also, but the battle is the same, against the natural forces that truly shape us. That is the true god, if you must use that word. Humans are so weak; we want to be separate and special not-animals in a dirty world where the forces of our atoms reign supreme. Somewhere they used to say that the heavenly spheres sung the music of truth.

It may be a "baby out with the bath water" conundrum, which we tend to do in a panic when confronted with conflict. But we should keep the ideas of following laws of right, and the idea of a creator and a higher power, but throw away the antiquated poetry and the old dude on a throne. The concepts of right and wrong, obedience and punishment are not new; a new view needs to be broader and include more truth as we are discovering it. What happens when we discover on one of those, they now say billions, of planets just like Earth, another intelligent species? To crap with the Dude on a Throne idea. Or will it *prove* his existence? "The Glass Planet" is one exploration in fiction in a world with more questions than answers, where possibilities are endless and therefore reasonableness and free discourse needs to reign..

I, too, have moved on. I've read at least a thousand new books since I have written these stories. And I've come to believe there was a god named for each heavenly visitor that showed themselves. Real actual visitors that now, with the violence we showed them in the middle ages when we were solidifying our bible as human, rather than visitor, centric, only show themselves secretly and safely. And only to those that can accept off-world visitations from Angels without spazing out and being able to keep it secret; look at at what they did to Saint Joan for telling the truth about visiting angels. The growing powers of the church needed to have control over information, and anyone admitting contact with these heavenly visitors were crucified. The bible stories are an actual account of these visitations from heavenly beings to our plane, to try to help us , or otherwise get stuff from here, our beautiful delicate Glass Planet of dreams. But for 2000 years we have been deep in the process of rejecting them and their history here. As it says in the ancient bible story, the Original Origin story of the apocrypha and the Nag Hammadi library, we have eaten from the Tree of the Knowledge of Good and Evil Men and we now are aware of the tyranny of rulers and want to throw off the power of the authorities over us and our destiny as sovereign beings on this planet. The story has been perverted and suffers now as a poor metaphor for right and wrong. Raging misogyny can be reversed if we see that Eve did not come from Adams rib. But was made by a group of angels like Adam was, made to be a partner, to help educate poor Adam in the dirt, and to rise above the tyranny of the rulers (including the raging maniacal angel, Yaldobaoth who made Adamantine Adam from dirt to be his slave). Words of the Plajarens say Gabriel was Jesus' father of Mary Magdalain, and when earthings tried to kill this child-man of the stars, Gabriel became enraged, visited again and punished us by forcing us to eat his flesh, thus the first communion was created, shown to the followers of Joseph of Aramathea, Jesus adoptive brother who now resided in England, thus the separation of the Roman and the Anglican churches. One followed Joseph of Aramathea to Angle-terra, and the other stayed in Rome with Peter and Paul. And that our long history with the visitations of "Angels" my be off-world visitors. That would explain a lot of things, kind of a unified field theory of sorts.

New Reading List 2023:

The Nag Hammadi Library
The Essence of the Notes prepared by Maurice Osborn
The Lancelot Grail Reader edited by Norris J. Lacy
Communion and Transformation by Whitley Strieber
The Alien Hoax of Religion
The original Origin Story of the ancient Bible by NM Reed
The Grail was a Gift of the Gods; ibid

**Continue reading with from the Authors:**
Glass Planet 2: Demon's Child
Glass Planet 3: Apocalypse
Glass Planet 4: Sky Door: Gabriel's Return

**On the subject nonfiction:**
The Original Origin Story of the ancient Bible
The Grail Was a Gift from the Gods
The Alien Hoax of Religion

## Bibliography for the Glass Planet series.

My curiosity started with the Holy Bible; I was not raised religious, which is maybe why I've been able to look with such a different view point.. My sheer curiosity for those old strange stories was as old as speech for me. I don't watch TV so I had no knowledge of the new wave of alien beliefs and study. I had no way of knowing that I was so not alone in my questioning the origins of the god myths around the world, and that the answer may lay in ancient experiences with extra-terrestrials. As a child, I had been gathering little bits here and there, and it was time for me to delve into them, as on some level I think I knew I was dying of cancer and I needed to make it good and deep, no matter how embarrassing. I didnt care what people thought; I needed to find out.

    I have struggled with the concept of putting down a bibliography and have poopooooed it many times. I thought maybe the authors of those books would not want me using them as proofs for my thesis, being the subject matter it was. And at first I thought it would be only a few really obvious books. But with each addition to the Glass Planet list of stories, the book stack became rather large. And with 2 stacks on either side of me, this is daunting; I should have done it earlier. 28 books in this direct bibliography for the stories of the Glass Planet; and ironically, I will start with a movie.

    The very first book of GP, The Clear Beings, was most definitely inspired by the movie, Planet of the Apes. I watched that movie one exhausted day, and with that image of the Statue of Liberty half buried in centuries of sand on the ancient coast of Manhattan, I stood up and wrote the first story, The Clear Beings, about beings stranded on another planet, ours, but way in the past. And they weren't humans, but as you would come to find out, they were proto-humans: our ancestors. It was a short story with a twisting short story ending. But after I wrote it, I had found that my human characters in the near past had come alive, and had a lot more to say.

And I had found that the Holy bible was still speaking to me. But it was running out of strange things and clues to tell me. And it occurred to me to look at its sources, at the sources in ancient scrolls that were now being translated, for the origins of the passages in the bible so I could find the things that they had taken out over the years. I bet there were a lot of strange secrets there.

And I was right. And that led to this stack of books. Amazon is a wonderful thing for finding all kinds of books, some of them long out of print are listed in private stores; most are a few dollars, but one was a hundred something upon my first search, but their algorithm must have found it in another store and listed it for a couple dollars. ( A note on my translations: I did my own translating; no where did I copy text. I read from several sources and then paraphrased in my own words, telling my own story's as I saw them.)

Here is my bibliography listed in order of importance, rather than alphabetical. The obvious and the oblique are listed last, for I would like to introduce a couple of these books that with the new translations are no longer so hard to read. And I think every body should read these. Not that I want to take the old religions down, but that we need to see their original words that describe some long-ago experience. And how those words are twisted and changed with translations; and how some of the pre-biblical forms are really very beautiful and fascinating.

"Eyewitness to Jesus": by Carsten Peter Thiede and Mathew D'Ancona c. 1952. The first book to scientifically discuss the possibility that people who wrote these old texts were actually contemporaries of Jesus. It demystified the bible phenomena and made us realize that we could *know* what happened then by studying these newly found ancient scrolls which were accounts contemporary to the living person, Jesus of Nazareth.

"The Apocryphal Gospels Tests and Translations" by Bart D. Ehrman and Zlatko Plese; Oxford University Press; ISBN 978-0-19-973210-4  Greek and Aramaic on the left and translations and text on the right. The Gospel of Mary can be found here. She was The Christ's best disciple. Also the birth of Jesus is found here in the Infancy Gospel of Thomas. The Gospel of Peter tells of the resurrection of Jesus, obviously extra-terrestrials.

"The Nag Hammadi Scriptures; The Revised ans Updated Translation of Sacred Gnostic Texts"; Edited by Marvin Mayer. "The Nature of Rulers" is fascinating. "On the Origin of the World" is astounding, the early Origin story; obviously extra-terrestrial in origin. "Thunder, Perfect Mind"  is a feminist poem, which might be a bit surprising for more than 2000 years ago.

"The Dead Sea Scroll Deception": Michael Biagent & Richardi Leigh. Inspiration for The Broken Scroll. The story of how they tried to persecute to hide the truth. (There is another work and I cant find it, it has a camel train on the front.)

"The Sacred Mushroom and the Cross";  1970 John M Allegro, although it was written far earlier than this, he dared years later to publish it.. The man whose life they ruined because he dared to translate the texts honestly. So he wrote this book about a small passage in the scriptures about sacred rights and native plants. This original passage in the scriptures has since been lost, although there are other hints hidden, and this book became famous after he wrote in in the 60's, which shows you how pivotal the things are that they are trying to hide from us. The publisher actually issued an apology for publishing this book, and the book has numerous defensive postures, indicating the severity of their attack on him.

"Lost Scriptures: books that did not make it into the New Testament"; Bart D. Ehrman. Adam: The book of John. "The Hymn of the Pearl".

"The Divine Comedy" by Dante Alighieri. The classical work of death and punishments, as written in the ancient texts of Revelations. Where all these words cross: Armageddon, Apocalypse, apocrypha, Revelation in the vivid story in the Apocryphal Gospels. I cant which story it is in right now; you're going to have to read "Stone Temple Nightmare".

Those are the main influences.

Secondary influences:

"Waterless Mountain": Laura Adams Armer. A sweet story about Native American life in the mysterious desert.

"Song of Heyoehkah": Hyemeyohsts Storm. Classic work of Native American spiritualism and symbolic writings. These stories are a very advanced form of subconscious symbolism that pervades the Native American cultures. That they know and acknowledge that their religion is based on subconscious and symbolic belief systems is something Christians and other one-god religions could learn from.

"The Mists of Avalon": Marion Zimmer Bradley. The great modern de-mystifyer and mystify-er at the same time. The book that illustrates how to rewrite historical works so they easily fit a different religious paradigm.

"Communion: A True Story" by Whitley Strieber. This story shows how a physical encounter with a terrifying and awe-inspiring extra-terrestrial reality would manifest as a spiritual experience.

"The Key of Solomon the King; by King Solomon: Translated from Ancient Manuscripts in the British Museum" by Samuel Liddell and MacGregor Mathers. This work is so strange and symbolic, that we cant help but feel inferior and mystified by the depth and complexity of our ancestors thousands of years ago, that appear to have had a much deeper and satisfying relationship with mystical secrets of the natural world. So much so that it begs that they must have had contacts with entities much great and more advanced than we foolishly fancy our selves to be today.

"Alcoholics Anonymous": c 1939 on up. A great a mystical under-rated book of healing, with many mystical secrets to life. The surrendering to a greater power, what ever that may be which may be written into our genes from our original experiences with entities not from this sphere.

More related texts and discussions of ancient texts:

"The Gnostic Gospels": Elaine Pagels 1979

"Dead Sea Scrolls: The Untold Story". Kenneth Hanson, Ph. D.1997 Some great pictures.

"The Dead Sea Scrolls and the Christian Myth"; John M. Allegro. Great pictures and discussion of the Dead Sea find.

"Lost Christianities: The Battle for Scriptures and Faiths we Never Knew"  Bart D. Ehrman Time-line of ancient Pre-Christian religions, some pictures.

"The Lost Gospel of Judas Iscariot: A new Look at the Betrayer and the Betrayed". In the ancient paintings, Judas is made to look like a dark hairy brute, and Jesus is painted to look like a clear being with light coming from his head. It appears from the ancient gospel that Judas came to deliver Jesus from this sphere, and was not the enemy, but His savior. I never really got into this theme but there are a lot of books on the subject.

"The Lost Gospel: The Quest for the Gospel of Judas Iscariot" by Herbert Krosney. Beautifully done with color pictures.

"The Gnostics" by Tobias Churton. Gnosis means knowledge. The writers of much of the ancient scrolls of the Nag Hammadi and the Dead Sea. Black and white diagrams and illustrations, discussions.

**Bibliography for the Glass Planet series.**

My curiosity started with the Holy Bible; I was not raised religious, which is maybe why I've been able to look with such a different view point.. My sheer curiosity for those old strange stories was as old as speech for me. I don't watch TV so I had no knowledge of the new wave of alien beliefs and study. I had no way of knowing that I was so not alone in my questioning the origins of the god myths around the world, and that the answer may lay in ancient experiences with extra-terrestrials. As a child, I had been gathering little bits here and there, and it was time for me to delve into them, as on some level I think I knew I was dying of cancer and I needed to make it good and deep, no matter how embarrassing. I didnt care what people thought; I needed to find out.

I have struggled with the concept of putting down a bibliography and have poopooooed it many times. I thought maybe the authors of those books would not want me using them as proofs for my thesis, being the subject matter it was. And at first I thought it would be only a few really obvious books. But with each addition to the Glass Planet list of stories, the book stack became rather large. And with 2 stacks on either side of me, this is daunting; I should have done it earlier. 28 books in this direct bibliography for the stories of the Glass Planet; and ironically, I will start with a movie.

The very first book of GP, The Clear Beings, was most definitely inspired by the movie, Planet of the Apes. I watched that movie one exhausted day, and with that image of the Statue of Liberty half buried in centuries of sand on the ancient coast of Manhattan, I stood up and wrote the first story, The Clear Beings, about beings stranded on another planet, ours, but way in the past. And they weren't humans, but as you would come to find out, they were proto-humans: our ancestors. It was a short story with a twisting short story ending. But after I wrote it, I had found that my human characters in the near past had come alive, and had a lot more to say.

And I had found that the Holy bible was still speaking to me. But it was running out of strange things and clues to tell me. And it occurred to me to look at its sources, at the sources in ancient scrolls that were now being translated, for the origins of the passages in the bible so I could find the things that they had taken out over the years. I bet there were a lot of strange secrets there.

And I was right. And that led to this stack of books. Amazon is a wonderful thing for finding all kinds of books, some of them long out of print are listed in private stores; most are a few dollars, but one was a hundred something upon my first search, but their algorithm must have found it in another store and listed it for a couple dollars. ( A note on my translations: I did my own translating; no where did I copy text. I read from several sources and then paraphrased in my own words, telling my own story's as I saw them.)

Here is my bibliography listed in order of importance, rather than alphabetical. The obvious and the oblique are listed last, for I would like to introduce a couple of these books that with the new translations are no longer so hard to read. And I think every body should read these. Not that I want to take the old religions down, but that we need to see their original words that describe some long-ago experience. And how those words are twisted and changed with translations; and how some of the pre-biblical forms are really very beautiful and fascinating.

"Eyewitness to Jesus": by Carsten Peter Thiede and Mathew D'Ancona c. 1952. The first book to scientifically discuss the possibility that people who wrote these old texts were actually contemporaries of Jesus. It demystified the bible phenomena and made us realize that we could *know* what happened then by studying these newly found ancient scrolls which were accounts contemporary to the living person, Jesus of Nazareth.

"The Apocryphal Gospels Tests and Translations" by Bart D. Ehrman and Zlatko Plese; Oxford University Press; ISBN 978-0-19-973210-4  Greek and Aramaic on the left and translations and text on the right. The Gospel of Mary can be found here. She was The Christ's best disciple. Also the birth of Jesus is found here in the Infancy Gospel of Thomas. The Gospel of Peter tells of the resurrection of Jesus, obviously extra-terrestrials.

"The Nag Hammadi Scriptures; The Revised ans Updated Translation of Sacred Gnostic Texts"; Edited by Marvin Mayer. "The Nature of Rulers" is fascinating. "On the Origin of the World" is astounding, the early Origin story; obviously extra-terrestrial in origin. "Thunder, Perfect Mind" is a feminist poem, which might be a bit surprising for more than 2000 years ago.

"The Dead Sea Scroll Deception": Michael Biagent & Richardi Leigh. Inspiration for The Broken Scroll. The story of how they tried to persecute to hide the truth. (There is another work and I cant find it, it has a camel train on the front.)

"The Sacred Mushroom and the Cross"; 1970 John M Allegro, although it was written far earlier than this, he dared years later to publish it.. The man whose life they ruined because he dared to translate the texts honestly. So he wrote this book about a small passage in the scriptures about sacred rights and native plants. This original passage in the scriptures has since been lost, although there are other hints hidden, and this book became famous after he wrote in in the 60's, which shows you how pivotal the things are that they are trying to hide from us. The publisher actually issued an apology for publishing this book, and the book has numerous defensive postures, indicating the severity of their attack on him.

"Lost Scriptures: books that did not make it into the New Testament"; Bart D. Ehrman. Adam: The book of John. "The Hymn of the Pearl".

"The Divine Comedy" by Dante Alighieri. The classical work of death and punishments, as written in the ancient texts of Revelations. Where all these words cross: Armageddon, Apocalypse, apocrypha, Revelation in the vivid story in the Apocryphal Gospels. I cant which story it is in right now; you're going to have to read "Stone Temple Nightmare".

Those are the main influences.

Secondary influences:

"Waterless Mountain": Laura Adams Armer. A sweet story about Native American life in the mysterious desert.

"Song of Heyoehkah": Hyemeyohsts Storm. Classic work of Native American spiritualism and symbolic writings. These stories are a very advanced form of subconscious symbolism that pervades the Native American cultures. That they know and acknowledge that their religion is based on subconscious and symbolic belief systems is something Christians and other one-god religions could learn from.

"The Mists of Avalon": Marion Zimmer Bradley. The great modern de-mystifyer and mystify-er at the same time. The book that illustrates how to rewrite historical works so they easily fit a different religious paradigm.

"Communion: A True Story" by Whitley Strieber. This story shows how a physical encounter with an terrifying and awe-inspiring extra-terrestrial reality would manifest as a spiritual experience.

"The Key of Solomon the King; by King Solomon: Translated from Ancient Manuscripts in the British Museum" by Samuel Liddell and MacGregor Mathers. This work is so strange and symbolic, that we cant help but feel inferior and mystified by the depth and complexity of our ancestors thousands of years ago, that appear to have had a much deeper and satisfying relationship with mystical secrets of the natural world. So much so that it begs that they must have had contacts with entities much great and more advanced than we foolishly fancy our selves to be today.

"Alcoholics Anonymous": c 1939 on up. A great a mystical under-rated book of healing, with many mystical secrets to life. The surrendering to a greater power, what ever that may be which may be written into our genes from our original experiences with entities not from this sphere.

More related texts and discussions of ancient texts:

"The Gnostic Gospels": Elaine Pagels 1979

"Dead Sea Scrolls: The Untold Story". Kenneth Hanson, Ph. D.1997 Some great pictures.

"The Dead Sea Scrolls and the Christian Myth"; John M. Allegro. Great pictures and discussion of the Dead Sea find.

"Lost Christianities: The Battle for Scriptures and Faiths we Never Knew" Bart D. Ehrman Time-line of ancient Pre-Christian religions, some pictures.

"The Lost Gospel of Judas Iscariot: A new Look at the Betrayer and the Betrayed". In the ancient paintings, Judas is made to look like a dark hairy brute, and Jesus is painted to look like a clear being with light coming from his head. It appears from the ancient gospel that Judas came to deliver Jesus from this sphere, and was not the enemy, but His savior. I never really got into this theme but there are a lot of books on the subject.

"The Lost Gospel: The Quest for the Gospel of Judas Iscariot" by Herbert Krosney. Beautifully done with color pictures.

"The Gnostics" by Tobias Churton. Gnosis means knowledge. The writers of much of the ancient scrolls of the Nag Hammadi and the Dead Sea. Black and white diagrams and illustrations, discussions.

**N. M. Reed** & **McCarthy Preston** are the co-authors of many books, and the producers of the children's series, the Littlest Coyote, and are married life-partners. They live in the mountains on a small ranch with lots of animals and books.

**Continue reading with from the Authors:**
Glass Planet 2: Demon's Child
Glass Planet 3: Apocalypse
Glass Planet 4: Sky Door: Gabriel's Return
**On the subject nonfiction:**
The Original Origin Story of the ancient Bible
The Grail Was a Gift from the Gods
The Alien Hoax of Religion
**What's It Gonna Be, Captain?:**
    **The Belerophon and the Crystal Sphere**
    **The Rescue of the CSS Galactic Empress and the Lament Cube**
    **The Green Man Horror**
    **Starship Revanant**
**The Oak Grove of Maeve: Cupped Hands, Magic Tears**
**The Adventures of Elf and Troll**
**The Saga of Elf and Troll: The Tattered Unicorn**
**The Dueling Wizards of Simpletown**
**The Worrisome War of the Whimsical Wizards**
**Dungeons for Dollars: Wizards 2**
**Romancing the Scroll** Historical Fiction
**Home Is Where the Horse Is:** surviving the Jackson Butte Fire 2015; also published in 2023 as **A Safer Place to Be: True story of Fire Survival, a girl and her horses**
    **Wind In My Mane 1, and 2: Cross Country Horseback Riding Stories**
    **The Littlest Coyote** series of illustrated children's stories

**NMReedBooks.com**

**StevensPressLLC.com**

**Walmart and Barnes&Noble online**

**and on social media by book title and author**

Made in the USA
Columbia, SC
17 November 2023